Speedwriting® Dictionary

LANDMARK SERIES
SECONDARY EDITION

Speedwriting® Dictionary

LANDMARK SERIES
SECONDARY EDITION

THE *Speedwriting* DIVISION OF
The Bobbs-Merrill Company, Inc.
INDIANAPOLIS

Copyright © 1977, 1975 by the Bobbs-Merrill Company, Inc.
Printed in the United States of America
All rights reserved. No part of this book shall be reproduced or transmitted in any form or by any means, electronic or mechanical, including photocopying, recording, or by any information or retrieval system, without written permission from the Publisher:

   The Bobbs-Merrill Company, Inc.
   4300 West 62nd Street
   Indianapolis, Indiana 46268

First Edition
Second Printing—1977

Library of Congress Catalog Card Number: 76-45551
ISBN 0-672-98358-3

INTRODUCTION

Speedwriting Dictionary contains shorthand outlines for over 20,000 words, all arranged in alphabetical order. Each word is divided at the syllable breaks preferred for word division in typing, not necessarily *phonetic* word division.

The rules followed in these word divisions are:

1. Divide words only between syllables: *blas/pheme,* not *blasph/eme.*
2. Retain at least two letters of a word on the first line, preferably three or more: *abomi/nable* or *abomina/ble,* not *a/bominable.*
3. Carry over three or more letters of a word to the second line: *bus/ily,* not *busi/ly.*
4. Divide hyphenated words at the hyphen only: *teen-/ager,* not *teen-a/ger.*
5. Divide after the double letter when a syllable is added to a complete word ending in a double letter: *small/est,* not *smal/lest.*
6. Divide between vowels when they constitute two one-letter syllables coming together: *idi/ocy,* not *id/iocy; apothe/osis,* not *apoth/eosis.*
7. Divide after a one-letter syllable that occurs within a word: *bio/scope,* not *bi/oscope.*

8. Do not divide a proper noun, a contraction, an abbreviation, or a number: *America,* not *A/mer/i/ca; shouldn't,* not *should/n'/t; intro,* not *in/tro; 2,812,* not *2,/812.*

9. Do not divide a word of five letters or fewer: *abode,* not *a/bode.*

Included in this dictionary are the almost 13,000 words in the updated high-frequency American business vocabulary prepared by Morris Mellinger (Chicago State College, 1970).

Consistency, rather than brevity of outline, has been the guideline for the shorthand outlines in this dictionary. Writing outlines differently, not consistent with the rules, makes for a long list of shortcuts, which adds to the amount of learning and decreases one's writing speed. Remember, shortcuts are valuable only for high-frequency words.

Some of the outlines are followed by a second outline in parentheses. For example, the pronunciation of the word depends upon whether it is used as a verb or an adjective so both outlines are given. The outline for *aluminum* is written according to the shorthand principle and is followed with the chemical abbreviation in parentheses.

The appendices beginning on page 333 include: a Summary of Principles, a Summary of Brief Forms, a Summary of Standard Abbreviations, and a Summary of Geographical Terms—which includes the states, a selection of American cities, the Canadian provinces and territories, and a selection of Canadian cities.

The authority for word divisions here is Webster's *Third New International Dictionary* (G. & C. Merriam Company, Springfield, Massachusetts, 1969).

Speedwriting® Dictionary

LANDMARK SERIES
SECONDARY EDITION

a *a*
aback *abc*
aba/cus *abcr*
abaft *abf*
aba/lone *ablne*
aban/don *ab — n*
aban/doned *ab — n̄*
aban/don/ing *ab — n*
aban/don/ment *ab — n-*
abase *abs*
abase/ment *abs-*
abash *abS*
abata/ble *abab*
abate *aba*
abate/ment *aba-*
abbe *aba*
ab/bess *ab'*
ab/bey *abe*
ab/bot *abl*
ab/bre/vi/ate *aBva*
ab/bre/vi/a/tion *aBvy*

ab/bre/vi/a/tional *aBvyl*
ab/di/cate *abdca*
ab/di/ca/tion *abdcy*
ab/do/men *abdm*
ab/dom/i/nal *abdml*
ab/duct *abdc*
ab/duc/tion *abdcy*
ab/duc/tor *abdc'*
ab/er/ra/tion *aBy*
abet *abl*
abey/ance *aba/*
abhor *abho*
ab/hor/rence *abho/*
ab/hor/rent *abho-*
abide *abd*
abili/ties *ab))*
abil/ity *ab)*
ab/ject *abjc*
ab/jec/tion *abjcy*
ab/ju/ra/tion *abjy*
ab/jure *abju*

ab/sten/tion

Word	Shorthand	Word	Shorthand
ablaze		above-mentioned	
able		above-numbered	
able-bodied		above-referred	
abloom		abrade	
ab/lu/tion		abra/sion	
ably		abra/sive	
ab/ne/gate		abreast	
ab/ne/ga/tion		abridge	
ab/nor/mal		abridg/ment	
ab/nor/mal/ity		aboard	
ab/nor/mally		ab/ro/gate	
aboard		ab/ro/ga/tion	
abode		abrupt	
abol/ish		abruptly	
abol/ished		abrupt/ness	
abol/ish/ment		ab/scess	
abo/li/tion		ab/scond	
abo/li/tion/ism		ab/sence	
abo/li/tion/ist		ab/sen/ces	
abomi/na/ble		ab/sent	
abomi/nate		ab/sen/tee	
abomi/na/tion		ab/sen/tee/ism	
ab/origi/nal		ab/so/lute	
ab/origi/nes		ab/so/lutely	
abort		ab/so/lu/tion	
abor/tion		ab/so/lut/ism	
abor/tive		ab/solve	
abound		ab/sorb	
about		ab/sorbed	
above		ab/sor/bent	
above-average		ab/sorb/ing	
above/board		ab/sorp/tion	
above-captioned		ab/sorp/tive	
above-described		ab/stain	
above-entitled		ab/stainer	
above-enumerated		ab/ste/mi/ous	
above-listed		ab/sten/tion	

Word	Shorthand	Word	Shorthand
ab/sten/tions	absys	ac/cepta/ble	xpb
ab/sti/nence	absn/	ac/cep/tance	xp/
ab/sti/nent	absn-	ac/cep/ta/tion	xpy
ab/stract	abSc	ac/cepted	xp̄
ab/stracts	abScs	ac/cept/ing	xp̱
ab/strac/tion	abScy	ac/cepts	xps
ab/surd	abSd	ac/cess	x'
ab/surd/ity	abSd)	ac/ces/si/bil/ity	xsb)
abun/dance	ab—/	ac/ces/si/ble	xsb
abun/dant	ab— -	ac/ces/sion	xsy
abuse	abz (abs)	ac/ces/so/ries	xsys
abused	abz̄	ac/ces/sory	xsy
abus/ing	abẕ	ac/ci/dence	xd/
abu/sive	absv	ac/ci/dent	xd-
abu/sively	absvl	ac/ci/den/tal	xd-l
abu/sive/ness	absv'	ac/ci/den/tally	xd-l̄
abut	abt	accident-free	xd-fe
abut/ment	abt-	ac/ci/dents	xd--
abut/tal	abtl	ac/claim	aca
abysm	abz	ac/cla/ma/tion	acy
abys/mal	abzl	ac/cli/mate	acl
abyss	ab'	ac/cli/ma/tize	aclz
aca/demic	acdc	ac/co/lade	acld
aca/de/mi/cian	acdy	ac/com/mo/date	akda
acad/emy	acde	ac/com/mo/dated	akdā
ac/cede	xd	ac/com/mo/dat/ing	akda̱
ac/cel/er/ant	xl-	ac/com/mo/da/tion	akdy
ac/cel/er/ate	xla	ac/com/mo/da/tions	akdys
ac/cel/er/ated	xlā	ac/com/mo/da/tive	akdav
ac/cel/er/at/ing	xla̱	ac/com/mo/da/tor	akda
ac/cel/er/a/tion	xly	ac/com/pa/nied	acō
ac/cel/er/a/tor	xla	ac/com/pa/nies	acos
ac/cent	x-	ac/com/pa/ni/ment	aco-
ac/cen/tu/ate	xca	ac/com/pa/nist	aco,
ac/cen/tu/a/tion	xcy	ac/com/pany	aco
ac/cept	xp	ac/com/pa/ny/ing	aco̱
ac/cept/a/bil/ity	xpb)	ac/com/plice	akps

acme

Word	Shorthand	Word	Shorthand
ac/com/plish		ac/cu/rately	
ac/com/plished		ac/cursed	
ac/com/plish/ing		ac/cu/sa/tion	
ac/com/plish/ment		ac/cu/sa/tive	
ac/com/plish/ments		ac/cuse	
ac/cord		ac/cused	
ac/cor/dance		ac/cuser	
ac/cor/dant		ac/cus/tom	
ac/corded		ac/cus/tomed	
ac/corder		ace	
ac/cord/ing		acer/bity	
ac/cord/ingly		ace/tate	
ac/cor/dion		ace/tic	
ac/cost		ace/tone	
ac/count		acety/lene	
ac/count/a/bil/ity		ache	
ac/count/a/ble		achieve	
ac/coun/tancy		achieved	
ac/coun/tant		achieve/ment	
ac/coun/tants		achieve/ments	
ac/count/ing		achiev/ing	
ac/counts		ach/ing	
ac/credit		ach/ro/matic	
ac/cred/i/ta/tion		acid	
ac/cred/ited		acidic	
ac/cre/tion		acid/ify	
ac/crual		acid/ity	
ac/crue		ac/id/proof	
ac/crued		acidu/late	
ac/cu/mu/late		acidu/lous	
ac/cu/mu/lated		ac/knowl/edge	
ac/cu/mu/lat/ing		ac/knowl/edged	
ac/cu/mu/la/tion		ac/knowl/edges	
ac/cu/mu/la/tive		ac/knowl/edg/ing	
ac/cu/mu/la/tor		ac/knowl/edg/ment	
ac/cu/racy		ac/knowl/edg/ments	
ac/cu/rate		acme	

adapted

acne
aco/lyte
aco/nite
acorn
acous/tic
acous/ti/cal
ac/quaint
ac/quaint/ance
ac/quaint/ances
ac/quainted
ac/quaint/ing
ac/qui/esce
ac/qui/es/cense
ac/qui/es/cent
ac/quire
ac/quired
ac/quir/ing
ac/qui/si/tion
ac/qui/si/tions
ac/quis/i/tive
ac/quit
ac/quit/tal
acre
acre/age
acres
ac/rid
acrid/ity
ac/ri/mo/ni/ous
ac/ri/mony
ac/ro/bat
ac/ro/batic
ac/ro/nym
acrop/o/lis
across
across-the-board
acros/tic
acrylic

act
acted
act/ing
ac/tinic
ac/tion
ac/tion/a/ble
action-packed
ac/tions
ac/ti/vate
ac/ti/vated
ac/tive
ac/tively
ac/tiv/i/ties
ac/tiv/ity
actor
ac/tors
ac/tress
acts
ac/tual
ac/tu/al/ity
ac/tu/ally
ac/tu/ar/ial
ac/tu/ary
ac/tu/ate
acu/ity
acu/men
acute
acutely
acute/ness
ad
adage
ada/mant
adapt
adapta/bil/ity
adapta/ble
ad/ap/ta/tion
adapted

5

adapter
adapt/a/ble
add
added
ad/denda
ad/den/dum
ad/dict
ad/dic/tion
add/ing
ad/di/tion
ad/di/tional
ad/di/tion/ally
ad/di/tive
ad/di/tives
addle
ad/dress
ad/dressed
ad/dressee
ad/dresses
ad/dress/ing
ad/dress/o/graph
adds
ad/duce
ade/noid
adept
ad/e/quacy
ad/e/quate
ad/e/quately
ad/here
ad/hered
ad/her/ence
ad/her/ent
ad/he/sion
ad/he/sive
ad/he/sives
adieu
ad in/fi/ni/tum

ad/ja/cent
ad/jec/tive
ad/join
ad/join/ing
ad/joins
ad/journ
ad/journed
ad/journ/ment
ad/judge
ad/ju/di/cate
ad/ju/di/ca/tion
ad/junct
ad/ju/ra/tion
ad/jure
ad/just
ad/just/a/ble
ad/justed
ad/juster
ad/just/ing
ad/just/ment
ad/just/ments
ad/ju/tant
ad lib
adman
ad/min/is/ter
ad/min/is/tered
ad/min/is/ter/ing
ad/min/is/ters
ad/min/is/trate
ad/min/is/tra/tion
ad/min/is/tra/tions
ad/min/is/tra/tive
ad/min/is/tra/tor
ad/min/is/tra/tors
ad/mi/ra/ble
ad/mi/ral
ad/mi/rals

ad/mi/ralty	adrift
ad/mi/ra/tion	adroit
ad/mire	adroitly
ad/mired	ads
ad/mirer	ad/sorb
ad/mis/si/bil/ity	ad/sorp/tion
ad/mis/si/ble	adu/late
ad/mis/sion	adu/la/tion
ad/mis/sions	adu/la/tory
ad/mit	adult
ad/mits	adults
ad/mit/tance	adul/ter/ant
ad/mit/ted	adul/ter/ate
ad/mit/tedly	adul/ter/a/tion
ad/mit/ting	adul/ter/a/tor
ad/mix/ture	adul/terer
ad/mon/ish	adul/ter/ous
ad/mo/ni/tion	adul/tery
ad/moni/tory	adult/hood
ad nau/seam	ad/vance
ado	ad/vanced
adobe	ad/vance/ment
ado/les/cense	ad/vance/ments
ado/les/cent	ad/vances
adopt	ad/van/tage
adopted	ad/van/ta/geous
adopt/ing	ad/van/tages
adop/tion	ad/vent
adop/tions	ad/ven/ti/tious
adop/tive	ad/ven/ture
ador/a/ble	ad/ven/turer
ado/ra/tion	ad/ven/tures
adore	ad/ven/ture/some
adorn	ad/ven/tur/ous
adorn/ment	ad/verb
adrenal	ad/ver/bial
adren/a/line	ad/ver/sary

af/forded

ad/verse
ad/versely
ad/ver/sity
ad/vert
ad/ver/tise
ad/ver/tise/ment
ad/ver/tise/ments
ad/ver/tiser
ad/ver/tis/ers
ad/ver/tis/ing
ad/vice
ad/vis/a/bil/ity
ad/vis/a/ble
ad/vise
ad/viser
ad/vis/ers
ad/vise/ment
ad/vises
ad/vis/ing
ad/vi/sor
ad/vi/sory
ad/vo/cacy
ad/vo/cate
adz
aegis
aeon
aer/ate
aer/a/tion
aer/a/tor
aer/ial
aero/dy/nam/ics
aero/naut
aero/nau/tic
aero/nau/ti/cal
aero/nau/tics
aero/sol
aero/space

aero/sys/tems
aes/thete
aes/thetic
aes/thet/i/cally
afar
af/fa/bil/ity
af/fa/ble
af/fair
af/fairs
af/fect
af/fec/ta/tion
af/fected
af/fect/edly
af/fect/ing
af/fec/tion
af/fec/tion/ate
af/fects
af/fi/ance
af/fi/ant
af/fi/da/vit
af/fili/ate
af/fili/ated
af/fili/a/tion
af/fin/ity
af/firm
af/fir/ma/tion
af/fir/ma/tive
af/firms
affix
af/fixed
af/fix/ing
af/flict
af/flic/tion
af/flu/ence
af/flu/ent
af/ford
af/forded

af/ford/ing
af/fords
af/fray
af/front
af/ghan
afield
afire
aflame
afloat
afoot
afore/men/tioned
afore/said
afore/thought
afore/time
afoul
afraid
afresh
aft
after
af/ter/burner
af/ter/care
af/ter/ef/fect
af/ter/glow
af/ter/hours
af/ter/math
af/ter/most
af/ter/noon
af/ter/noons
af/ter/taste
af/ter/thought
af/ter/ward
again
against
agape
agate
age
age/less

age-old
aged
agen/cies
agency
agenda
agen/das
agent
agents
ag/glom/er/ate
ag/glom/er/a/tion
ag/glu/ti/nate
ag/gran/dize
ag/gran/dize/ment
ag/gra/vate
ag/gra/vated
ag/gra/va/tion
ag/gre/gate
ag/gre/ga/tion
ag/gres/sion
ag/gres/sive
ag/gres/sive/ness
ag/gres/sor
ag/grieve
ag/grieved
aghast
agile
ag/ilely
agil/ity
aging
agi/tate
agi/ta/tion
agi/ta/tor
aglow
ag/nos/tic
ago
agog
ago/nize

a la carte

agony
agrar/ian
agree
agreea/bil/ity
agreea/ble
agreed
agree/ing
agree/ment
agree/ments
agrees
ag/ri/cul/tural
ag/ri/cul/ture
ag/ro/chem/i/cals
aground
ague
ahead
ahoy
aid
aide
aid/ing
aids
ai/grette
ail
ai/le/ron
ail/ment
aim
aimed
aim/less
aims
air
air-actuated
air/base
air/borne
air/brake
air/brush
air/brushes
air-condition

air-conditioned
air-conditioning
air/craft
air/drome
air/drop
air ex/press
air/field
air/foil
air force
air/freight
air/lift
air/line
air/liner
air lines
air/mail
air/mailed
air-minded
air-operated
air/plane
air/planes
air/port
air/proof
air/ship
air/space
air/speed
air/strip
air/tight
air ven/ture
air/wave
air/way
air/ways
airy
aisle
ajar
akin
ala/bas/ter
a la carte

alac/rity
a la mode
alarm
alarmed
alarm/ist
alas
al/ba/tross
al/beit
al/bino
album
al/bums
al/bu/min
al/co/hol
al/co/holic
al/co/hol/ism
al/cove
al/der/man
ale
alert
alerted
alerts
al/fal/fa
al/ge/bra
al/ge/braic
al/ge/bra/i/cal
alias
alibi
alien
al/iena/ble
ali/en/ate
ali/en/ated
ali/en/a/tion
ali/en/ist
alight
align
align/ment
alignment-wise

alike
ali/ment
ali/men/tary
ali/men/ta/tion
ali/mony
alive
al/kali
al/ka/line
al/ka/loid
al/kyd
all
all-around
allay
all-cotton
all-day
al/le/ga/tion
al/lege
al/leges
al/le/giance
al/le/gori/cal
al/le/gory
al/ler/gic
al/lergy
al/le/vi/ate
al/le/vi/ates
al/le/via/tion
al/ley
al/leys
al/li/ance
al/lied
al/li/ga/tor
al/lit/era/tion
all-night
all-pro
al/lo/cate
al/lo/cated
al/lo/cat/ing

al/ways

al/lo/ca/tion	al/pha/bet/ize
al/lo/ca/tions	al/pine
al/lot	al/ready
al/lot/ted	also
al/lot/ment	altar
allow	alter
al/lowa/ble	al/tera/tion
al/low/ance	al/tera/tions
al/low/ances	al/ter/cate
al/owed	al/ter/ca/tion
al/low/ing	al/tered
al/lows	alter ego
alloy	al/ter/ing
al/loys	al/ter/nate
all right	al/ter/na/tive
all-time	al/ter/na/tives
al/lude	al/though
al/lure	al/tim/e/ter
al/lu/sion	al/ti/tude
al/lu/sive	al/ti/tudes
al/lu/vial	alto
al/lu/vium	al/to/gether
all-weather	al/tru/ism
all-wool	al/tru/ist
ally	al/tru/is/tic
alma mater	alum
al/ma/nac	alu/minum
al/mighty	alumna
al/mond	alum/nae
al/most	alumni
alms	alum/nus
aloft	al/ways
alone	
along	
along/side	
aloof	
aloud	

alp
al/paca
al/pha/bet
al/pha/bet/i/cal
al/pha/nu/meric

12

amount/ing

am
amal/gam
amal/gam/ate
amal/gam/a/tion
amanu/en/sis
amass
am/a/teur
amaze
amazed
amaz/ing
amaz/ingly
am/bas/sa/dor
amber
am/ber/gris
am/bi/dex/trous
am/bi/ence
am/bi/gu/ity
am/big/u/ous
am/bi/tion
am/bi/tions
am/bi/tious
am/biva/lent
am/biva/lence
amble
am/bro/sia
am/bu/lance
am/bu/la/tory
am/bus/cade
am/bush
ame/lio/rate
ame/lio/ra/tion
amen
ame/na/ble
amend
amen/da/tory
amended
amend/ing

amend/ment
amend/ments
amends
amen/ity
America
American
Americanization
American-made
American-owned
Americans
ame/thyst
amia/bil/ity
amia/ble
ami/ca/bil/ity
ami/ca/ble
amid
amid/ships
amidst
amiss
amity
am/me/ter
am/mo/nia
am/mo/nium
am/mu/ni/tion
am/ne/sia
am/nesty
amoeba
amoe/bic
among
amongst
amo/rous
amor/phous
amor/ti/za/tion
amor/tize
amount
amounted
amount/ing

13

amounts
am/per/age
am/pere
am/phib/ian
am/phibi/ous
am/phi/the/ater
ample
am/pli/fi/ca/tion
am/pli/fier
am/pli/fi/ers
amplify
am/pli/tude
am/ply
am/pu/tate
am/pu/ta/tion
am/pul
amu/let
amuse
amus/ing
an
anach/ro/nism
anach/ro/nis/tic
ana/gram
anal
an/al/ge/sia
ana/log/i/cal
analo/gous
ana/logue
anal/ogy
analy/ses
analy/sis
ana/lyst
ana/lysts
ana/lytic
ana/lyt/i/cal
ana/ly/za/tion
ana/lyze

ana/lyzed
ana/lyzer
ana/lyzes
ana/lyz/ing
an/ar/chism
an/ar/chist
an/ar/chy
anath/ema
an/a/tom/i/cal
anat/omy
an/ces/tor
an/ces/tors
an/ces/try
anchor
an/chor/age
an/chored
an/cho/rite
an/chors
an/chovy
an/cient
an/cil/lary
and
and/or
an/dante
and/iron
an/ec/dote
an/ec/dotes
ane/mia
ane/mic
ane/mom/e/ter
an/er/oid
an/es/the/sia
an/es/thetic
anes/the/tist
anes/the/tize
anew
angel

anger
angle
an/gler
an/gli/cize
an/grily
angry
an/guish
an/gu/lar
an/gu/lar/ity
ani/line
ani/mal
ani/mals
ani/mate
ani/mated
ani/ma/tion
ani/mos/ity
ani/mus
anise
ankle
an/klet
an/nals
an/neal
annex
an/nex/a/tion
an/ni/hi/late
an/ni/hi/la/tion
an/ni/hi/la/tor
an/ni/ver/sary
anno Domini
an/no/tate
an/no/ta/ted
an/no/ta/tion
an/no/ta/tor
an/nounce
an/nounced
an/nounce/ment
an/nounce/ments

an/nouncer
an/nounces
an/nounc/ing
an/noy
an/noy/ance
an/nual
an/nu/ally
an/nu/i/tant
an/nu/i/tants
an/nu/ities
an/nu/ity
annul
an/nul/ment
annum
an/nun/ci/ate
an/nun/ci/a/tion
an/nun/ci/a/tor
anode
ano/dized
ano/diz/ing
ano/dyne
anoint
anoma/lous
anom/aly
anon
ano/nym/ity
anon/y/mous
an/other
an/swer
an/swer/able
an/swered
an/swer/ing
an/swers
ant
ant/acid
an/tago/nism
an/tago/nist

15

ap/er/ture

an/tago/nis/tic a- gnsc
an/tago/nize a- gnz
ant/arc/tic a- rcc
an/te/ced/ent a- sd-
an/te/cham/ber a- Crb
an/te/date a-da
an/te/lope a- lp
ante/me/ri/dian a- rden (am)
an/tenna alna
an/ten/nas alnas
an/te/rior aly
an/te/room a-r
an/them al
an/thol/o/gies alljes
an/thol/ogy allje
an/thra/cite aTsi
an/thrax a⁺
an/thro/poid aTpyd
an/thro/pol/ogy aTplje
anti a-e
an/ti/bi/otic a- blc
an/ti/bi/ot/ics a- blcs
an/ti/body a- bde
antic a-c
an/tic/i/pate alspa
an/tic/i/pated alspā
an/tic/i/pat/ing alspa
an/tic/i/pa/tion alspj
an/tic/i/pa/tor alspa
an/ti/cli/max a- crx
anti-Communist a- kn,
anti/def/a/ma/tion a- dfn
an/ti/dote a-do
an/ti/freeze a- Fz
an/ti/his/ta/mine a- hsm
an/ti/mony a- me (Sb)
an/tip/a/thy alple

an/tip/o/des alpds
an/ti/quar/ian a- qyn
an/ti/quate a- qa
an/tique alc
an/tiques alcs
an/tiq/uity alq)
an/ti/sep/sis a- spss
an/ti/sep/tic a- spc
an/ti/so/cial a- sx
an/tith/e/sis attss
an/ti/thet/i/cal a- ttcl
an/ti/toxin a- txn
ant/ler a- l
ant/onym a- n
an/trum a
anvil avl
anx/i/ety agze)
anx/ious agx
anx/iously agx
any ne
any/body nebde
any/how nehr
any/more nero
any/one ne/
any/thing ne
any/time nētc
any/way necra
any/where necr
aorta ala
apart asl
apart/heid asla
apart/ment asl- (apl)
apart/ments asl-- (apls)
apa/thetic apttc
apa/thy aple
ape ap
ap/er/ture arc

16

ap/pli/ca/tions

apex
apha/sia
api/ces
aph/o/rism
api/ary
api/cal
apiece
aplomb
apoca/lypse
apoc/ry/phal
apo/gee
apolo/getic
apolo/gia
apolo/gies
apolo/gist
apolo/gize
apol/ogy
apo/plec/tic
apo/plexy
apos/tasy
apos/tate
a pos/te/ri/ori
apos/tle
apos/to/late
ap/os/tolic
apos/tro/phe
apos/tro/phize
apothe/cary
apothe/osis
Appalachian
ap/pall
ap/pa/ra/tus
ap/parel
ap/par/ent
ap/par/ently
ap/pa/ri/tion
ap/peal

ap/pealed
ap/peal/ing
ap/peals
ap/pear
ap/pear/ance
ap/pear/ances
ap/peared
ap/pear/ing
ap/pears
ap/pease
ap/peas/ment
ap/pel/lant
ap/pel/lants
ap/pel/late
ap/pel/la/tion
ap/pel/lee
ap/pend
ap/pen/dage
ap/pen/dec/tomy
ap/pended
ap/pen/di/ci/tis
ap/pen/dix
ap/per/tain
ap/pe/tite
ap/pe/tizer
ap/pe/tiz/ing
ap/plaud
ap/plause
apple
ap/ple/jack
ap/pli/ance
ap/pli/ances
ap/pli/ca/bil/ity
ap/pli/cant
ap/pli/cants
ap/pli/ca/tion
ap/pli/ca/tions

ap/ti/tude

ap/pli/ca/tor	apca	ap/pren/tices	aP-ss
ap/plied	apī	ap/pren/tice/ship	aP-ss
ap/plies	apis	ap/prise	aPz
apply	api	ap/proach	aPc
ap/ply/ing	api̱	ap/proach/able	aPcb
ap/point	apy-	ap/proaches	aPcs
ap/pointed	apy=	ap/proach/ing	aPc
ap/pointee	apy-e	ap/pro/ba/tion	aPby
ap/point/ing	apy=	ap/pro/ba/tive	aPbv
ap/point/ive	apy-v	ap/pro/ba/tory	aPbly
ap/point/ment	apy--	ap/pro/pri/ate	aPpel (aPpa)
ap/point/ments	apy---	ap/pro/pri/ated	aPpā
ap/por/tion	ayī	ap/pro/pri/ately	aPpell
ap/por/tioned	ay	ap/pro/pri/ate/ness	aPpel'
ap/por/tion/ment	ay-	ap/pro/pri/a/tion	aPpy
ap/po/site	apzi	ap/pro/pri/a/tions	aPpys
ap/po/si/tion	apzy	ap/proval	aPvl
ap/praisal	aPzl	ap/prov/als	aPvls
ap/prais/als	aPzls	ap/prove	aPv
ap/praise	aPz	ap/proved	aPv̄
ap/praised	aPz̄	ap/proves	aPvs
ap/praiser	aPz/	ap/prov/ing	aPv̱
ap/prais/ers	aPz//	ap/proxi/mate	apx
ap/prais/ing	aPẕ	ap/proxi/mated	apx̄
ap/pre/cia/ble	apb	ap/proxi/mately	apx
ap/pre/ci/ate	ap	ap/proxi/ma/tion	apxy
ap/pre/ci/ated	ap̄	ap/pur/te/nance	astn/
ap/pre/ci/ates	aps	ap/pur/te/nant	astn-
ap/pre/ci/a/tion	apy	apri/cot	ascl
ap/pre/cia/tive	apv	April	ap
ap/pre/hend	aPh—	a pri/ori	aPy
ap/pre/hend/ing	aPẖ—	apron	aPn
ap/pre/hen/si/ble	aPh/b	aprons	aPns
ap/pre/hen/sion	aPhy	ap/ro/pos	aPpo
ap/pre/hen/sions	aPhys	apse	aps
ap/pre/hen/sive	aPh/v	apt	ap
ap/pren/tice	aP-s	ap/ti/tude	apld

18

aqua
aq/ua/cade
aq/ua/lung
aq/ua/ma/rine
aq/ua/plane
aquar/ium
aquatic
aq/ue/duct
aque/ous
aq/ui/line
ara/besque
Arabic
ara/ble
ar/bi/ter
ar/bi/tra/ble
ar/bi/trar/ily
ar/bi/trary
ar/bi/trate
ar/bi/tra/tion
ar/bi/tra/tor
arbor
ar/bo/real
ar/bo/re/tum
arc
ar/cade
ar/cane
arch
ar/chaeo/log/i/cal
ar/chae/ol/o/gist
ar/chae/ol/ogy
ar/chaic
arch/an/gel
arch/bishop
arch/dea/con
arch/dio/cese
arch/duch/ess
arch/duke
arch/en/emy
archer
arch/ery
ar/che/type
ar/chi/pel/ago
ar/chi/tect
ar/chi/tects
ar/chi/tec/tural
ar/chi/tec/ture
ar/chi/trave
ar/chives
arch/ness
arch/way
arc/tic
ar/dent
ardor
ar/du/ous
are
area
areas
area/wide
arena
aren't
ar/gent
argon
ar/gosy
ar/got
ar/gu/able
ar/gue
ar/gu/ment
ar/gu/ments
ar/gu/men/ta/tive
ar/gyle
aria
arid
arise
arises

ar/tic/u/lat/ing

aris/ing	ar/rang/ing
ar/is/toc/racy	ar/rant
aris/to/crat	arras
aris/to/cratic	array
arith/me/tic	ar/rears
ar/ith/meti/cal	ar/rear/age
arith/me/ti/cian	ar/rest
ark	ar/rested
arm	ar/rests
ar/mada	ar/rival
ar/ma/dillo	ar/riv/als
ar/ma/ment	ar/rive
ar/ma/ture	ar/rived
arm/chair	ar/rives
arm/chairs	ar/riv/ing
armed	ar/ro/gance
arm/ful	ar/ro/gant
ar/mi/stice	ar/ro/gate
ar/mor	ar/row
ar/mory	ar/row/head
arm/pit	ar/royo
arm/rest	ar/se/nal
arms	ar/se/nate
army	ar/se/nic
aroma	arson
aro/matic	art
arose	ar/te/rial
around	ar/te/rio/scle/ro/sis
arouse	ar/tery
arouses	ar/te/sian
ar/peg/gio	art/ful
ar/raign	ar/thri/tis
ar/raign/ment	ar/ti/choke
ar/range	ar/ticle
ar/ranged	ar/ti/cles
ar/range/ment	ar/tic/u/late
ar/range/ments	ar/tic/u/lat/ing

ar/tic/u/la/tion
ar/ti/fact
ar/ti/fice
ar/ti/fi/cial
ar/ti/fi/ci/al/ity
ar/ti/fi/cially
ar/til/lery
ar/ti/san
art/ist
art/ists
ar/tis/tic
ar/tist/ry
art/less
arts
art/work
Aryan
as
as/bes/tos
as/cend
as/cend/ancy
as/cend/ant
as/cend/ing
as/cen/sion
ascent
as/cer/tain
as/cer/tain/able
as/cer/tained
as/cer/tain/ing
as/cetic
as/ceti/cism
ascor/bic
as/cribe
as/crip/tion
asep/sis
asep/tic
ash
ashamed
ashen
ashore
Asian
Asiatic
aside
asi/nine
asi/nin/ity
ask
asked
ask/ing
asks
askance
askew
aslant
asleep
as/para/gus
as/pect
as/pects
aspen
as/per/ity
as/per/sion
as/phalt
as/phal/tic
as/phyxia
as/phyxi/ate
as/phyx/i/ation
aspic
as/pi/rant
as/pi/rate
as/pi/ra/tion
as/pi/ra/tor
as/pire
as/pi/rin
as/sail
as/sail/ant
as/sas/sin
as/sas/si/nate

as/surer

as/sas/si/na/tion
as/sault
assay
as/sem/blage
as/sem/ble
as/sem/bled
as/sem/blers
as/sem/bling
as/sem/blies
as/sem/bly
as/sent
as/sert
as/serts
as/ser/tion
as/sert/ive
as/sess
as/sess/able
as/sessed
as/sess/ment
as/sess/ments
as/ses/sor
asset
as/sets
as/sev/er/ate
as/sev/er/a/tion
as/si/du/ity
as/sid/u/ous
as/sign
as/sign/able
as/sig/nate
as/sig/na/tion
as/signed
as/signee
as/signer
as/sign/ing
as/sign/ment
as/sign/ments

as/signs
as/simi/late
as/simi/la/tion
as/simi/la/tive
as/simi/la/tory
as/sist
as/sist/ance
as/sist/ant
as/sist/ants
as/sisted
as/sist/ing
as/size
as/so/ciate (noun)
as/so/ci/ate (verb)
as/so/ci/ated
as/so/ciates (noun)
as/so/ci/ates (verb)
as/so/ci/at/ing
as/so/cia/tion
as/so/cia/tions
as/so/cia/tive
as/so/nance
as/so/nant
as/sort
as/sorted
as/sort/ment
as/sort/ments
as/suage
as/sume
as/sumed
as/sum/ing
as/sump/tion
as/sur/ance
as/sure
as/sured
as/sured/ly
as/surer

as/sures
as/sur/ing
aster
as/ter/isk
astern
as/ter/oid
asthma
asth/matic
as/tig/matic
astig/ma/tism
as/ton/ish
as/ton/ish/ing
as/tound
as/tral
astray
astride
as/trin/gent
as/tro/jet
as/tro/labe
as/trol/o/ger
as/trol/ogy
as/tro/naut
as/tro/nauts
as/trono/mer
as/tro/nom/i/cal
as/tron/omy
as/tro/phys/ics
as/tute
asun/der
asy/lum
asym/met/ri/cal
at
ata/vism
ate
ate/lier
athe/ism
athe/ist
athe/is/tic
athe/naeum
ath/lete
ath/letic
athwart
Atlantic
atlas
at/mo/sphere
at/mo/spheric
atoll
atom
atomic
at/om/ize
at/om/izer
at/om/iz/ers
atone
atrium
atro/cious
atroc/ity
at/ro/phy
at/ro/pine
at/tach
at/ta/che
at/tached
at/taches
at/tach/ing
at/tach/ment
at/tach/ments
at/tack
at/tain
at/tain/able
at/tain/der
at/tained
at/tain/ing
at/tain/ment
at/tain/ments
at/tains

au/ric/u/lar

at/taint
attar
at/tempt
at/tempted
at/tempt/ing
at/tempts
at/tend
at/ten/dance
at/ten/dant
at/tended
at/tend/ing
at/ten/tion
at/ten/tive
at/ten/tive/ness
at/ten/u/ate
at/test
at/tes/ta/tion
at/tested
at/tests
attic
at/tire
at/ti/tude
at/ti/tudes
at/tor/ney
attorney-in-fact
at/tor/neys
at/tract
at/tracted
at/tract/ing
at/trac/tion
at/trac/tions
at/trac/tive
at/trac/tively
at/tracts
at/trib/ut/able
at/tri/bute (noun)
at/trib/ute (verb)

at/trib/u/ted
at/trib/utes
at/trib/u/tive
at/tri/tion
at/tune
au/burn
auc/tion
auc/tion/eer
au/da/cious
au/dac/ity
au/di/ble
au/di/ence
au/di/ences
au/dio
au/dio/phile
audit
au/dited
au/dit/ing
au/di/tion
au/di/tor
au/di/to/rium
au/di/tors
au/di/tory
au/ger
aug/ment
au gra/tin
au/gur
au/gury
August
aunt
aura
aural
au/re/ole
au/reo/my/cin
auric
au/ri/cle
au/ric/u/lar

au/rif/er/ous
au/rora
aus/pice
aus/pices
aus/pi/cious
aus/tere
aus/ter/ity
Australian
Austrian
au/then/tic
au/then/ti/cate
au/then/tic/ity
au/thor
au/thor/ess
au/thori/tar/ian
au/thori/ta/tive
au/thori/ties
au/thori/ty
au/tho/ri/za/tion
au/tho/ri/za/tions
au/tho/rize
au/tho/rized
au/tho/rizes
au/tho/riz/ing
au/thors
au/thor/ship
auto
au/to/bi/og/ra/phy
au/toc/racy
au/to/crat
au/to/cratic
au/to/graph
au/to/mate
au/to/mated
au/to/matic
au/to/mat/i/cally
au/to/mat/ing

au/to/ma/tion
au/tom/a/tize
au/tom/a/ton
au/to/mo/bile
au/to/mo/biles
au/to/mo/tive
au/to/nom/ic
au/tono/mous
au/ton/omy
au/topsy
au/to/sug/ges/tion
au/tumn
au/tum/nal
aux/il/iary
avail
avail/abil/ity
avail/able
ava/lanche
avant-garde
ava/rice
ava/ri/cious
avenge
ave/nue
ave/nues
aver
av/er/age
av/er/ag/ing
averse
aver/sion
avert
avian
avi/ary
avia/tion
avia/tor
avid
avid/ity
avi/on/ics

azure

av/o/cado
av/o/ca/tion
avoid
avoid/able
avoid/ance
avoided
avoid/ing
av/oir/du/pois
avow
avowedly
avun/cu/lar
await
await/ing
awake
awaken
awak/en/ing
award
award-winning
aware
aware/ness
awash
away
awe
awe/some
awe/stricken
awful
awhile
awk/ward
awl
awn/ing
awn/ings
awoke
awry
ax
axial
axiom
axi/om/atic

axis
axle
aye
aza/lea
azi/muth
Aztec
azure

B

bab/bitt	*bbt*	back/handed	*bch—*
bab/ble	*bb*	back/lash	*bcls*
babe	*bab*	back/log	*bclg*
ba/bies	*bbes*	back order	*bc O*
baby	*bbe*	back-ordered	*bc Ō*
baby-sitting	*bbest*	back-pedaled	*bcpdl*
bac/ca/lau/re/ate	*bclyt*	backs	*bcs*
bac/ca/rat	*bCa*	back/slide	*bcsd*
bac/cha/na/lia	*bcnla*	back tax	*bclx*
bache/lor	*bCl*	backup (noun; adj.)	*bcp*
ba/cilli	*bsli*	back up (verb)	*bcp*
ba/cil/lus	*bslc*	back/ward	*bcl d*
back	*bc*	back/ward/ness	*bcl d'*
back/bone	*bcbn*	bacon	*bcn*
backed	*bc̄*	bac/te/ria	*bcya*
backer	*bc*	bac/te/ri/cide	*bcysd*
back fat	*bcfl*	bac/te/ri/olo/gist	*bcyly,*
back/fire	*bcfr*	bac/te/ri/olo/gy	*bcylye*
back/gam/mon	*bcgm*	bad	*bd*
back/ground	*bcg—*	bade	*bd*
back/hand	*bch—*	badge	*by*

27

bands

Word	Shorthand	Word	Shorthand
bad/ger	by	balk	bc
bad/ges	bys	balky	bce
badi/nage	bdnz	ball	bal
badly	bdl	bal/lad	bld
bad/min/ton	bd-n	bal/ladry	blDe
bad/ness	bd'	bal/last	bl,
baf/fle	bfl	bal/le/rina	bdna
baf/fle/ment	bfl-	bal/let	bla
bag	bg	bal/lis/tic	blsc
baga/telle	bgll	bal/loon	bln
bag/gage	bgg	bal/lot	bll
bagged	bḡ	bal/lots	blls
bag/ging	bg	ball/room	blr
bag/pipe	bgpp	balls	bals
bags	bgs	bal/ly/hoo	blhu
bail	bal	balm	b—
bailee	bl	balmy	b—e
bai/liff	blf	balmi/ness	b—e'
bai/li/wick	blwc	balsa	blsa
bail/or	bl	bal/sam	bls—
bait	ba	bal/us/ter	blS
bake	bc	bal/us/trade	blSd
baked	bc̄	bam/boo	b-bu
Bakelite	bcli	bam/boo/zle	b-bzl
bak/ery	bcy	ban	bn
bake/shop	bcsp	banal	bnl
bak/ing	bc̱	ba/nal/ity	bnl)
bal/ance	bl/ (bal)	ba/nana	bnna
bal/anced	bl/	band	b—
bal/ances	bl//	ban/dage	b—-j
bal/anc/ing	bl/̱	ban/danna	b—-na
bal/cony	blke	band/box	b—-bx
bald	bld	ban/deau	b—-o
bal/der/dash	blDdS	ban/dit	b—-l
bale	bal	band/mas/ter	b— —S
bale/ful	blf	ban/dol/lier	b— le
bales	bals	bands	b— —

28

band shell
band/stand
bandy
bane
bane/ful
bang
ban/gle
ban/ish
ban/ish/ment
ban/is/ter
banjo
bank
bank/book
banker
bank/ers
bank/ing
bank/rupt
bank/ruptcy
banks
ban/ner
ban/ners
ban/quet
ban/quets
ban/shee
ban/tam
ban/ter
bap/tism
bap/tis/mal
bap/tis/tery
bap/tize
bar
barb
bar/bar/ian
bar/baric
bar/ba/rism
bar/bar/ity
bar/ba/rous

bar/be/cue
bar/ber
bar/ber shop
bar/bi/tu/rate
bar/ca/role
bard
bare
bare/back
bare/ness
bar/gain
bar/gain/ing
bar/gains
barge
barge/man
bari/tone
barium
bark
bar/keeper
bar/ken/tine
barker
bar/ley
bar/maid
barn
bar/na/cle
barn/stormer
barn/yard
baro/graph
bar/ome/ter
bar/ome/ters
baro/met/ric
baron
bar/on/ess
bar/onet
baronial
baroque
baro/scope
bar/racks

bar/ra/cuda	bcda
bar/rage	bj
bar/ra/try	bje
bar/rel	bl
bar/reled	bl-
bar/rels	bls
bar/ren	bn
bar/ri/cade	bcd
bar/rier	bj
bar/ring	bx
bar/ris/ter	bs-
bar/room	brr
bar/row	bo
bar/tender	brl—
bar/ter	b/
basal	bsl
bas/ally	bsl
ba/salt	bsll
base	bas
base/ball	bsbal
base/balls	bsbals
base/board	bsbd
based	ba,
base/less	bsl'
base/ment	bs—
base/ness	bs?
bases	bass
bash/ful	bsf
basic	bsc
ba/sics	bscs
ba/si/cally	bscl
ba/sil/ica	bslca
basin	bsn
ba/sins	bsns
basis	bss
bask	bsc
bas/ket	bscl
bas/ket/ball	bsclbal
bas/ket/ful	bsclf
bas/ket/like	bscllc
bas/ketry	bscje
bas/kets	bscls
basks	bscs
Basque	bsc
bas-relief	blf
bass	b?
bas/si/net	bsnl
bas/soon	bsn
baste	ba,
bas/tion	bsCn
bat	bl
batch	bC
batch/ing	bC-
bate	ba
ba/teau	blo
bath	bl
bathe	bal
ba/ther	bT
ba/thetic	bttc
bath/ing	bal-
ba/thos	bls
bath/room	blrn
bath/rooms	blrns
baths	bls
ba/tiste	ble,
baton	bln
bat/tal/ion	blln
bat/ten	bln
bat/ter	b/
bat/ter/ies	blys
bat/tery	bly
bat/tle	bll
bat/tle/field	bllfld
bat/tle/front	bllf—

bat/tle/ship
bau/ble
bawl
bay
bay/o/net
bayou
ba/zaar
ba/zooka
be
beach
beach/comber
bea/con
bead
bea/dle
beads
bea/gle
beak
beaker
beam
beams
bean
beans
bear
bear/able
bear/ing
bear/ings
bears
beast
beast/li/ness
beastly
beat
beater
be/atific
be/ati/fi/ca/tion
be/ati/tude
beats
beau

beau/te/ous
beau/ti/cian
beau/ti/fi/ca/tion
beau/ti/ful
beauty
bea/ver
be/calm
be/came
be/cause
beck
beckon
be/cloud
be/come
be/comes
be/com/ing
bed
bed/cham/ber
be/devil
bed/lam
bed/ouin
be/drag/gle
bed/room
bed/rooms
beds
bed/spreads
bed/time
bee
beech
beech/nut
beef
beef/eat/ers
beef/steak
bee/hive
been
beer
beet
bee/tle

bend

be/fall	bfal	belch	bec
be/fore	bf	be/lea/guer	blg
be/fore/hand	bfh—	bel/fry	belfe
be/fore/time	bfti	Belgian	belgn
be/friend	bf—	belie	ble
be/fud/dle	bfdl	be/lief	blef
beg	bg	be/liefs	blefs
began	bg	be/lieve	ble
beget	bgt	be/lieved	ble̅
be/get/ter	bg	be/liever	ble/
beg/gar	bg/	be/liev/ers	ble//
beg/garly	bgl	be/lieves	bles
beg/gary	bgy	be/lit/tle	bell
begin	bg	bell	bell
be/gin/ner	bg/	bell-ringer	blrg/
be/gin/ning	bg	bel/la/donna	bldna
be/gins	bgs	bel/li/cose	blcs
begot	bgt	bel/lig/er/ence	blg/
be/grime	bgi	bel/lig/er/ent	blg⊥
be/grudge	bgj	bel/low	blo
be/guile	bgl	belly	bl
begun	bgn	be/long	blg
be/half	bhf	be/longed	blg̅
be/have	bha	be/long/ing	blg
be/hav/ior	bha/	be/long/ings	blg
be/held	bhl	be/longs	blgs
be/hest	bh,	be/loved	blv̅
be/hind	bhi—	below	blo
be/hold	bhol	below-listed	blol;
be/hoove	bhu	belt	bel
be/hooves	bhus	belt/ing	bel
beige	bay	belts	bels
being	b	bel/ve/dere	blvde
be/ings	b	be/moan	bm
be/la/bor	bl̄b	bench	bc
be/lated	bla̅	benches	bcs
be/lay	bla	bend	b—

32

bend/ing
be/neath
bene/dict
bene/dic/tion
bene/fac/tor
bene/fac/tress
bene/fice
be/nefi/cence
be/nefi/cent
bene/fi/cial
bene/fi/ci/ar/ies
bene/fi/ci/ary
bene/fit
ben/e/fited
bene/fit/ing
bene/fits
be/nevo/lence
be/nevo/lent
be/nighted
be/nign
be/nig/nancy
be/nig/nant
be/nig/nity
beni/son
bent
ben/zine
ben/zo/ate
ben/zoin
be/queath
be/quest
be/quests
be/reave
be/reft
be/rets
beri/beri
berry
ber/serk

berth
beryl
be/ryl/lium
be/seech
be/side
be/sides
be/siege
be/sought
best
bes/tial
bes/ti/al/ity
be/stir
best-known
best-looking
best-qualified
best/sellers
best/selling
be/stow
bet
be/took
be/tray
be/trayal
be/tray/ing
be/troth
be/trothal
bet/ter
better-known
bet/ter/ment
better-stocked
be/tween
be/twixt
bevel
bev/er/age
bev/er/ages
bevy
be/wail
be/ware

be/wil/der
be/wil/der/ing
be/wil/der/ment
be/witch
bey
be/yond
bi/an/nual
bias
bi/be/lot
Bible
Bib/li/cal
bib/li/og/ra/pher
bib/li/og/ra/phy
bib/li/o/phile
bibu/lous
bi/cam/eral
bi/car/bon/ate
bi/cen/ten/nial
bi/ceps
bi/chlo/ride
bi/chro/mate
bicker
bi/cus/pid
bi/cy/cle
bi/cy/cles
bi/cy/clist
bid
bide
bid/ding
bi/en/nial
bier
bi/fo/cal
bi/fur/cate
big
biga/mist
biga/mous
big/amy

big/ger
big/gest
big/ness
bigot
big/otry
big shot
big/wig
bi/kini
bi/lat/eral
bile
bilge
bi/lin/gual
bil/ious
bilk
bill
bill/board
bill/boards
bill/book
billed
bil/let
bill/fold
bil/liard
bil/liards
bill/ing
bill/ings
bil/lion
bil/lion/aire
bil/lionth
bil/low
bill/poster
bills
billy
bi/me/talic
bi/monthly
bin
bi/nary
bin/au/ral

bind
binder
bind/ery
bind/ing
bingo
bin/na/cle
bin/oc/u/lar
bi/no/mial
bio/chemi/cal
bio/chem/is/try
bi/og/ra/pher
bio/graphic
bio/graphi/cal
bi/og/ra/phy
bio/log/i/cal
bi/ol/ogy
bi/opsy
bi/par/ti/san
bi/par/tite
biped
bi/plane
bi/ra/cial
birch
bird
birdie
birds
bird's-eye
birth
birth/day
birth/mark
birth/place
birth/right
birth/stone
bis/cuit
bi/sect
bishop
bis/muth

bison
bisque
bis/tro
bit
bite
bits
bit/ter
bit/ter/sweet
bi/tu/men
bi/tu/mi/nous
bi/valve
biv/ouac
bi/weekly
bi/zarre
black
black/board
blacken
black/guard
black/mail
black/out
bladder
blade
blades
blam/able
blame
blamed
blame/less
blame/wor/thy
blanch
bland
blan/dish
blan/dish/ment
blank
blan/ket
blank/ing
blank/ness
blanks

blow/out

blare	ba
blar/ney	bne
blasé	bza
blas/pheme	bsfe
blas/phe/mous	bsfx
blas/phemy	bsfre
blast	b,
bla/tancy	bl/
bla/tant	bl-
blather	b
blaze	bz
bla/zon	bzn
bleach	bec
bleak	bec
bleary	by
bleat	be
bled	bd
bleed	bd
blem/ish	bns
blem/ishes	bnss
blench	bc
blend	b—
blend/ing	b—=
blends	b— —
bless	b'
blessed	b,
bless/ed/ness	bsd'
bless/ing	b,_
bless/ings	b,=
blest	b,
blew	bu
blight	be
blind	be—
blinder	be/
blind/fold	be—fol
blindly	be—l
blinds	be— —
blink	bg
blinker	bg/
bliss	b'
bliss/ful	bsf
blis/ter	bs
blithe	bl
blitz	bls
bliz/zard	bzd
bloat	bo
block	bc
block/ade	bcd
block/bus/ter	bcbs
block/head	bchd
block/house	bchs
block/ing	bc_
blocks	bcs
blond	b—
blood	bd
blood/hound	bdh—
bloodi/est	bde,
blood/ily	bdl
bloodi/ness	bde'
blood/less	bdl'
blood/shed	bdsd
blood/shot	bdsl
blood/stain	bdsn
bloom	bu
blooper	bp
blos/som	bs
blot	bl
blotch	bc
blot/ter	b/
blouse	bus
blow	bo
blower	bo/
blown	bn
blow/out	boou

blow/torch	
blowzy	
blub/ber	
blub/bery	
blu/cher	
bludg/eon	
blue	
blue/jacket	
blue/print	
bluff	
blun/der	
blun/der/buss	
blunt	
bluntly	
blunt/ness	
blur	
blurb	
blurt	
blush	
blus/ter	
blus/ter/ous	
boa	
boar	
board	
board/ing	
board/ing/house	
boards	
board/walk	
boast	
boast/ful	
boasts	
boat	
boat/builder	
boat/ing	
boat/own/ers	
boats	
bob	
bob/bin	
bob/sled	
bode	
bod/ice	
bodi/less	
bodily	
bod/kin	
body	
body/guard	
Boer	
bog	
bogey	
bog/gle	
bogus	
boil	
boiler	
boils	
boil/ing	
bois/ter/ous	
bold	
bolder	
bold/face	
boldly	
bold/ness	
bo/lero	
boll	
Bolshevik	
bol/ster	
bolt	
bolts	
bolus	
bomb	
bom/bard	
bom/bard/ier	
bom/bard/ment	
bom/bast	
bom/bas/tic	

bosses

bom/ba/zine
bomb/sight
bona fide
bo/nanza
bond
bond/age
bonded
bond/holder
bond/ing
bonds
bone
boned
bones
bon/fire
bon/net
bonny
bonus
bo/nuses
booby
booby trap
boo/dle
book
book/binder
book/case
booked
book/ing
book/keeper
book/keepers
book/keep/ing
book/let
book/lets
book/mo/bile
books
book/shelf
book/shelves
book/stores
boom

boom/er/ang
boon
boon/dog/gle
boor
boor/ish
boost
booster
boot/black
booth
booths
boot/leg
boot/less
booty
booze
bo/racic
bo/rate
borax
bor/der
bor/der/line
bor/ders
bore
bo/real
bored
bore/dom
boric
bor/ing
born
borne
boron (B)
bor/ough
bor/row
bor/rower
bor/row/ing
bosh
bosom
boss
bosses

Word	Shorthand	Word	Shorthand
bo/tani/cal		bou/tique	
bot/a/nist		bou/ton/niere	
botany		bo/vine	
botch		bow	(bo)
both		bowd/ler/ize	
bother		bowel	
both/ered		bower	
both/ers		bow/knot	
both/er/some		bowl	
bot/tle		bowler	
bot/tle/necks		bowl/ing	
bot/tlers		bow/string	
bot/tles		box	
bot/tom		box/car	
bot/tom/less		boxed	
bou/doir		boxer	
bouf/fant		boxes	
bough		boy	
bought		boy/cott	
bouil/lon		boy/hood	
boul/der		boy/ish	
bou/le/vard		boys	
bounce		brace	
bound		brace/let	
bounda/ries		braces	
bound/ary		bracket	
bounded		brack/ets	
bounder		brack/ish	
bound/less		brad	
boun/te/ous		brag	
boun/ti/ful		brag/ga/do/cio	
bounty		brag/gart	
bou/quet		braid	
bour/geois		braille	
bour/geoi/sie		brain	
bourse		brain/less	
bout		brains	

brev/ity

brain/wash
braise
brake
brakes
bram/ble
bran
branch
branches
brand
brand/ing
bran/dish
brandy
brass
bras/sard
bras/siere
brat
bra/vado
brave
brav/ery
brav/est
bravo
bra/vura
brawl
brawn
brawni/est
brawny
bray
bra/zen
bra/zier
Brazilian
breach
bread
breads
breadth
bread/win/ner
break
break/able

break/age
break/down (noun)
break down (verb)
breaker
break/fast
break/fasts
break/ing
break/neck
breaks
break/through
break/throughs
break/water
breast
breast/bone
breast-feed
breast-feeding
breath
breath/able
breathe
breather
breath/ing
breath/less
breath/tak/ing
bred
breech
breed
breed/ers
breed/ing
breeds
breeze
breeze/way
breezy
breth/ren
breve
bre/vet
bre/viary
brev/ity

40

brew	bu
brewed	bu-
brewer	bu/
brew/ery	buy
brew/ing	bu_
briar	be/
bribe	beb
brib/ery	bby
bric-a-brac	bcbc
brick	bc
brick/bat	bcbt
brick/layer	bcla/
bricks	bcs
brick/yard	bcyd
bridal	bdl
bride	bd
bride/groom	bdgu
brides/maid	bdsnd
bridge	by
bridge/head	byhd
bridges	bys
bridge/work	byh-c
bri/dle	bdl
brief	bef
brief/case	bfcs
briefed	bef-
briefly	bfl
brig	bg
bri/gade	bgd
briga/dier	bgde
brig/and	bg—
brig/an/tine	bg-n
bright	be
brighten	ben
brighter	be/
brightly	bel
bright/ness	be'
bril/liance	bl/
bril/liancy	bl/
bril/liant	bl-
bril/lian/tine	bl-n
bril/liantly	bl-l
brim	bn
brim/ful	bnf
brim/ming	bn_
brim/stone	bnsn
brin/dle	b—l
brine	bn
bring	bq
bring/ing	bq_
brings	bqs
brink	bq
briny	bine
bri/oche	beS
bri/quette	bcl
brisk	bsc
bris/ket	bscl
briskly	bscl
bris/tle	bsl
British	bUS
broach	boC
broad	bd
broad/cast	bdc,
broad/casted	bdc,-
broad/cast/ers	bdcSs
broad/cast/ing	bdc,_
broad/cloth	bdcl
broaden	bdn
broad/ened	bdn-
broader	bd/
broadly	bdl
broad-minded	bdn-—
broad/side	bdsd
broad/sword	bdSd

Word	Shorthand
broad/tail	bdll
bro/cade	bcd
broc/coli	bcl
bro/chette	bSl
bro/chure	bSu
bro/chures	bSus
brogue	bog
broil	byl
broke	boc
bro/ken	ben
bro/ker	bc
bro/ker/age	bCj
bro/kers	bc//
bro/mate	b-a
bro/mide	b-d
bro/midic	b-dc
bro/mine	b-m
bron/chial	bqel
bron/chi/tis	bqls
bronco	bqo
bronze	bnz
brooch	boC
brood	bd
brook	bc
brook/let	bcll
broom	bu
broom/stick	busc
broth	bl
brother	b-
broth/er/hood	b-hd
brother-in-law	b-nla
broth/erly	b-l
broth/ers	b-s
brougham	bo
brought	bl
brou/haha	bhha
brow	b-
brow/beat	b-be
brown	b-n
brownie	b-ne
brown/stone	b-nsn
browse	b-z
bruin	bun
bruise	bz
bruises	bzs
bruit	bu
brunch	bC
bru/net	bnl
brunt	b-
brushes	bSs
brush/work	bSl-c
brusque	bsc
bru/tal	bul
bru/tal/ity	bul)
bru/tal/ize	bulz
brute	bu
bub/ble	bb
bu/bonic	bbnc
buc/ca/neer	bcne
buck	bc
bucket	bcl
buckle	bcl
buck/ler	bcl
buck/ram	bC-
bu/col/ic	bclc
bud	bd
Buddhism	bdz-
Buddhist	bd,
budge	bj
bud/get	bjl
bud/get/ary	bjly
bud/geted	bjl
bud/get/ing	bjl
bud/gets	bjls

buff bf	bull/fight blft
buf/falo bflo	bull/frog blfg
buffed bf	bul/lion bln
buf/fer bf	bull/ock blc
buf/fet bft (bfa)	bull's-eye blse
buf/foon bfn	bully bl
buf/foon/ery bfny	bul/rush blrS
bug bg	bul/wark bll rc
bug/a/boo bgbu	bum bm
bug/bear bgba	bum/ble bmb
buggy bge	bum/ble/bee bmbbe
bugle bgl	bump bmp
build bld	bumped bmp̄
builder bld	bump/ing bmp
build/ers bld/	bump/kin bmcn
build/ing bld	bump/tious bmx
build/ings bld̄	bumpy bmpe
builds blds	bun bn
build-up (noun) bldp	bunch bC
buildup (verb) bldp	bun/combe bnco
built blt	bun/dle b—l
built-in bltn	bun/dles b—ls
bulb blb	bung bg
bul/bous blbs	bun/ga/low bglo
bulbs blbs	bun/gle bgl
bulge blj	bun/ion bnyn
bulk blc	bunk bg
bulk/head blchd	bunker bg
bulky blce	bun/kum bnk
bull bl	bun/nies bnes
bull/dog bldg	bunny bne
bull/doze bldz	bun/ting b=
bull/dozer bldz	buoy bue
bul/let blt	buoy/ancy by/
bul/le/tin bltn	buoy/ant by-
bul/le/tin board bltnBd	bur/den Bdn
bul/le/tins bltns	bur/dened Bdn̄

43

buy

bur/dens	Bdns	burst	B,
bur/den/some	Bdns	burst/ing	B₂
bur/dock	Bdc	bury	by
bu/reau	Bu	bus	bs
bu/reau/cracy	BuCse	bush	bS
bu/reau/crat	BuCt	bushel	bSl
bu/reau/crats	BuCts	bush/els	bSls
bu/reaus	Bus	bush/ing	bS₂
bu/rette	Bt	bush/wacker	bSwc
bur/geon	Bgn	bus/ier	bz
bur/geon/ing	Bgn₂	busi/est	bz₃
burgher	Bg	bus/ily	bzl
bur/glar	Bg	busi/ness	bs
bur/glar/ize	Bgz	busi/ness/man	bsm
bur/glary	Bgy	busi/ness/men	bsm
Burgundy	Bg—e	bust	b,
bur/ial	byl	bus/tle	bsl
bur/ied	by	busy	bz
burl	Bl	but	b
bur/lap	Blp	butcher	bc
bur/lesque	Blsc	butch/ery	bcy
burly	Bl	but/ler	bll
Burmese	Bmz	butte	bu
burn	Bn	but/ter	b
burned	Bn	but/ter/cup	btcp
burner	Bn	but/ter/fat	btft
burn/ing	Bn₂	but/ter/fly	btfe
bur/nish	BnS	but/ter/milk	btmc
bur/noose	Bns	but/ter/nut	btnt
burn out	Bnou	but/tery	bty
burns	Bns	but/tocks	btcs
burnt	B-	but/ton	btn
burp	Bp	but/ton/hole	btnhl
burr	b	but/tress	bt'
bur/row	Bo	butts	bs
bur/sar	Bs	buxom	bxm
bur/si/tis	Bsls	buy	b

buyer
buy/ers
buy/ing
buzz
buz/zard
by
by/gone
by/law
by/laws
by/pass
by/passes
by/road
by/stander

cab *cb*
cabal *cbal*
cab/a/lis/tic *cblsc*
ca/bana *cbna*
cab/a/ret *cBa*
cab/bage *cbj*
cabin *cbn*
cabi/net *cbnt*
cabi/net/maker *cbntrc*
cabi/nets *cbnts*
cab/ins *cbns*
cable *cb*
ca/ble/gram *cbg*
ca/boose *cbs*
ca/booses *cbss*
cab/rio/let *cBla*
cabs *cbs*
cab/stand *cbs—*
cacao *ccu*
cache *cs*
ca/chet *csa*

cackle *ccl*
ca/copho/nous *ccfnx*
ca/coph/ony *ccfne*
cacti *ccu*
cac/tus *ccx*
cad *cd*
ca/daver *cdv*
ca/dav/er/ous *cdvx*
cad/die *cde*
ca/dence *cd/*
ca/denza *cdnza*
cadet *cdt*
cadge *cj*
cad/mium *cdres (Cd)*
cadre *cDe*
ca/du/ceus *cdsx*
café *cfa*
ca/fe/te/ria *cflya*
caf/feine *cfn*
cage *caj*
ca/hoots *chus*

cam/ou/flage

cais/son	csn
cais/sons	csns
ca/jole	cjl
Cajun	cjn
cake	cc
cakes	ccs
cala/bash	clbs
cala/boose	clbs
ca/lami/tous	clmx
ca/lam/ity	cl)
cal/care/ous	clcx
cal/ci/fi/ca/tion	clsfc/
cal/cify	clsf
cal/ci/mine	clsmn
cal/ci/na/tion	clsn/
cal/cine	clsn
cal/cite	clst
cal/cium	clse (Ca)
cal/cu/late	clcla
cal/cu/lated	clclā
cal/cu/lat/ing	clcla/
cal/cu/la/tion	clcl/
cal/cu/la/tions	clcl/s
cal/cu/la/tor	clcla
cal/cu/la/tors	clcla//
cal/cu/lus	clclx
cal/dron	cldn
cal/en/dar	cl—/
calf	cf
calf/skin	cfscn
cali/ber	clb
cali/brate	clBa
cali/brated	clBā
cali/bra/tor	clBa/
cal/ico	clco
cali/per	clp
ca/liph	clf
cal/is/then/ics	clstncs
calk	cc
call	cl
called	cē
cal/ler	cl
cal/lig/ra/phy	clgfe
cal/ling	cl
cal/los/ity	cls)
cal/lous	clx
cal/low	clo
cal/lus	clx
calm	cm
calmly	cml
calm/ness	cm'
calo/mel	clml
ca/lo/ric	cLc
calo/rie	cly
calo/ries	clys
ca/lum/ni/ate	clmna
ca/lum/nia/tor	clmna/
ca/lum/ni/ous	clmnx
cal/umny	clmne
calves	cvz
calyx	clx
ca/ma/ra/de/rie	cmdy
cam/ber	cmb
cam/bric	cmBc
came	k
camel	cml
ca/mel/lia	cmla
cameo	cmo
cam/era	cma
cam/era/man	cma—
cam/eras	cmas
cami/sole	cmsl
camo/mile	cmml
cam/ou/flage	cmfz

camp
cam/paign
cam/paigns
camp/ers
camp ground
cam/phor
camp/ing
cam/pus
cam/puses
can
Canadian
canal
ca/nal/boat
ca/nal/iza/tion
ca/napé
ca/nard
ca/nary
can/cel
can/cel/la/tion
can/celed
can/cel/ing
can/cer
can/cer/ous
can/de/la/bra
can/de/la/brum
can/did
can/di/dacy
can/di/date
can/di/dates
can/didly
can/did/ness
can/dle
can/dle/light
can/dle/stick
can/dor
candy
cane

ca/nine
can/is/ter
can/is/ters
can/ker
can/ker/ous
can/ner
can/nery
can/ni/bal
can/ni/bal/is/tic
can/ni/est
can/nily
can/ni/ness
can/ning
can/non
can/non/eer
can/not
canny
canoe
canon
ca/noni/cal
can/on/ize
can/opy
can't
can/ta/loupe
can/tan/ker/ous
can/tata
can/teen
can/ter
can/ti/cle
can/ti/le/ver
canto
can/ton
can/ton/ment
can/tor
can/vas
can/vass
can/vass/ing

card/board

can/yon	cyn	cap/tious	cpx
cap	cp	cap/ti/vate	cpva
ca/pa/bili/ties	cpb))	cap/ti/va/tion	cpvy
ca/pa/bil/ity	cpb)	cap/tive	cpv
ca/pa/ble	cpb	cap/tiv/ity	cpv)
ca/pa/bly	cpb	cap/tor	cp
ca/pa/cious	cpx	cap/ture	cpC
ca/pa/cious/ness	cpx '	cap/tured	cpC⁻
ca/paci/ties	cps))	car	cr
ca/paci/tor	cps	ca/rafe	Cf
ca/pac/ity	cps)	cara/mel	Crl
cape	cap	cara/pace	Cps
caper	cp	carat	Cl
cap/il/lary	cply	cara/van	Cvn
capi/tal	cap	cara/van/sary	Cv/y
capi/tal/ism	capz	cara/vel	Cvl
capi/tal/ist	cap,	cara/way	Cwa
capi/tal/iza/tion	capzy	car/bide	Cbd
capi/tal/ize	capz	car/bine	Cbn
capi/tal/ized	capz⁻	car/bo/hy/drate	CbhDa
capi/tal/izes	capzs	car/bolic	Cblc
capi/tol	cap	car/bon	Cbn
ca/pitu/late	cpCla	car/bo/na/ceous	Cbnx
ca/pitu/la/tion	cpCly	car/bon/ate	Cbna
capon	cpn	car/bonic	Cbnc
cap/ping	cp	car/bon/if/er/ous	CbnAr
ca/price	cps	car/bon/ize	Cbnz
ca/pri/cious	csx	Carborundum	CB—
ca/pri/cious/ness	csx '	car/boy	Cby
cap/size	cpsz	car/bun/cle	Cbgl
cap/stan	cpsn	car/bu/retor	CBa
cap/sule	cpsl	car/cass	Cc '
cap/sules	cpsls	car/casses	Cc ''
cap/tain	cpn	car/cino/gen	Csnyn
cap/tains	cpns	car/ci/noma	Cnra
cap/tion	cpy	card	Cd
cap/tioned	cpy⁻	card/board	CdBd

50

cash

card case
car/diac
car/di/gan
car/di/nal
car/dio/graph
care
cared
ca/reen
ca/reer
ca/reers
care/free
care/ful
care/fully
care/ful/ness
care/less
care/less/ness
ca/ress
caret
care/worn
cargo
cari/bou
cari/ca/ture
car/ies
car/il/lon
car/mine
car/nage
car/nal
car/na/tion
car/ne/lian
car/ni/val
car/nivo/rous
carol
car/ols
carom
ca/rotid
ca/rouse
car/pen/ter

car/pen/try
car/pet
car/pet/ing
car/riage
car/rier
car/ri/ers
car/ries
car/rion
car/rot
car/rou/sel
carry
car/ry/all
car/ry/ing
cart
cart/age
carte blanche
car/tel
Cartesian
car/ti/lage
car/ti/lagi/nous
car/to/gra/phic
car/tog/ra/phy
car/ton
car/toned
car/toon
car/toon/ist
car/toons
car/tridge
carve
cas/cade
cas/caded
case
case harden
ca/sein
case/ment
cases
cash

51

cat/tle

cash/book cSbc
cashed cS
ca/shew cSu
cash/ier cSe
cash/ing cS
cash/mere czre
cas/ing cas
ca/sino csno
cask csc
cas/ket cscl
cas/ket/ing cscl
casque csc
cas/se/role cSl
cas/sia cSa
cas/sock csc
cast c,
cas/ta/net csnl
cast/away csava
caste c,
cas/tel/lated cslā
cas/ters cSs
cas/ti/gate csga
cas/ti/ga/tion csgj
cast/ing c,
cas/tle csl
cast/off (noun) csof
cast-off (adj.) csof
cas/trate cSa
ca/sual czul
ca/su/alty czul)
ca/su/ist czu
ca/su/istry czu-Se
cat cl
cata/clysm clcz
cata/comb clco
cata/lepsy cllpse
cata/lep/tic cllpc

cata/log cal
cata/logs cals
ca/taly/sis clss
cata/lytic cllc
cata/ma/ran cl m
cata/pult clpll
cata/ract crc
ca/tas/tro/phe clSfe
ca/tas/tro/phes clSfes
cata/strophic clSfc
catch cC
catch/all cCal
catcher cC
catches cCs
catch/ing cC
catch/word cC rd
cate/chism clcz
cate/chize clcz
cate/gori/cal clgcl
cate/go/ries clgys
cate/gory clgy
cate/go/rize clgz
cater ca
ca/terer cT
ca/ter/ing ca
cat/er/pil/lar clpl
cat/er/waul crval
ca/thar/sis cTas
ca/thar/tic cTc
ca/the/dral clDl
cathe/ter cl
cath/ode cld
catho/lic cllc
Catholicism cllsz
ca/tholi/cize cllsz
cat/nip clnp
cat/tle cll

catty-corner
cat/walk
Caucasian
cau/cus
cau/dal
caught
caul/dron
cau/li/flower
caulk
causal
cau/sa/tion
caus/ative
cause
caused
cau/se/rie
cau/ses
caus/ing
cause/way
caus/tic
cau/teri/za/tion
cau/ter/ize
cau/tery
cau/tion
cau/tion/ary
cau/tioned
cau/tious
cav/al/cade
cava/lier
cav/alry
cavil
cave
cav/ern
cav/ern/ous
cav/iar
cav/ity
ca/vort
cease

ceased
cease/less
ceases
cedar
cede
ceil/ing
ceil/ings
Celanese
cele/brant
cele/brate
cele/brated
cele/brat/ing
cele/bra/tion
cele/bra/tor
ce/leb/ri/ties
ce/leb/rity
ce/ler/ity
cel/ery
ce/les/tial
celi/bacy
celi/bate
cell
cel/lar
cel/lar/ette
cel/list
cel/lo
cel/lo/phane
cel/lu/lar
Celluloid
cel/lu/lose
Celt
ce/ment
ce/men/ta/tion
ceme/tery
ceno/taph
cen/sor
cen/so/ri/ous

chal/lis

cen/sor/ship s/rš
cen/sur/able s/rb
cen/sure sc
cen/sus s/x
cent c
cen/taur s-o
cen/tavo s-vo
cen/te/nary s-ny
cen/ten/nial s-nel
cen/ter s-
cen/ter/piece s-rps
cen/ters s-//
cen/ti/grade s-gd (C)
cen/ti/gram s-g
cen/ti/li/ter s-le
cen/time s-e
cen/ti/me/ter s-re
cen/ti/me/ters s-rell
cen/ti/pede s-pd
cen/tral s-rl
cen/tral/iza/tion s-rlz)
cen/tral/ize s-rlz
cen/tral/ized s-rlz
cen/tral/iz/ing s-rlz
cen/trally s-rl
cen/trifu/gal s-rfgl
cen/tripe/tal s-rptl
cen/tu/ries sCys
cen/tu/rion s-yn
cen/tury sCy
ce/phalic sflc
ce/ramic src
ce/real syl
cere/bral SBl
cere/brate SBa
cere/mo/nial Smel
cere/mo/ni/ous Smx

cere/mony Sme
ce/rise So
cer/tain Stn
cer/tainly Stnl
cer/tainty Stn)
cer/tifi/cate Cerl
cer/tifi/cates Cerls
cer/ti/fi/ca/tion Cerly
cer/ti/fied Cert
cer/tify Cert
cer/ti/fy/ing Cert
cer/ti/tude Sttd
ce/ru/lean Slen
cer/vi/cal Svcl
cer/vix Svr
cess s'
ces/sa/tion ssj
ces/sion sj
cess/pit sspt
cess/pool sspl
chafe Caf
chaff Cf
cha/grin Sgn
cha/grined Sgn
chain Cn
chair Ca
chair/lift Calf
chair/man Can-
chair/men Cam
cha/let Sla
chal/ice Cls
chalk Cc
chal/lenge Clj
chal/lenged Clj
chal/lenges Cljs
chal/leng/ing Clj
chal/lis Cls

cham/ber
cham/ber/lain
cham/ber/maid
cha/me/leon
cham/ois
chamo/mile
champ
cham/pagne
cham/pion
cham/pi/on/ship
chance
chan/cel
chan/cel/lor
chan/cery
chan/ces
chan/de/lier
chan/dler
chan/dlery
change
change/abil/ity
change/able
changed
change/less
change/ling
change over (verb)
change/over (noun)
changes
chang/ing
chan/nel
chan/nels
chan/son
chant
chan/teuse
chaos
cha/otic
chap
cha/peau

chapel
chap/eron
chap/lain
chap/let
chap/ter
chap/ters
char
char/ac/ter
char/ac/ter/is/tic
char/ac/ter/is/tics
char/ac/ter/iza/tion
char/ac/ter/ize
cha/rade
char/coal
charge
charge/able
charged
charge d'af/faires
char/ges
char/ging
char/iot
chari/oteer
chari/is/matic
chari/ta/ble
chari/ties
char/ity
char/la/tan
charm
char/nel
chart
charted
char/ter
char/tered
char/treuse
chart room
char/woman
chary

cir/cum/scrib/ing

Christian *csCn*
Christianity *csCn)*
Christly *csl*
Christmas *Krs*
Christmastide *Krsld*
chro/matic *crlc*
chrome *co*
chro/mium *cre* (*cr*)
chromo *cro*
chro/mo/some *crso*
chronic *cnc*
chroni/cle *cncl*
chro/no/graph *cngf*
chro/no/logi/cal *cnlgcl*
chro/no/logi/cally *cnlgcl*
chro/nol/ogy *cnlge*
chro/nome/ter *cnm*
chro/no/met/ric *cnmtc*
chrysa/lis *csls*
chry/san/the/mum *csnlm*
chryso/lite *csli*
chubby *Cbe*
chuck *Cc*
chuckle *Ccl*
chuk/ker *Cc*
chum *Cn*
chump *Cnp*
chunk *Cq*
church *CrC*
church/goer *CrCg*
church/war/den *CrCrdn*
churl *Crl*
churl/ish *Crls*
churn *Crn*
chute *Su*
chut/ney *Clne*
ci/cada *scde*

ci/ca/trix *sct*
cider *sd*
cigar *sgr*
ciga/rette *sgt*
ciga/rettes *sgts*
cinch *sC*
cin/cho/na *sCna*
cinc/ture *sgC*
cin/der *s*
cin/ema *snra*
cin/na/bar *snbr*
cin/na/mon *snm*
ci/pher *sf*
cir/cle *Scl*
cir/cled *Scl*
cir/cuit *Scl*
cir/cuitous *Sculs*
cir/cuitry *Scute*
cir/cu/lar *Scl*
cir/cu/lar/iza/tion *Scdzj*
cir/cu/lar/ize *Scdz*
cir/cu/late *Scla*
cir/cu/lated *Scla*
cir/cu/lat/ing *Scla*
cir/cu/la/tion *Sclj*
cir/cu/la/tive *Sclv*
cir/cu/la/tor *Scla*
cir/cu/la/tory *Sclly*
cir/cum/cise *Sksz*
cir/cum/ci/sion *Sksj*
cir/cum/fer/ence *Skf/*
cir/cum/flex *Skf*
cir/cum/lo/cu/tion *Sklcj*
cir/cum/navi/gate *Sknvga*
cir/cum/navi/ga/tor *Sknvga*
cir/cum/scribe *SkscB*
cir/cum/scrib/ing *Skscb*

classes

cir/cum/spect	claim
cir/cum/stance	claim/ant
cir/cum/stan/ces	claimed
cir/cum/stan/tial	claim/ing
cir/cum/stan/ti/ate	clair/voy/ance
cir/cum/vent	clair/voy/ant
cir/cum/ven/tion	clam
cir/cus	clam/ber
cir/rho/sis	clam/mi/ness
cir/rus	clammy
cis/tern	clamor
cita/del	clam/or/ing
ci/ta/tion	clam/or/ous
cite	clamp
cit/ies	clan
cit/ing	clan/des/tine
citi/zen	clang
citi/zenry	clan/gor
citi/zen/ship	clank
ci/trate	clan/nish
cit/ric	clap
cit/ron	clap/per
cit/ron/ella	claque
cit/rus	claret
city	clari/fi/ca/tion
city/wide	clari/fied
civet	clari/fies
civic	clari/fy
civil	clari/fy/ing
ci/vil/ian	clari/net
ci/vil/ity	clar/ion
civi/li/za/tion	clar/ity
civi/lize	clash
civi/lized	clasp
civ/illy	class
clack	classed
clad	classes

clock

clas/sic	cleft
clas/si/cal	clem/ency
clas/si/fi/able	clem/ent
clas/si/fi/ca/tion	clench
clas/si/fi/ca/tions	clere/story
clas/si/fied	clergy
clas/sify	cler/gy/man
clas/si/fying	cleric
class/mate	cleri/cal
class/room	clerk
clat/ter	clever
clause	cli/ché
claus/tro/pho/bia	click
clavi/cle	cli/ent
cla/vier	cli/en/tele
claw	cliff
clay	cli/mate
clean	cli/max
cleaned	climb
cleaner	climb/ing
clean/ing	clime
clean/li/ness	clinch
cleanly	cling
cleanse	clinic
cleanup	clini/cal
clear	cli/ni/cian
clear/ance	cli/ni/cians
clearer	clink
clear/est	clip
clear/ing	clip/per
clear/ing/house	clip/ping
clearly	clips
clear/ness	clique
cleat	clo/aca
cleave	cloak
cleaver	cloche
clef	clock

Word	Shorthand	Word	Shorthand
clock/wise		clown	
clod		clown/ish	
clod/hop/per		cloy	
clog		club	
clogged		club/foot	
cloi/sonné		club room	
clois/ter		cluck	
clop		clue	
close (noun, verb)		clump	
close (adj.)		clum/sier	
closed		clum/sily	
closely		clum/si/ness	
close/ness		clumsy	
close out (verb)		clung	
close/out (noun)		clus/ter	
closer		clutch	
closet		clut/ter	
close-up		clut/tered	
clos/ing		coach	
clo/sure		coach/man	
clot		co/ad/ju/tant	
cloth		co/ad/ju/tor	
clothe		co/agu/late	
clothed		co/agu/la/tion	
clothes		coal	
clothes/pin		co/alesce	
cloth/ier		co/ales/cent	
cloth/ing		coal bin	
clo/ture		coal box	
cloud		coal field	
cloud burst		co/ali/tion	
cloud/less		coarse	
cloudy		coarsen	
clout		coarse/ness	
clove		coast	
clo/ven		coastal	
clo/ver		coaster	

coif/fure

coast/line	csli	cod/ify	cdf
coat	co	cod/ing	cd̄
coated	cō	co-ed	cod̄
coat/ing	co̱	co/ef/fi/cient	cefs-
coat/tail	coll	co/erce	cos
co/au/thor	cat	co/er/cion	cOl
coax	cox	co/er/cive	cOsv
co/ax/ial	cxel	co/eval	covl
cob	cb	co/ex/ist	cx,
co/balt	cbll (Co)	cof/fee	cfe
cob/ble	cb	cof/fee/pot	cfepl
co/bra	cBa	cof/fer	cf
cob/web	cbwb	cof/fin	cfn
co/caine	ccn	cog	cg
coc/cyx	ccsx	co/gency	cy/
cochi/neal	cCnel	co/gent	cj-
cock	cc	co/gently	cj-l
cocka/too	cclu	cogi/tate	cgta
cocka/trice	ccto	cogi/ta/tion	cgly
cockle	ccl	co/gnac	cnyc
cock/ney	ccne	cog/nate	cgna
cock/pit	ccpl	cog/ni/tion	cgny
cock/sure	ccsu	cog/ni/zance	cgnz/
cock/tail	ccl	cog/ni/zant	cgnz-
cocoa	cco	cog/no/men	cgnm
co/co/nut	ccnl	cog/wheel	cgwl
co/coon	ccn	co/habit	chbl
cod	cd	co/heir	ca
cod/dle	cdl	co/here	che
code	cd̄	co/her/ence	che/
coded	cd̄	co/her/ent	che-
co/de/fen/dant	cdf— -	co/he/sion	chy
co/deine	cdn	co/he/sive	chsv
codex	cdx	co/hort	cHl
cod/ger	cy	coif	qf
codi/cil	cdsl	coif/feur	qf
codi/fi/ca/tion	cdfcy	coif/fure	qfu

coil
coils
coin
co/in/cide
co/in/ci/dence
co/in/ci/den/tal
co/in/sure
co/ition
coke
col/an/der
cold
colder
cold/est
cold/ness
colic
coli/seum
co/li/tis
col/labo/rate
col/labo/rated
col/labo/rat/ing
col/labo/ra/tion
col/labo/ra/tor
col/lage
col/lapse
col/lapsed
col/laps/ible
col/lar
col/lar/band
col/lar/bone
col/lars
col/late
col/lat/eral
col/lat/ing
col/la/tion
col/league
col/leagues
col/lect

col/lected
col/lect/ible
col/lect/ing
col/lec/tion
col/lec/tive
col/lec/tively
col/lec/tor
col/leen
col/lege
col/leges
col/le/giate
col/lide
col/lid/ing
col/lie
col/lier
col/liery
col/li/sion
col/lo/dion
col/loid
col/lo/quial
col/lo/qui/al/ism
col/lo/quy
col/lu/sion
co/logne
colon
colo/nel (col)
colo/nelcy
co/lo/nial
co/lonic
colo/nist
colo/ni/za/tion
col/on/nade
col/ony
colo/phon
color
col/or/ation
colo/ra/tura

com/mis/er/ate

color-blind	cLbc—	com/fort/ably	kflb
col/ored	cl⁻	com/forter	kf,
col/or/ful	cdf	com/fort/less	kfll'
col/or/ings	cl=	comic	kc
col/or/less	cdl'	comi/cal	kcl
co/los/sal	clsl	com/ing	k
co/los/sus	clsx	comma	ka
colt	coll	com/mand	k—
col/umn	cl	com/man/dant	k— -
co/lum/nar	clm	com/man/deer	k— e
col/um/nist	cl,	com/mander	k—J
coma	cra	com/mand/ing	k—=
coma/tose	crlo	com/mand/ment	k—--
comb	co	com/mando	k—o
com/bat	kbl	com/memo/rate	k ra
com/ba/tant	kbl-	com/memo/rat/ing	k ra
com/bat/ing	kbl	com/memo/ra/tion	k y
com/bat/ive	kbv	com/memo/ra/tive	k w
com/bi/na/tion	kbny	com/mence	k/
com/bine	kbm	com/mence/ment	k/-
com/bined	kbm⁻	com/menc/ing	k/
com/bin/ing	kbm	com/mend	k—
com/bus/ti/ble	kbsb	com/mend/able	k—b
com/bus/tion	kbsCn	com/men/da/tion	k—y
come	k	com/men/da/tory	k— ly
come back (verb)	kbc	com/men/su/ra/ble	k/rb
come/back (noun)	kbc	com/men/su/rate	k/ra
co/me/dian	kden	com/ment	k-
com/edy	kde	com/men/tary	k-y
come/li/ness	kl'	com/men/ta/tor	k-a
comely	kl	com/ment/ing	k-=
co/mes/ti/ble	ksb	com/merce	ko
comet	kl	com/mer/cial	kx
come/up/pance	kp/	com/mer/cial/iza/tion	kxy
com/fit	kfl	com/mer/cially	kx
com/fort	kfl	com/min/gle	kgl
com/fort/able	kflb	com/mis/er/ate	ksa

com/mis/era/tion
com/mis/sar
com/mis/sar/iat
com/mis/sary
com/mis/sion
com/mis/sion/aire
com/mis/sioner
com/mis/sion/ing
com/mit
com/mit/ment
com/mit/tee
com/mode
com/mo/di/ous
com/modi/ties
com/mod/ity
com/mo/dore
com/mon
com/moner
com/monly
com/mon/place
com/mon/wealth
com/mo/tion
com/mu/nal
com/mune
com/mu/ni/ca/ble
com/mu/ni/cant
com/mu/ni/cate
com/mu/ni/cated
com/mu/ni/cat/ing
com/mu/ni/ca/tion
com/mu/ni/ca/tor
com/mu/nion
com/mu/ni/que
com/mu/nism
com/mu/nist
com/mu/ni/ties
com/mu/nity

com/mu/ta/tion
com/mute
com/muted
com/muter
com/pact
com/pa/nies
com/pan/ion
com/pan/ion/able
com/pan/ion/ship
com/pany
com/pa/ra/ble
com/pa/ra/bly
com/para/tive
com/pare
com/pared
com/pari/son
com/part/ment
com/part/men/tal/ize
com/pass
com/pas/sion
com/pas/sion/ate
com/pati/bil/ity
com/pati/ble
com/pa/triot
com/pel
com/pelled
com/pell/ing
com/pen/dium
com/pen/sate
com/pen/sated
com/pen/sa/tion
com/pen/sa/tory
com/pete
com/pe/tence
com/pe/tency
com/pe/tent
com/pet/ing

com/pe/ti/tion
com/peti/tive
com/peti/tively
com/peti/tor
com/pi/la/tion
com/pile
com/piled
com/piler
com/pil/ing
com/pla/cence
com/pla/cency
com/pla/cent
com/plain
com/plain/ant
com/plainer
com/plaint
com/plai/sance
com/ple/ment
com/ple/men/tal
com/ple/ment/ing
com/plete
com/pleted
com/pletely
com/plete/ness
com/plet/ing
com/ple/tion
com/plex
com/plex/ion
com/plexi/ties
com/plex/ity
com/pli/ance
com/pli/ant
com/pli/cate
com/pli/cated
com/pli/ca/tion
com/plic/ity
com/plied

com/pli/ment
com/pli/men/tary
com/pli/ments
com/ply
com/ply/ing
com/po/nent
com/port
com/port/ment
com/pose
com/posed
com/pos/ite
com/po/si/tion
com/posi/tor
com/post
com/po/sure
com/pound
com/pounded
com/pre/hend
com/pre/hen/si/ble
com/pre/hen/sion
com/pre/hen/sive
com/press
com/pressed
com/presses
com/press/ible
com/pres/sion
com/pres/sor
com/prise
com/prised
com/prises
com/pro/mise
comp/troller
com/pul/sion
com/pul/sory
com/punc/tion
com/put/able
com/pu/ta/tion

com/pute	con/cili/ate
com/puted	con/cili/a/tion
com/puter	con/cili/atory
com/put/ing	con/cise
com/rade	con/clave
con	con/clude
con/cate/na/tion	con/clu/sion
con/cave	con/clu/sive
con/cav/ity	con/clu/sively
con/ceal	con/coct
con/cealed	con/coc/tion
con/cede	con/comi/tant
con/ceit	con/cord
con/ceited	con/cor/dance
con/ceiv/able	con/cor/dant
con/ceiv/ably	con/cor/dat
con/ceive	con/course
con/ceived	con/crete
con/cen/trate	con/cretely
con/cen/trated	con/cu/bine
con/cen/trat/ing	con/cur
con/cen/tra/tion	con/cur/rence
con/cen/tra/tor	con/cur/rent
con/cen/tric	con/cus/sion
con/cept	con/demn
con/cep/tion	con/dem/na/tion
con/cern	con/dem/na/tory
con/cerned	con/den/sa/tion
con/cern/ing	con/dense
con/cert	con/densed
con/certed	con/denser
con/cer/tina	con/dens/ing
con/certo	con/de/scend
con/ces/sion	con/de/scend/ing
con/ces/sion/aire	con/de/scend/ing
conch	con/de/scen/sion
con/cierge	con/dign

con/geal

con/di/ment
con/di/tion
con/di/tional
con/di/tion/ing
con/dole
con/do/lence
con/do/min/ium
con/done
con/dor
con/duce
con/du/cive
con/duct
con/duc/tion
con/duc/tor
con/duit
con/duits
cone
con/fabu/la/tion
con/fec/tion
con/fec/tioner
con/fec/tion/ery
con/fed/er/acy
con/fed/er/ate
con/fed/er/ation
con/fer
con/feree
con/fer/ence
con/fer/ences
con/ferred
con/fess
con/fes/sion
con/fes/sor
con/fetti
con/fide
con/fi/dence
con/fident
con/fi/den/tial

con/fi/den/ti/al/ity
con/fi/den/tially
con/figu/ra/tion
con/fine
con/fined
con/fine/ment
con/firm
con/fir/ma/tion
con/firm/a/tive
con/firmed
con/firm/ing
con/fis/cate
con/fis/ca/tion
con/fla/gra/tion
con/flict
con/flict/ing
con/flic/tion
con/flu/ence
con/flu/ent
con/form
con/for/mance
con/for/ma/tion
con/form/ist
con/for/mity
con/found
con/frere
con/front
con/fronted
con/front/ing
con/fuse
con/fused
con/fusedly
con/fus/ing
con/fu/sion
con/fu/ta/tion
con/fute
con/geal

68

con/ge/nial
con/ge/nial/ity
con/geni/tal
con/ge/ries
con/gest
con/ges/tion
con/ges/tive
con/glom/er/ate
con/glom/era/tion
con/gratu/late
con/gratu/lated
con/gratu/lat/ing
con/gratu/la/tion
con/gratu/la/tory
con/gre/gate
con/gre/ga/tion
con/gress
con/gres/sio/nal
con/gress/man
con/gress/men
con/gru/ent
con/gru/ity
con/gru/ous
conic
coni/cal
co/ni/fer
co/nif/er/ous
con/jec/tural
con/jec/ture
con/join
con/jugal
con/ju/gate
con/ju/ga/tion
con/junc/tion
con/junc/tiva
con/junc/ture
con/jure

con/jurer
con/nect
con/nected
con/nect/ing
con/nec/tion
con/nec/tive
con/nec/tor
con/nip/tion
con/niv/ance
con/nive
con/nois/seur
con/no/ta/tion
con/no/ta/tive
con/note
con/nu/bial
con/quer
con/quered
con/queror
con/quest
con/san/guine/ous
con/san/guin/ity
con/science
con/sci/en/tious
con/sci/en/tiously
con/scious
con/scious/ness
con/script
con/scrip/tion
con/se/crate
con/se/cra/tion
con/secu/tive
con/secu/tively
con/sen/sus
con/sent
con/se/quence
con/se/quences
con/se/quent

con/sult/ing

con/se/quen/tial
con/se/quently
con/ser/va/tion
con/ser/va/tive
con/ser/va/tory
con/serve
con/serv/ing
con/sider
con/sid/er/able
con/sid/er/a/bly
con/sid/er/ate
con/sid/er/ation
con/sid/ered
con/sid/er/ing
con/sign
con/signee
con/sign/ees
con/sign/ment
con/signor
con/sist
con/sisted
con/sis/tency
con/sis/tent
con/sis/tently
con/so/la/tion
con/so/la/tory
con/sole
con/sol/i/date
con/sol/i/dated
con/sol/i/da/tion
con/somme
con/so/nance
con/so/nant
con/sort
con/sor/tium
con/spec/tus
con/spic/u/ous

con/spic/u/ously
con/spir/acy
con/spir/a/tor
con/spire
con/sta/ble
con/stab/u/lary
con/stancy
con/stant
con/stantly
con/stel/la/tion
con/ster/na/tion
con/sti/pate
con/sti/pa/tion
con/stit/u/ency
con/stit/u/ent
con/sti/tute
con/sti/tu/tion
con/sti/tu/tional
con/sti/tu/tion/ally
con/strain
con/straint
con/strict
con/stric/tion
con/stric/tor
con/struct
con/struc/tion
con/struc/tive
con/strue
con/strued
con/sul
consul/ar
con/sul/ate
con/sult
con/sul/tant
con/sul/ta/tion
con/sulted
con/sult/ing

con/sume
con/sumed
con/sumer
con/sum/mate
con/sum/mated
con/sum/ma/tion
con/sump/tion
con/sump/tive
con/tact
con/tacted
con/tact/ing
con/ta/gion
con/ta/gious
con/tain
con/tained
con/tainer
con/tain/ing
con/tami/nant
con/tami/nate
con/tami/nated
con/tami/na/tion
con/temn
con/tem/plate
con/tem/plated
con/tem/plat/ing
con/tem/pla/tion
con/tem/po/ra/ne/ous
con/tem/po/raries
con/tem/po/rary
con/tempt
con/tempt/ible
con/temp/tu/ous
con/tend
con/tent
con/ten/tion
con/ten/tious
con/tent/ment

con/ter/mi/nous
con/test
con/tes/tant
con/tested
con/text
con/tex/ture
con/ti/gu/ity
con/tigu/ous
con/ti/nence
con/ti/nent
con/ti/nen/tal
con/tin/gency
con/tin/gent
con/tin/ual
con/tinu/ally
con/tinu/ance
con/tinu/ation
con/tinue
con/tin/ued
con/tinu/ing
con/ti/nu/ity
con/tinu/ous
con/tinu/ously
con/tinuum
con/tort
con/tor/tion
con/tor/tion/ist
con/tour
con/tra/band
con/tra/cep/tion
con/tract
con/trac/tile
con/tract/ing
con/trac/tion
con/trac/tor
con/trac/tual
con/tra/dict

con/vince

- con/tra/dic/tion
- con/tra/dic/tory
- con/tralto
- con/trap/tion
- con/tra/ri/ety
- con/trari/ness
- con/trari/wise
- con/trary
- con/trast
- con/tra/vene
- con/tra/ven/tion
- con/tre/temps
- con/trib/ute
- con/trib/uted
- con/trib/ut/ing
- con/tri/bu/tion
- con/tri/bu/tions
- con/tribu/tor
- con/tribu/tors
- con/tribu/tory
- con/trite
- con/tri/tion
- con/triv/ance
- con/trive
- con/trol
- con/trolled
- con/trol/ler
- con/troll/ing
- con/tro/ver/sial
- con/tro/versy
- con/tro/vert
- con/tu/ma/cious
- con/tu/mely
- con/tuse
- con/tu/sion
- co/nun/drum
- con/va/lesce
- con/va/les/cence
- con/va/les/cent
- con/va/lesc/ing
- con/vec/tion
- con/vec/tor
- con/vene
- con/ve/nience
- con/ve/nient
- con/ve/niently
- con/ven/ing
- con/vent
- con/ven/ti/cle
- con/ven/tion
- con/ven/tional
- con/ven/tion/al/ity
- con/ven/tion/eer
- con/verge
- con/ver/gence
- con/ver/sant
- con/ver/sa/tion
- con/ver/sa/tional
- con/ver/sa/tion/al/ist
- con/verse
- con/ver/sion
- con/vert
- con/verted
- con/vert/ers
- con/vert/ible
- con/vert/ing
- con/vex
- con/vey
- con/vey/ance
- con/veyed
- con/veyor
- con/vict
- con/vic/tion
- con/vince

con/vinc/ing
con/vinc/ingly
con/viv/ial
con/vivi/al/ity
con/vo/ca/tion
con/voke
con/vo/lu/tion
con/voy
con/vulse
con/vul/sion
con/vul/sive
cook
cook/ery
cook/ies
cooky
cool
cool/ant
cooler
cool/est
coo/lie
coolly
cool/ness
coop
co-op
coo/per
co/op/er/ate
co/op/er/ated
co/op/er/ates
co/op/er/at/ing
co/op/er/ation
co/op/era/tive
co/op/era/tively
co-opt
co/or/di/nate
co/or/di/nated
co/or/di/nat/ing
co/or/di/na/tion

co/or/di/na/tor
cope
coped
co/pi/ous
cop/per
cop/per/head
cop/per/plate
cop/pice
co/pra
copse
cop/ula
copu/la/tive
copy
copy/book
copy/holder
copy/ing
copy/ist
copy/right
copy/righted
co/quetry
co/quette
coral
cord
cord/age
cor/dial
cor/dial/ity
cor/dially
cor/don
cor/du/roy
core
co/re/spon/dent
cork
cork/screw
cor/mo/rant
corn
corn/cob
cor/nea

cos/mo/poli/tan

cor/ner	cor/re/la/tion
cor/nered	cor/rel/a/tive
cor/ner/stone	cor/re/spond
cor/ner/wise	cor/re/sponded
cor/net	cor/re/spon/dence
corn/field	cor/re/spon/dent
cor/nice	cor/re/spond/ing
corn/stalk	cor/re/spond/ingly
corn/starch	cor/ri/dor
cor/nu/co/pia	cor/ri/dors
co/rolla	cor/robo/rate
cor/ol/lary	cor/robo/ra/tion
co/rona	cor/rode
cor/onary	cor/ro/sion
coro/na/tion	cor/ro/sive
coro/ner	cor/ru/gate
coro/net	cor/ru/gated
cor/po/ral	cor/ru/ga/tion
cor/po/rate	cor/rupt
cor/por/ra/tion	cor/rupt/ible
cor/po/real	cor/rup/tion
corps	cor/sage
corpse	cor/sair
cor/pu/lence	cor/set
cor/pu/lent	cor/tege
cor/pus	cor/tex
cor/pus/cle	cor/ti/sone
cor/ral	cor/us/cate
cor/rect	cor/us/ca/tion
cor/rected	cor/vette
cor/rect/ing	co/sine
cor/rec/tion	cos/metic
cor/rec/tional	cos/met/ics
cor/rec/tive	cos/me/tolo/gist
cor/rectly	cos/mic
cor/re/late	cos/mol/ogy
cor/re/lat/ing	cos/mo/poli/tan

cos/mopo/lite
cos/mos
cost
cost/ing
costly
cos/tume
cos/tumer
cot
co/te/rie
cot/tage
cot/tages
cot/ton
cot/tons
couch
cou/gar
cough
could
couldn't
coun/cil
coun/cil/man
coun/sel
coun/sel/ing
coun/selor
count
count/down
coun/te/nance
counter
coun/ter/act
coun/ter/bal/ance
coun/ter/claim
coun/ter/feit
coun/ter/feiter
coun/ter/ir/ri/tant
coun/ter/mand
coun/ter/pane
coun/ter/part
coun/ter/point

coun/ter/sign
coun/ter/sue
count/ess
coun/ties
count/ing
count/less
coun/tries
coun/try
coun/try/side
county
coup
coup d'etat
coupe
cou/ple
cou/pled
cou/pler
cou/plet
cou/pon
cour/age
cou/ra/geous
cou/ra/geously
cou/rier
course
court
cour/te/ous
cour/te/ously
cour/te/san
cour/te/sies
cour/tesy
court/house
court/ier
court/room
court/ship
cousin
cove
cove/nant
cover

cover

75

cre/ative

cov/er/age
cov/er/all
cov/er/ing
cov/er/let
co/vert
covet
cov/et/ous
covey
cow
cow/ard
cow/ard/ice
cow/bo
cower
cowl
cowl/ing
co-worker
cox/comb
cox/swain
coy
coy/ote
coy/otes
cozen
cozy
crab
crab apple
crack
cracked
cracker
crackle
crack/pot
cra/dle
craft
crafts/man
crafts/man/ship
crafty
crag
cram

cramp
cramped
cran/berry
crane
cra/nial
cra/nium
crank
cranki/ness
cranky
cranny
crash
crass
crate
cra/ter
crat/ing
cra/vat
crave
cra/ven
crawl
cray/fish
crayon
craze
cra/zily
cra/zi/ness
crazy
creak
cream
creamer
cream/ery
creamy
crease
creased
creases
cre/ate
cre/at/ing
cre/ation
cre/ative

76

cre/atively	crewel
cre/ativ/ity	crib
cre/ator	crib/bage
crea/ture	cricket
cre/dence	crime
cre/den/tial	crimi/nal
credi/bil/ity	crimi/nally
credi/ble	crimi/nol/ogy
credit	crimp
cred/it/able	crim/son
cred/ited	cringe
cred/it/ing	crin/kle
credi/tor	crino/line
credo	crip/ple
cre/du/lity	cri/ses
credu/lous	cri/sis
creed	crisp
creek	criss/cross
creel	cri/te/ria
creep	cri/te/rion
cre/mate	critic
cre/ma/tory	criti/cal
Creole	criti/cally
creo/sote	criti/cize
crepe	criti/cized
crept	cri/tique
cre/pus/cu/lar	croak
cre/scendo	cro/chet
cres/cent	crock
cress	crock/ery
crest	croco/dile
crest/fallen	cro/cus
cre/ta/ceous	crone
cre/tonne	crony
cre/vasse	crook
crev/ice	croon
crew	crooner

cue

crop cp
crop/per cp
crop/ping cp
cro/quet cca
cross c'
crosses c"
cross/ing c'
cross/over csO
cross/ques/tion csq
cross/road csrd
cross/walk csw
cross/word cswd
crotch cC
crotch/ety cC)
crouch cuC
croup cup
crou/pier cpe
crou/ton ctn
crow co
crow/bar cobr
crowd cwd
crowded cwd
crown cwn
cru/cial cx
cru/ci/ble csb
cru/ci/fix csfx
cru/ci/fix/ion csfxy
cru/cify csf
crude cd
crudely cdl
cru/dity cd)
cruel cul
cru/elly cul
cru/elty cul)
cruet cul
cruise cz
cruiser cz

crul/ler cl
crumb c
crum/ble crb
crum/pet cpt
crum/ple crp
crunch cC
cru/sade csd
cru/sad/ers csd//
crush cS
crust c,
crus/ta/cean csy
crutch cC
crutches cCs
crux cx
cry cu
cry/ing cu
crypt cp
cryp/tic cpc
cryp/to/gram cpg
cryp/tog/ra/phy cpgfe
crys/tal csl
crys/tal/line csln
crys/tal/lize cslz
cub cb
cub/by/hole cbhl
cube cub
cubic cbc
cu/bi/cle cbcl
cub/ist cb,
cu/bit cbt
cuck/old ccol
cuckoo ccu
cu/cum/ber ckb
cud cd
cud/dle cdl
cud/gel cgl
cue cu

cuff	cf	cu/ra/tor	Ca
cuffed	cf̄	curb	Cb
cui/sine	gzn	curb/line	Cbli
cul-de-sac	cldsc	curb/stone	Cbsn
cu/li/nary	clny	curd	Cd
cull	cl	cur/dle	Cdl
cul/mi/nate	clma	cure	cu
cul/mi/na/tion	clmy	cu/rette	cul
cul/pa/bil/ity	clpb)	cur/few	Cfu
cul/pa/ble	clpb	cur/ing	cu̱
cul/prit	cept	cu/rio	cyo
cult	clt	cu/ri/osi/ties	cys))
cul/ti/vate	cltva	cu/ri/os/ity	cys)
cul/ti/va/tion	cltvy	cu/ri/ous	cyx
cul/ti/va/tor	cltva	curl	Cl
cul/tur/al	clCrl	curli/cue	Clcu
cul/tur/ally	clCrl	curly	Cl
cul/ture	clC	cur/rent	C-
cul/vert	clVt	cur/rently	C-l
cum/ber/some	kBsn	cur/rency	C/
cum/brous	kBx	cur/ricu/lum	Ccl
cum/mer/bund	Kb—	curry	cy
cu/mu/la/tion	crly	cur/ry/comb	cyco
cu/mu/la/tive	crlv	curse	Cs
cu/mu/lus	crlx	cur/sive	Csv
cu/nei/form	cnf	cur/sory	Csy
cun/ningly	cnl	curt	Ct
cup	cp	cur/tail	Ctl
cup/bearer	cpba	cur/tain	Ctn
cup/board	cBd	curtsy	Ctse
cup/ful	cpf	cur/va/ture	CvC
Cupid	cpd	curve	Cv
cu/pid/ity	cpd)	curved	Cv̄
cu/pola	cpla	cur/vi/lin/ear	Cvlne
cur	c	cush/ion	Cy
cur/able	cub	cush/ioned	cȳ
cu/rate	Ca	cusp	CS

cus/pi/dor
cus/tard
cus/to/dial
cus/to/dian
cus/tody
cus/tom
cus/tom/ar/ily
cus/tom/ary
cus/tomer
cut
cut-and-dried
cute
cu/ti/cle
cut/lass
cut/lery
cut/let
cut off (verb)
cut/off (noun)
cut out (verb)
cut/out (noun)
cut/ter
cut/throat
cut/ting
cy/ana/mide
cy/anic
cya/nide
cy/ano/gen
cya/no/sis
cycle
cy/clome/ter
cy/clone
cy/clo/rama
cy/clo/tron
cyl/in/der
cy/lin/dri/cal
cym/bal
cynic
cyni/cal
cyni/cism
cy/no/sure
cy/press
cyst
cys/tic
cys/toid
cy/tol/ogy
czar
cza/rina
Czech

D

dab	daisy
dab/ble	dale
dachs/hund	dal/li/ance
Dacron	dally
dac/tyl	dam
dad	dam/age
daddy	dam/age/able
dado	dam/aged
daf/fo/dil	dam/ages
daft	dam/ag/ing
dag/ger	dama/scene
da/guerreo/type	dam/ask
dahlia	dame
dai/lies	damn
daily	dam/na/ble
dain/tily	dam/na/tion
dain/ti/ness	damp
dainty	dampen
dairy	damper
dairy/man	dam/sel
dais	dance

deaf/ness

dancer	dV	date/line	dale
dan/de/lion	d— len	dat/ing	da̅
dan/der	d—/	datum	dt̅
dan/dle	d—l	daub	db
dan/druff	d—rf	daugh/ter	d
dandy	d—e	daughter-in-law	dṉla
Dane	dn	daunt	d-
dan/ger	dj	daunt/less	d-l'
dan/ger/ous	dJr	dau/phin	dfn
dan/ger/ously	dJr	dav/en/port	dvnsl
dan/gers	dj//	davit	dvl
dan/gle	dgl	daw/dle	ddl
dank	dg	dawn	dn
dan/seuse	dnsz	day	d
dap/per	dp	day/break	dBc
dap/ple	dp	day/dream	dDe
dare	da	day/light	dli
dare/devil	dadvl	day/light sav/ing time	dli sv li
dar/ing	da̅	day/time	dli (DST)
dark	Dc	daze	dz
darken	Dcn	daz/zle	dzl
dark/en/ing	Dcn̲	daz/zling	dzl̲
darker	Dc⁄	dea/con	dcn
dark/est	Dc,	de/ac/ti/vate	dacva
dark/ness	Dc'	dead	dd
dark/room	Dcr	dead/beat	ddbe
dar/ling	Dlg	deaden	ddn
darn	Dn	dead/head	ddhd
darned	Dn̅	dead/line	ddli
dart	Dl	dead/li/ness	ddl'
dash	dS	dead/lock	ddlc
dash/board	dSBd	deadly	ddl
das/tard	dSd	dead/weight	ddwa
das/tardly	dSdl	dead/wood	ddwd
data	dla	deaf	df
date	da	deafen	dfn
dated	da̅	deaf/ness	df'

deal
dealer
deal/er/ship
deal/ing
dealt
dean
dear
dearer
dearly
dearth
death
death/bed
death/blow
death/less
death/like
deathly
death/watch
de/ba/cle
debar
de/bark
de/bar/ka/tion
de/base
de/bat/able
de/bate
de/bauch
de/bauch/ery
de/ben/ture
de/bili/tate
de/bil/ity
debit
debo/nair
de/bris
debt
debtor
debug
de/bunk
debut

debu/tante
de/cade
de/ca/dence
de/ca/dent
de/cal/co/ma/nia
deca/logue
de/camp
de/cant
de/canter
de/capi/tate
de/cath/lon
decay
de/cease
de/ceased
de/ce/dent
de/ceit
de/ceit/ful
de/ceiv/able
de/ceive
de/ceiver
de/cel/er/ate
December
de/cency
de/cent
de/cen/tral/ize
de/cen/tral/ized
de/cep/tion
de/cep/tive
deci/bel
de/cide
de/cided
de/cid/edly
de/cid/ing
de/cidu/lous
deci/mal
deci/mate
de/ci/pher

def/er/ence

de/ci/sion	dsy	dedi/cate	ddca
de/ci/sive	dssv	dedi/ca/tion	ddcy
deck	dc	de/duce	dds
de/claim	dca	de/duc/ible	ddsb
de/claimer	dca/	de/duct	ddc
de/clar/able	dcb	de/ducted	ddc̄
dec/la/ra/tion	dcy	de/duct/ible	ddcb
de/clara/tive	dcv	de/duct/ing	ddc̱
de/clara/tory	dcly	de/duc/tion	ddcy
de/clare	dec	deed	dd
de/clar/ing	dec̱	deem	de
de/clen/sion	dcy	deemed	dē
de/clin/able	dcnb	deep	dep
dec/li/na/tion	dcny	deeper	dp
de/cline	dcn	deep/est	dp,
de/clin/ing	dcṉ	deeply	dpl
de/cliv/ity	dcv)	deer	de
de/code	dcd	de/face	dfs
dé/col/leté	dclla	de facto	dfco
de/com/pose	dkpz	de/fal/cate	dflca
de/com/po/si/tion	dkpzy	de/fal/ca/tion	dflcy
de/com/pres/sion	dkcy	defa/ma/tion	dfy
de/con/tami/nate	dklma	de/fame	dfa
decor	dco	de/fault	dfll
deco/rate	dCa	de/fea/si/ble	dfzb
deco/rat/ing	dCa̱	de/feat	dfe
deco/ra/tion	dCy	de/feated	dfē
deco/ra/tor	dCa/	de/fect	dfc
de/co/rous	dCx	de/fec/tive	dfcv
de/co/rum	dC	de/fec/tor	dfc/
decoy	dcy	de/fend	df—
de/crease	dCs	de/fen/dant	df——
de/creas/ing	dCs̱	de/fender	df—/
de/cree	dCe	de/fense	df/
de/crepit	dCpl	de/fen/sive	df/v
decry	dCc	defer	df
de/cum/bent	dkb-	def/er/ence	dfl

def/er/en/tial
de/fer/ment
de/fi/ance
de/fi/ant
de/fi/ciency
de/fi/cient
defi/cit
de/file
de/file/ment
de/fin/able
de/fine
de/fined
de/fin/ing
defi/nite
defi/nitely
defi/ni/tion
de/fini/tive
de/flate
de/fla/tion
de/flect
de/flec/tion
de/form
de/for/mity
de/fraud
de/fray
de/funct
defy
de/gen/er/acy
de/gen/er/ate
de/gen/er/ation
deg/ra/da/tion
de/grade
de/gree
de/hy/drate
deice
de/icer
deify

deign
de/ities
deity
de/jec/tion
de/jure
de/lay
de/lec/ta/ble
dele/gate
dele/ga/tion
de/lete
de/leted
dele/te/ri/ous
de/le/tion
delft
de/lib/er/ate
de/lib/era/tion
deli/cacy
deli/cate
deli/ca/tes/sen
de/li/cious
de/light
de/light/ful
de/lin/eate
de/lin/eated
de/line/ation
de/line/ator
de/lin/quen/cies
de/lin/quency
de/lin/quent
de/liri/ous
de/lir/ium
de/liver
de/liv/er/ance
de/liv/eries
de/liv/er/ing
de/liv/ery
dell

de/part/men/tal

delta
de/lude
del/uge
de/lu/sion
de/luxe
delve
de/mag/ne/tize
dema/gogue
de/mand
de/mand/ing
de/mar/cate
de/mar/ca/tion
de/mean
de/mea/nor
de/ment
de/men/tia
de/merit
demi/god
demi/john
de/mise
demi/tasse
de/mo/bi/lize
de/moc/racy
demo/crat
demo/cratic
de/mog/ra/pher
de/mol/ish
demo/li/tion
demon
de/mone/tize
de/mo/naic
de/monic
dem/on/strate
dem/on/strated
dem/on/stra/tion
de/mon/stra/tive
dem/on/stra/tor

de/mor/al/ize
de/mote
de/mot/ing
demur
de/mure
de/mur/rage
de/mur/rer
den
de/nial
de/nied
de/nier
deni/grate
denim
deni/zen
de/nomi/na/tion
de/nomi/na/tor
de/note
de/noue/ment
de/nounce
dense
den/sity
dent
den/tal
den/ti/frice
den/tist
den/tistry
den/ture
de/nude
de/nun/ci/ate
de/nun/cia/tion
de/nun/cia/tory
deny
de/odor/ant
de/odor/izes
de/part
de/part/ment
de/part/men/tal

de/scry

de/par/ture
de/pend
de/pend/abil/ity
de/pend/able
de/pend/ent
de/pend/ing
de/pict
de/pict/ing
de/pic/tion
de/pila/tory
de/plete
de/ple/tion
de/plor/able
de/plore
de/ploy
de/po/nent
de/popu/late
de/popu/la/tion
de/port
de/por/ta/tion
de/port/ment
de/pose
de/posit
de/pos/it/ing
de/po/si/tion
de/posi/tor
de/posi/tory
depot
de/prave
de/prav/ity
dep/re/cate
dep/re/ca/tory
de/pre/ci/ate
de/pre/ci/at/ing
de/pre/cia/tion
dep/re/da/tion
de/press

de/pres/sant
de/pres/sion
de/pri/va/tion
de/prive
de/priv/ing
depth
depu/ta/tion
de/pute
depu/tize
dep/uty
de/rail
de/range
derby
dere/lict
dere/lic/tion
de/ride
de/ri/sion
de/ri/sive
deri/va/tion
de/riva/tive
de/rive
der/ma/tol/ogy
dero/gate
de/roga/tory
der/rick
der/vish
de/salt/ing
des/cant
de/scend
de/scen/dant
de/scend/ing
de/scent
de/scribe
de/scrib/ing
de/scrip/tion
de/scrip/tive
de/scry

de/ter/mi/na/tion

dese/crate	dsCa	de/spond/ent	ds— —
dese/cra/tion	dsCy	des/pot	dsl
de/seg/re/gate	dsgga	des/potic	dslc
des/ert	dzl	des/po/tism	dsly
de/serter	dz	des/sert	dzl
de/ser/tion	dzy	des/ti/na/tion	dsny
de/serve	dzv	des/tine	dsn
de/serv/ing	dzv_	des/tined	dsn̄
des/ic/cant	dsc-	des/ti/nies	dsnes
des/ic/cate	dsca	des/tiny	dsne
des/ic/ca/tion	dscy	des/ti/tute	dslu
de/sid/er/ata	dsDla	des/ti/tu/tion	dsly
de/sid/er/atum	dsDl	de/stroy	dSy
de/sign	dzın	de/stroyer	dSy
des/ig/nate	dzgna	de/struct	dSc
des/ig/nated	dzgnā	de/struc/tion	dScy
des/ig/na/tion	dzgny	de/struc/tive	dScv
de/signer	dzın	de/struc/tor	dSc
de/sign/ing	dzın	des/ul/tory	dslly
de/sir/abil/ity	dzıb)	de/tach	dlC
de/sir/able	dzıb	de/tach/ment	dlC-
de/sire	dzı	de/tail	dll
de/sir/ous	dzıx	de/tail/ing	dll_
de/sist	dz,	de/tain	dln
desk	dsc	de/tect	dlc
deso/late	dsll	de/tect/ing	dlc_
deso/la/tion	dsly	de/tec/tion	dlcy
de/spair	dsa	de/tec/tive	dlcv
de/spair/ing	dsa_	de/tec/tor	dlc
des/per/ado	dSdo	de/ten/tion	dly
des/per/ate	dSl	deter	de
des/per/ation	dSy	de/ter/gent	dT-
de/spi/ca/ble	dscb	de/te/rio/rate	dtlja
de/spise	dsz	de/te/rio/rat/ing	dtlja̱
de/spite	dsı	de/te/rio/ra/tion	dtly
de/spoil	dsyl	de/ter/min/able	d⌐mb
de/spond	ds—	de/ter/mi/na/tion	d⌐my

de/ter/mine
de/ter/min/ing
de/ter/rent
de/test
de/test/able
de/tes/ta/tion
de/throne
deti/nue
deto/nate
deto/na/tion
deto/na/tor
de/tour
de/tract
de/trac/tion
det/ri/ment
det/ri/men/tal
deuce
dev/as/tate
dev/as/ta/tion
de/velop
de/vel/oper
de/vel/op/ing
de/vel/op/ment
de/vel/op/men/tal
de/vi/ant
de/vi/ate
de/via/tion
de/vice
devil
dev/il/ish
dev/il/ment
de/vi/ous
de/vise
de/vi/tal/ize
de/void
de/volve
de/vote

devo/tee
de/vo/tion
de/vour
de/vout
dew
dewy
dex/ter/ity
dex/ter/ous
dex/trose
dhow
dia/be/tes
dia/betic
dia/ble/rie
dia/bolic
dia/boli/cal
dia/criti/cal
dia/dem
di/ag/nose
di/ag/nos/ing
di/ag/no/sis
di/ag/nos/tic
di/ag/nos/ti/cian
di/ago/nal
dia/gram
dia/gram/matic
dial
dia/lect
di/al/ing
di/ame/ter
dia/met/ric
dia/met/ri/cally
dia/mond
dia/per
di/apha/nous
dia/phragm
di/ar/rhea
dia/ries

di/lu/tion

diary
dia/thermy
dia/tonic
dia/tribe
dice
di/chot/omy
dicker
dicta
Dictaphone
dic/tate
dic/ta/tion
dic/ta/tor
dic/ta/to/rial
dic/ta/tor/ship
dic/tion
dic/tio/nar/ies
dic/tio/nary
dic/tum
did
di/dac/tic
didn't
die
di/elec/tric
diemaker
die/sel
diet
di/etary
di/etetic
di/eti/tian
dif/fer
dif/fer/ence
dif/fer/ences
dif/fer/ent
dif/fer/en/ti/ate
dif/fer/ently
dif/fi/cult
dif/fi/cul/ties

dif/fi/culty
dif/fi/dence
dif/fi/dent
dif/frac/tion
dif/fuse
dif/fus/ers
dif/fu/sion
dig
di/gest
di/gest/ible
di/ges/tion
dig/ger
dig/ging
digit
digi/tal
digi/talis
dig/nify
dig/ni/tary
dig/nity
di/gress
di/gres/sion
di/gres/sive
dike
di/lapi/date
di/lapi/dated
di/lapi/da/tion
di/late
di/la/tion
dila/tory
di/lemma
dil/et/tante
dili/gence
dili/gent
dili/gently
dil/ly/dally
di/lute
di/lu/tion

dim
dime
di/men/sion
di/min/ish
dimi/nu/tion
di/minu/tive
di/minu/tively
dim/ity
dimly
dim/mer
dim/ple
din
dine
diner
dingy
din/gus
din/ing
din/ner
di/no/saur
dint
dio/cese
diode
di/ox/ide
dip
diph/the/ria
diph/thong
di/plex
di/ploma
di/plo/macy
dip/lo/mat
dip/lo/matic
dip/per
dire
di/rect
di/rect/ing
di/rec/tion
di/rec/tive

di/rectly
di/rec/tor
di/rec/to/ries
di/rec/tory
dire/ful
dirge
diri/gi/ble
dirt
dirti/ness
dirty
dis/abili/ties
dis/abil/ity
dis/able
dis/abling
dis/abuse
dis/ad/van/tage
dis/ad/van/taged
dis/ad/van/tages
dis/af/fect
dis/agree
dis/al/low
dis/ap/pear
dis/ap/pear/ance
dis/ap/pear/ing
dis/ap/point
dis/ap/point/ing
dis/ap/point/ment
dis/ap/pro/ba/tion
dis/ap/prove
dis/arm
dis/ar/range
dis/ar/ray
dis/as/sem/ble
dis/as/sem/bly
dis/as/so/ci/ate
di/sas/ter
di/sas/trous

dis/avow
dis/band
disbar
dis/be/lief
dis/be/lieve
dis/burse
dis/burse/ment
dis/burs/ing
disc
dis/card
dis/card/ing
dis/cern
dis/cern/ible
dis/cern/ment
dis/charge
dis/charg/ing
dis/ci/ple
dis/ci/plin/ary
dis/ci/pline
dis/claim
dis/claimer
dis/close
dis/clos/ing
dis/clo/sure
dis/color
dis/com/bobu/late
dis/com/fit
dis/com/fi/ture
dis/com/fort
dis/com/mode
dis/com/pose
dis/com/po/sure
dis/con/cert
dis/con/nect
dis/con/so/late
dis/con/tent
dis/con/tinu/ance

dis/con/tinue
dis/cord
dis/co/theque
dis/count
dis/cour/age
dis/course
dis/cour/te/ous
dis/cover
dis/cov/erer
dis/cov/eries
dis/cov/er/ing
dis/cov/ery
dis/credit
dis/creet
dis/creetly
dis/crep/an/cies
dis/crep/ancy
dis/cre/tion
dis/crimi/nate
dis/crimi/nat/ing
dis/crimi/na/tion
dis/cur/sive
dis/cuss
dis/cussed
dis/cuss/ing
dis/cus/sion
dis/dain
dis/ease
dis/em/bark
dis/em/body
dis/en/chant
dis/en/cum/ber
dis/en/gage
dis/en/tan/gle
dis/es/teem
dis/fa/vor
dis/fig/ure

dis/fran/chise
dis/gorge
dis/grace
dis/grace/ful
dis/grun/tle
dis/guise
dis/gust
dish
dis/ha/bille
dis/heart/en
di/shevel
dis/hon/est
dis/hon/or
dish/washer
dis/il/lu/sion
dis/in/cli/na/tion
dis/in/fect
dis/in/genu/ous
dis/in/herit
dis/in/te/grate
dis/in/ter
dis/in/ter/ested
dis/join
dis/joint
dis/junc/tion
disk
dis/like
dis/lo/cate
dis/lodge
dis/loyal
dis/mal
dis/man/tle
dis/mast
dis/may
dis/mem/ber
dis/miss
dis/mount

dis/obe/di/ent
dis/obey
dis/or/der
dis/or/ga/ni/za/tion
dis/or/ga/nize
dis/own
dis/par/age
dis/par/rate
dis/par/ity
dis/pas/sion/ate
dis/patch
dis/patches
dis/pel
dis/pen/sary
dis/pense
dis/penser
dis/perse
dispirit
dis/place
dis/place/ment
dis/play
dis/play/able
dis/play/ing
dis/pleas/ant
dis/please
dis/plea/sure
dis/port
dis/posal
dis/pose
dis/pos/ing
dis/po/si/tion
dis/pos/sess
dis/pro/por/tion
dis/prove
dis/pu/ta/tious
dis/pute
dis/qual/ify

dis/quali/fy/ing
dis/quiet
dis/qui/si/tion
dis/re/gard
dis/re/gard/ing
dis/re/pair
dis/repu/ta/ble
dis/re/pute
dis/re/spect
dis/robe
dis/rupt
dis/sat/is/fac/tion
dis/sat/is/fied
dis/sect
dis/sem/ble
dis/semi/nate
dis/semi/na/tion
dis/sen/sion
dis/sent
dis/ser/ta/tion
dis/ser/vice
dis/si/dent
dis/simi/lar
dis/simu/late
dis/si/pate
dis/si/pa/tion
dis/so/ci/ate
dis/solu/ble
dis/so/lute
dis/solve
dis/so/nance
dis/so/nant
dis/suade
dis/sua/sion
dis/taff
dis/tance
dis/tances

dis/tant
dis/taste
dis/taste/ful
dis/tem/per
dis/tend
dis/ten/sion
dis/till
dis/til/late
dis/tiller
dis/till/ery
dis/tinct
dis/tinc/tion
dis/tinc/tive
dis/tinctly
dis/tin/guish
dis/tin/guish/ing
dis/tort
dis/tract
dis/traint
dis/traught
dis/tress
dis/trib/ute
dis/trib/ut/ing
dis/tri/bu/tion
dis/tribu/tive
dis/tribu/tor
dis/trict
dis/trict/ing
dis/trust
dis/turb
dis/turbed
dis/turb/ing
dis/unite
dis/unity
dis/use
ditch
dither

ditto
di/ur/nal
diva
divan
dive
di/verge
di/ver/gence
di/vers
di/verse
di/ver/si/fi/ca/tion
di/ver/sify
di/ver/sion
di/ver/sity
di/vert
di/vest
di/vide
divi/dend
di/vider
di/vid/ing
divi/na/tion
di/vine
di/vin/ity
di/visi/bil/ity
di/visi/ble
di/vi/sion
di/vi/sional
di/vorce
divot
di/vulge
diz/zi/ness
dizzy
do
doc/ile
do/cil/ity
dock
docket
doc/tor

doc/toral
doc/tor/ate
doc/trine
docu/ment
docu/men/tary
docu/men/ta/tion
docu/ment/ing
dod/der
dodge
doe
does
doesn't
dog
doge
dog/gerel
dogma
dog/matic
doily
doing
dol/drums
dole
dole/ful
doll
dol/lar
dolly
dol/man
dolor
do/lor/ous
dol/phin
dolt
do/main
dome
do/mes/tic
do/mes/ti/cally
do/mes/ti/cate
do/mes/tic/ity
domi/cile

drain/age

domi/nant
domi/nate
domi/na/tion
domi/neer
do/min/ion
dom/ino
don
do/nate
do/na/tion
done
don/key
donor
don't
doom
dooms/day
door
door/way
Doppler
dor/mant
dor/mer
dor/mi/tory
dor/sal
dory
dos/age
dose
dos/sier
dot
dot/age
dote
dou/ble
dou/blet
dou/bling
dou/bloon
dou/bly
doubt
doubt/ful
doubt/less

dough
dough/boy
dough/nut
dove
dove/tail
dowa/ger
dowel
dower
down
down/cast
down/fall
down/hill
down/pour
down/range
down/right
down/stairs
down/town
down/ward
downy
dowry
dox/ol/ogy
doze
dozen
dozer
drab
drachma
draft
drafts/man
drafts/men
drag
drag/net
drago/man
dragon
drag/on/fly
dra/goon
drain
drain/age

drain/pipe
dram
drama
dra/matic
dra/mati/cally
drama/tist
drama/tize
drank
drape
drap/er/ies
drap/ery
dras/tic
dras/ti/cally
draw
draw/back
draw/bridge
drawer
draw/ing
drawl
drawn
dray
dread
dread/ful
dread/nought
dream
dreamer
dream/ily
drear/ily
dreary
dredge
dreg
drench
dress
dresser
dress/ing
dress/maker
drew

drib/ble
dried
drier
drift
drift/wood
drill
drill/ing
drink
drink/able
drinker
drink/ing
drip
drive
drivel
driven
driver
drive/way
driv/ing
driz/zle
droll
droll/ery
drome/dary
drone
drool
droop
droop/ing
drop
drop/out
drop/ping
dropsy
dross
drought
drove
drown
drowsi/ness
drowsy
drub

97

dusk

word	shorthand	word	shorthand
drudge	df	duke	duc
drudg/ery	dfy	duke/dom	dcd
drug	dg	dul/cet	dlst
drug/gist	dg,	dul/ci/mer	dls
drug/store	dgs	dull	dl
drum	d	dull/ard	dld
drum/stick	drsc	dull/ness	dl'
drunk	dg	duly	dul
drunk/ard	dgd	dumb	d
drunken	dgn	dumb/bell	drbl
dry	dr	dumb/waiter	drwa
dryad	drd	dummy	dre
dryer	dr	dump	drp
dryly	drl	dump/ling	drpg
dry/ness	dr'	dun	dn
dual	dul	dunce	d/
dub	db	dune	dn
du/bi/ous	dbr	dun/ga/rees	dges
ducal	dcl	dun/geon	dgn
ducat	dcl	dunk	dg
duch/ess	dc'	duo/deci/mal	dudsl
duchy	dce	duo/de/nal	dudnl
duck	dc	duo/de/num	dudn
duck/ling	dcg	dupe	dup
duct	dc	du/plex	dpx
duc/tile	dcl	du/pli/cate	dpca (dpcl)
dud	dd	du/pli/cat/ing	dpca
dude	dd	du/pli/ca/tion	dpcj
dud/geon	dgn	du/pli/ca/tor	dpca
due	du	du/plic/ity	dps)
duel	dul	du/ra/bil/ity	Db)
du/el/ist	dul,	du/ra/ble	Db
du/enna	duna	du/rance	D/
duet	dul	du/ra/tion	D1
du/fer	df	du/ress	D'
dug	dg	dur/ing	du
dug/out	dgou	dusk	dsc

dust
dustcloth
duster
dusty
Dutch
du/ti/able
du/ties
du/ti/ful
duty
dwarf
dwell
dweller
dwell/ing
dwin/dle
dye
dye/stuff
dyke
dy/namic
dy/na/mite
dy/namo
dy/nasty
dys/en/tery
dys/pep/sia
dys/pep/tic

each ec
eager eg
ea/gerly egl
ea/ger/ness eg'
eagle egl
ear E
ear/drum ED
earl El
ear/lier El
ear/li/est El,
early El
ear/mark Ex
earn En
earned En̄
ear/nest En,
ear/nestly Ensl
earn/ing En_
earn/ings En̄
ear/ring Erg
ear/shot ESt
earth El
earthly Ell

earth/quake Elqc
earth/ward Elrd
ease ez
easel ezl
ease/ment ez-
eases ezs
eas/ier ez
easi/est ez,
eas/ily ezl
eas/ing ez
east E
Easter E/
east/ern Ern
east/ward Elrd
easy ez
easy/go/ing ezg
eat el
eat/ing el_
eaves evz
ebb eb
ebo/ny ebne
ebul/lient ebl-

ef/figy

ec/cen/tric
ec/cen/tric/ity
ec/cle/si/as/tic
eche/lon
echo
echoed
echoes
eclair
eclat
eclec/tic
eclipse
eco/nomic
eco/nom/i/cal
eco/nom/i/cally
eco/nom/ics
econo/mies
econo/mist
econo/mists
econo/mize
economy
ec/stasy
ec/static
ecu/men/i/cal
ecu/men/i/cism
ec/zema
eddy
edge
edge/ways
edi/ble
edict
edi/fi/ca/tion
edi/fice
edify
edit
ed/ited
ed/it/ing
edi/tion

edi/tions
edi/tor
edi/to/rial
edi/to/ri/ally
edi/to/ri/als
edi/tors
edu/cate
edu/cat/ing
edu/ca/tion
edu/ca/tional
edu/ca/tor
edu/ca/tors
educe
eel
ee/rie
ef/face
ef/face/ment
ef/fect
ef/fect/ed
ef/fect/ing
ef/fec/tive
ef/fec/tively
ef/fec/tive/ness
ef/fects
ef/fec/tual
ef/fec/tu/ate
ef/fec/tu/a/tion
ef/fem/i/nate
ef/fer/vesce
ef/fer/ves/cent
ef/fete
ef/fi/ca/cious
ef/fi/cacy
ef/fi/ciency
ef/fi/cient
ef/fi/ciently
ef/figy

ef/flo/res/cent
ef/flu/vium
ef/fort
ef/forts
ef/fron/tery
ef/ful/gent
ef/fu/sion
ef/fu/sive
e.g.
egg
egg/head
egg/nog
egg/plant
eggs
ego
ego/ist
ego/tism
ego/tist
ego/tis/ti/cal
egre/gious
egress
Egyptian
ei/der
eight
eighth
either
ejacu/late
eject
ejec/tion
eke
elabo/rate
elabo/rated
elabo/ra/tion
elapse
elapsed
elas/tic
elas/tic/ity

elate
ela/tion
elbow
elder
el/derly
el/dest
elect
elected
elect/ing
elec/tion
elec/tions
elec/tion/eer
elec/tive
elec/tor
elec/toral
elec/tor/ate
elec/tric
elec/tri/cal
elec/tri/cally
elec/tri/cian
elec/tric/ity
elec/tri/fi/ca/tion
elec/tri/fied
elec/trify
elec/tro
elec/tro/car/dio/gram
elec/tro/car/dio/grams
elec/tro/car/dio/graphic
elec/tro/cute
elec/tro/cu/tion
elec/trode
elec/tro/dy/nam/ics
elec/trol/y/sis
elec/tro/lyte
elec/tro/mag/net
elec/tron
elec/tronic

elec/tron/ics
elec/tro/plate
elec/tros
elec/tro/scope
elec/tro/type
elects
ele/gance
ele/gant
ele/giac
elegy
ele/ment
ele/men/tal
ele/men/tary
ele/ments
ele/phant
ele/phants
ele/phan/tine
ele/vate
ele/va/tion
ele/va/tor
ele/va/tors
elf
elves
elicit
elide
eli/gi/bil/ity
eli/gi/ble
elim/i/nate
elim/i/nated
elim/i/nates
elim/i/nat/ing
elim/i/na/tion
eli/sion
elite
elixir
elk
ell

el/lipse
el/lip/sis
el/lip/ti/cal
elm
elo/cu/tion
elon/gate
elon/ga/tion
elope
elo/quence
elo/quent
else
else/where
elu/ci/date
elu/ci/da/tion
elude
eludes
elu/sive
Elysium
ema/ci/ate
ema/ci/a/tion
ema/nate
ema/nat/ing
ema/na/tion
eman/ci/pate
eman/ci/pa/tion
eman/ci/pa/tor
emas/cu/late
em/balm
em/bank/ment
em/bargo
em/bark
em/bar/ka/tion
em/barked
em/bark/ing
em/bar/rass
em/bar/rasses
em/bar/rass/ment

104

em/bassy	émi/gré
em/bel/lish	emi/nence
ember	emi/nent
em/bez/zle	emi/nently
em/bit/ter	emir
em/bla/zon	em/is/sary
em/blem	emit
em/blem/atic	emol/lient
em/blems	emolu/ment
em/bod/i/ment	emote
em/body	emo/tion
em/bolden	emo/tional
em/boss	emo/tions
em/bossed	em/pa/thy
em/brace	em/pen/nage
em/bra/sure	em/peror
em/bro/cate	em/pha/sis
em/broi/der	em/pha/size
em/broi/dery	em/pha/sized
em/broil	em/pha/sizes
em/bryo	em/pha/siz/ing
em/bry/onic	em/phatic
emcee	em/phat/i/cally
emend	em/pire
em/er/ald	em/pir/i/cal
em/er/alds	em/ploy
emerge	em/ployed
emer/gen/cies	em/ployee
emer/gency	em/ployer
emer/gent	em/ploy/ers
emer/i/tus	em/ploy/ing
emer/sion	em/ploy/ment
em/ery	em/ploys
emetic	em/po/rium
emi/grant	em/power
emi/grate	em/press
emi/gra/tion	empty

empty

105

emu
emu/late
emu/la/tion
emul/si/fier
emul/sify
emul/sion
en/able
en/abled
en/ables
en/abling
enact
en/acted
en/act/ment
enamel
enam/eler
en/amor
en/camp
en/case
en/ceinte
en/chant
en/chant/ment
en/chant/ress
en/cir/cle
en/clave
en/close
en/closed
en/clos/ing
en/clo/sure
en/clo/sures
en/co/mium
en/com/pass
en/com/passed
en/com/pass/ing
en/core
en/coun/ter
en/coun/tered
en/cour/age

en/cour/aged
en/cour/age/ment
en/cour/ag/ing
en/croach
en/croached
en/croach/ing
en/croach/ment
en/crust
en/crus/ta/tion
en/cum/ber
en/cum/brance
en/cyc/lical
en/cy/clo/pe/dia
en/cy/clo/pe/dias
end
en/dan/ger
en/dan/gered
en/dear
en/dear/ment
en/deavor
en/deav/ored
en/deav/or/ing
en/deav/ors
ended
en/demic
end/ing
en/dive
end/less
en/dorse
en/dorsed
en/dorse/ments
en/dorses
endow
en/dow/ment
en/dur/ance
en/dure
en/dur/ing

enema
ene/mies
enemy
en/er/getic
en/er/gize
en/ergy
en/er/vate
en/fee/ble
en/fold
en/force
en/force/able
en/forced
en/force/ment
en/forcer
en/forces
en/fran/chise
en/gage
en/gaged
en/gage/ment
en/gages
en/gen/der
en/gine
en/gi/neer
en/gi/neer/ing
en/gi/neers
en/gines
English
en/grain
en/grave
en/graver
en/grav/ings
en/gross
en/hance
en/hance/ment
enigma
enig/matic
en/join

enjoy
en/joy/able
en/joyed
en/joy/ing
en/joy/ment
en/joys
en/large
en/larged
en/large/ment
en/larg/ing
en/lighten
en/light/en/ing
en/light/en/ment
en/list
en/list/ing
en/liven
en/mity
en/no/ble
ennui
enor/mity
enor/mous
enough
en/quiry
en/rage
en/rap/ture
en/rich
en/riched
en/roll
en/rolled
en/roll/ing
en/roll/ment
en/roll/ments
en route
en/sconce
en/sem/ble
en/shrine
en/shroud

en/sign
en/sile
en/slave
en/slaved
en/slave/ment
en/snare
en/snarl
ensue
en/sued
en/su/ing
en/sure
en/tab/la/ture
en/tail
en/tailed
en/tan/gle
enter
en/tered
en/teric
en/ter/ing
en/ter/prise
en/ter/pris/ing
en/ter/tain
en/ter/tainer
en/ter/tain/ing
en/ter/tain/ment
en/thrall
en/throne
en/thuse
en/thused
en/thu/si/asm
en/thu/si/as/tic
en/thu/si/as/ti/cally
en/tice
en/tire
en/tirely
en/ti/tle
en/ti/tled

en/ti/tles
en/tity
en/tomb
en/to/molo/gist
en/to/mol/ogy
en/trails
en/trance
en/trances
en/trant
en/treat
en/treaty
en/trée
en/trench
en/trenched
en/tre/pre/neur
en/trust
entry
enu/mer/ate
enu/mera/tion
enu/mera/tor
enun/ci/ate
enun/ci/ated
enun/cia/tion
enun/cia/tor
en/velop
en/ve/lope
en/ve/lopes
en/vel/op/ment
en/vi/able
en/vied
en/vi/ous
en/vi/ron/ment
en/vi/ron/men/tal
en/vis/age
en/vis/aged
en/vi/sion
envoy

er/ratic

envy	nve
en/zyme	nzi
ep/au/let	epll
ephem/eral	ef l
epic	epc
epi/cure	epcu
epi/cu/rean	epcyn
epi/cy/cle	epscl
epi/demic	epdc
epi/der/mis	epd~
epi/glot/tis	epgls
epi/gram	epg
epi/graph	epgf
epi/lepsy	eplpse
epi/lep/tic	eplpc
epi/logue	eplg
epis/co/pal	epscp
Episcopalian	epscplen
epi/sode	epsd
epis/tle	epsl
epi/taph	eplf
epi/thet	eptt
epit/ome	eptre
epit/o/mize	eplz
ep/och	epc
epoxy	epve
equa/ble	eqb
equal	eql
equal/ity	eql)
equal/iza/tion	eqlzj
equal/ize	eqlz
equal/ized	eqlz-
equal/iz/ing	eqlz
equally	eql
equals	eqls
equa/nim/ity	eqn)
equate	ega
equat/ing	ega
equa/tion	eqj
equa/tor	ega
equa/to/rial	eqlyl
eques/trian	eqsen
equi/an/gu/lar	eqagl
equi/dis/tant	eqds-
equi/lat/eral	eqlrl
equi/lib/rium	eqlBe
equi/nox	eqnx
equip	eqp
equip/ment	eqp-
equipped	eqp
equip/ping	eqp
eq/ui/ta/ble	eqlb
eq/uity	eq)
equiva/lent	eqvl-
equivo/cal	eqvcl
equivo/cate	eqvca
equivo/ca/tor	eqvca
era	Ea
eradi/cate	erdca
erase	ers
eraser	ers
era/sure	erS
ere	E
erect	erc
erected	erc-
erec/tion	ercj
er/mine	Em
erode	erd
ero/sion	ey
erotic	erlc
err	E
er/rand	E—
er/rant	E-
er/ratic	Elc

er/rata
er/ra/tum
erred
er/ro/ne/ous
er/ro/ne/ously
error
er/rors
er/satz
eru/dite
eru/di/tion
erupt
erup/tion
es/ca/la/tor
es/ca/la/tors
es/ca/pade
es/cape
es/caped
es/chew
es/cort
es/corted
es/crow
es/cutch/eon
Eskimo
eso/teric
es/pe/cial
es/pe/cially
es/pi/o/nage
es/pla/nade
es/pouse
es/prit
es/quire
essay
es/says
es/sence
es/sen/tial
es/sen/tially
es/sen/tials

es/tab/lish
es/tab/lished
es/tab/lish/ment
es/tab/lish/ments
es/tate
es/teem
es/ti/ma/ble
es/ti/mate
es/ti/mated
es/ti/mates
es/ti/mat/ing
es/ti/ma/tion
es/ti/mat/ors
Estonian
estop
es/trange
es/tro/gen
es/tu/ary
et al
et cet/era
etch
eter/nal
ether
ethe/real
ethic
ethi/cal
eth/ics
Ethiopian
eth/nic
ethyl
eti/quette
ety/mol/o/gist
ety/mol/ogy
eu/ca/lyp/tus
eu/gen/ics
eu/lo/gize
eu/logy

eu/phe/mism
eu/pho/ni/ous
eu/pho/ria
eu/reka
European
evacu/ate
evacu/ation
evade
evalu/ate
evalu/ated
evalu/at/ing
evalu/ation
evalu/ations
eva/nes/cent
evan/gelic
evan/ge/lism
evan/ge/list
evapo/rate
evapo/rated
evapo/ra/tion
evapo/rator
eva/sion
eva/sive
eva/sive/ness
eve
even
evened
eve/ning
eve/nings
evenly
even-numbered
event
event/ful
even/tual
even/tu/ally
even/tu/ate
ever

ev/er/more
every
ev/ery/body
ev/ery/day
ev/ery/one
ev/ery/thing
ev/ery/where
evict
evicted
evic/tion
evi/dence
evi/denced
evi/dent
evi/dently
evil
evil-minded
evil/ness
evince
evis/cer/rate
evoca/tive
evo/ca/tor
evoke
evoked
evokes
evo/lu/tion
evolve
evolves
ewe
ewer
ex/ac/er/bate
ex/ac/er/ba/tion
exact
ex/act/ing
ex/actly
ex/ag/ger/ate
ex/ag/ger/a/tion
ex/ag/ger/a/tor

ex/cuses

- exalt
- exam
- ex/am/i/na/tion
- ex/am/i/na/tions
- ex/am/ine
- ex/am/ined
- ex/am/iner
- ex/am/in/ers
- ex/am/in/ing
- ex/am/ple
- ex/am/ples
- exams
- ex/as/per/ate
- ex/as/per/a/tion
- ex/ca/vate
- ex/ca/vated
- ex/ca/vat/ing
- ex/ca/va/tion
- ex/ceed
- ex/ceeded
- ex/ceed/ing
- ex/ceed/ingly
- ex/ceeds
- excel
- ex/cel/lence
- ex/cel/lent
- ex/cel/lently
- ex/cel/sior
- ex/cept
- ex/cept/ing
- ex/cep/tion
- ex/cep/tional
- ex/cep/tion/ally
- ex/cep/tions
- ex/cerpt
- ex/cess
- ex/ces/sive

- ex/change
- ex/change/able
- ex/changed
- ex/changes
- ex/chang/ing
- ex/che/quer
- ex/cise
- ex/ci/sion
- ex/cit/able
- ex/ci/ta/tion
- ex/cite
- ex/cited
- ex/cite/ment
- ex/cit/ing
- ex/claim
- ex/cla/ma/tion
- ex/clam/a/tory
- ex/clude
- ex/cluded
- ex/clud/ing
- ex/clu/sion
- ex/clu/sive
- ex/clu/sively
- ex/com/mu/ni/cate
- ex/com/mu/ni/ca/tion
- ex/co/ri/ate
- ex/crete
- ex/cre/tion
- ex/cru/ci/at/ing
- ex/cul/pate
- ex/cul/pa/tory
- ex/cur/sion
- ex/cur/sive
- ex/cus/able
- ex/cuse
- ex/cused
- ex/cuses

exe/cra/ble
exe/crate
exe/cute
exe/cuted
exe/cut/ing
exe/cu/tion
exe/cu/tioner
ex/ec/u/tive
ex/ec/u/tives
ex/ec/u/tor
ex/ec/utors
ex/ec/u/to/rial
ex/ec/u/trix
ex/em/plar
ex/em/plary
ex/em/plify
ex/empt
ex/empted
ex/emp/tion
ex/emp/tions
ex/er/cise
ex/er/cised
ex/er/cises
exert
ex/ert/ing
ex/er/tion
ex/ha/la/tion
ex/hale
ex/haust
ex/hausted
ex/haust/ing
ex/haus/tion
ex/haus/tive
ex/hibit
ex/hib/ited
ex/hi/bi/tion
ex/hib/i/tor

ex/hib/i/tors
ex/hil/a/rate
ex/hil/a/rat/ing
ex/hil/a/ra/tion
ex/hort
ex/hor/ta/tion
ex/hume
exi/gency
exile
exist
ex/isted
ex/ist/ence
ex/ist/ing
ex/ists
ex/is/ten/tial
exit
exo/dus
ex/of/fi/cio
ex/on/er/ate
ex/or/bi/tant
ex/or/cise
ex/o/teric
ex/o/ther/mic
ex/otic
ex/pand
ex/panded
ex/pand/ing
ex/panse
ex/pan/sion
ex/parte
ex/pa/ti/ate
ex/pa/tri/ate
ex/pect
ex/pec/tant
ex/pec/ta/tion
ex/pected
ex/pect/ing

ex/po/si/tions

ex/pec/to/rant
ex/pec/to/rate
ex/pects
ex/pe/di/ency
ex/pe/di/ent
ex/pe/dite
ex/pe/dited
ex/pe/dites
ex/pe/di/tion
ex/pe/di/tion/ary
ex/pe/di/tious
ex/pe/di/tiously
expel
ex/pend
ex/pend/ing
ex/pen/di/ture
ex/pen/di/tures
ex/pense
ex/penses
ex/pen/sive
ex/pe/ri/ence
ex/pe/ri/enced
ex/pe/ri/ences
ex/pe/ri/enc/ing
ex/per/i/ment
ex/per/i/men/tal
ex/per/i/men/tally
ex/per/i/men/ta/tion
ex/per/i/ments
ex/pert
ex/perts
ex/per/tise
ex/pi/ate
ex/pi/a/tion
ex/pi/a/tory
ex/pi/ra/tion
ex/pire

ex/pired
ex/pires
ex/pir/ing
ex/plain
ex/plained
ex/plain/ing
ex/pla/na/tion
ex/pla/na/tions
ex/plan/a/tory
ex/ple/tive
ex/pli/ca/ble
ex/plicit
ex/plic/itly
ex/plode
ex/plodes
ex/ploit
ex/ploi/ta/tion
ex/plo/ra/tion
ex/plo/ra/tions
ex/plor/a/tory
ex/plore
ex/plored
ex/plorer
ex/plor/ing
ex/plo/sion
ex/plo/sive
ex/plo/sives
ex/po/nent
ex/port
ex/ported
ex/porter
ex/pose
ex/posé
ex/posed
ex/poses
ex/po/si/tion
ex/po/si/tions

ex post facto
ex/pos/tu/late
ex/po/sure
ex/po/sures
ex/pound
ex/press
ex/pressed
ex/presses
ex/pres/sion
ex/pres/sions
ex/pres/sive
ex/pres/sively
ex/press/way
ex/pro/pri/ate
ex/pul/sion
ex/punge
ex/pur/gate
ex/qui/site
ex/tant
ex/tem/po/ra/ne/ous
ex/tem/pore
ex/tem/po/rize
ex/tend
ex/tended
ex/tend/ers
ex/tend/ing
ex/tends
ex/ten/sion
ex/ten/sions
ex/ten/sive
ex/ten/sively
ex/tent
ex/tenu/ate
ex/tenu/ation
ex/te/rjor
ex/te/ri/ors
ex/ter/mi/nate

ex/ter/mi/na/tion
ex/ter/mi/na/tor
ex/ter/nal
ex/ter/nal/ize
ex/ter/nally
ex/tinct
ex/tinc/tion
ex/tin/guish
ex/tin/guished
ex/tin/guisher
ex/tin/guish/ing
ex/tir/pate
extol
ex/tolled
ex/tort
ex/tor/tion
extra
ex/tract
ex/trac/tion
ex/trac/tor
ex/tracts
ex/tra/dite
ex/tra/di/tion
ex/tra/ne/ous
ex/tra/or/di/nar/ily
ex/tra/or/di/nary
ex/tras
ex/trav/a/gance
ex/trav/a/gant
ex/trav/a/ganza
ex/treme
ex/tremely
ex/trem/ist
ex/trem/ity
ex/tri/cate
ex/trin/sic
ex/tro/vert

eye/wit/nesses

ex/trude
ex/truded
ex/tru/sion
ex/tru/sions
exu/ber/ant
exu/da/tion
exude
exult
eye
eye/ball
eye-catching
eye/lash
eye/let
eye/lid
eyes
eye/sight
eye/wit/ness
eye/wit/nesses

f

fable	fac/sim/ile
fab/ric	fact
fab/ri/cate	fac/tion
fab/ri/cat/ing	fac/ti/tious
fab/ri/ca/tion	fac/tor
fab/ri/ca/tor	fac/to/ries
fab/rics	fac/tory
fabu/lous	facts
fa/cade	fac/tual
face	fac/ulty
faces	fad
facet	fade
fac/ets	fad/ing
fa/ce/tious	fagot
fa/cial	Fahrenheit
fac/ile	fa/ience
fa/cil/i/tate	fail
fa/cil/i/tat/ing	failed
fa/cil/i/ties	fail/ing
fa/cil/ity	faille
fac/ing	fail/ure

fail/ures
faint
faintly
fair
fairly
fairs
fairy
fairy/land
fait ac/com/pli
faith
faith/ful
fake
faker
fak/ing
fal/con
fall
fal/lacy
fallen
fal/li/ble
fall/ing
fal/low
false
false/hood
fal/setto
fal/si/fi/ca/tion
fal/si/fier
fal/sify
fal/ter
fame
famed
fa/mil/iar
fa/mil/iar/ity
fa/mil/iar/ize
fa/mil/iar/iz/ing
fa/mil/iarly
fam/i/lies
fam/ily

fam/ine
fam/ish
fa/mous
fa/mously
fan
fa/natic
fa/nat/i/cism
fan/ci/ful
fancy
fan/fare
fan/fares
fang
fan-jet
fan/tail
fan/tas/tic
fan/tasy
far
far/away
farce
fare
fares
fare/well
far/fetched
fa/rina
farm
farmer
farm/house
farm/ing
far-reaching
far/rier
far/row
far/see/ing
far/sighted
far/ther
far/thest
far/thing
fas/ci/nate

fas/ci/nat/ing
fas/ci/na/tion
fas/ci/na/tor
fas/cism
fash/ion
fash/ion/able
fast
fasten
fas/tened
fas/tener
faster
fas/tidi/ous
fast/ness
fat
fatal
fa/tal/ist
fa/tal/ity
fa/tally
fate
fate/ful
fa/ther
fa/ther/hood
father-in-law
fa/ther/land
fa/ther/less
fathom
fa/tigue
fat/ness
fatty
fatu/ous
fau/cet
fault
fault/less
faulty
faux pas
favor
fa/vor/able

fa/vor/ably
fa/vored
fa/vor/ing
fa/vor/ite
fa/vor/ites
fawn
faze
fe/alty
fear
fear/fully
fear/less
fear/some
fea/si/bil/ity
fea/si/ble
feast
feat
feather
feath/ers
feath/er/weight
fea/ture
fea/tured
fea/tur/ing
feb/ri/fuge
February
fe/cund
fe/cun/dity
fed
fed/eral
fed/er/ate
fed/er/ated
fed/er/a/tion
fed/er/a/tions
fee
fee/ble
feed
feed/back
feed/ers

119

fewer

feed/ing	fern
feeds	fern/ery
feel	fe/ro/cious
feeler	fe/roc/ity
feel/ing	fer/ret
feel/ingly	fer/ric
feels	fer/rous
fees	fer/rule
feet	ferry
feign	fer/ry/boat
feint	fer/tile
fe/lici/tate	fer/til/ity
fe/lic/ity	fer/til/ize
fe/line	fer/ti/lizer
fell	fer/til/izers
fel/low	fer/vent
fel/low/man	fer/vid
fel/low/ship	fer/vor
felon	fes/ter
fe/lo/ni/ous	fes/ti/val
fel/ony	fes/ti/vals
felt	fes/tive
fe/male	fes/tivi/ties
fe/males	fes/tiv/ity
femi/nine	fes/toon
femi/nin/ity	fetch
femur	fete
fen	fetid
fence	fe/tish
fenced	fet/ter
fencer	feud
fences	feu/dal
fend	feu/dal/ism
fender	fever
fer/ment	fe/ver/ish
fer/men/ta/tion	few
fer/ment/ers	fewer

fey
fez
fi/ancé
fi/an/cée
fi/asco
fiat
fib
fiber
fiber glass
fi/brous
fickle
fic/tion
fic/ti/tious
fid/dle
fi/del/ity
fid/get
fi/du/ciary
field
fields
fiend
fiend/ish
fierce
fiercely
fierce/ness
fiery
fi/esta
fife
fif/teenth
fifth
fif/ti/eth
fight
fighter
fight/ing
fig/ment
figu/ra/tive
fig/ure
fig/ured

fig/ure/head
fig/ures
fila/ment
fil/bert
filch
file
filed
files
fil/ial
fili/bus/ter
fili/gree
fil/ings
Filipino
fill
filled
fil/let
fill/ing
film
films
film/strips
filmy
fil/ter
fil/ters
filth
filthi/ness
filthy
fil/trate
fin
fi/na/gle
final
fi/nale
fi/nal/ist
fi/nal/iza/tion
fi/nal/ized
fi/nance
fi/nanced
fi/nan/cial

fixa/tion

fi/nan/cially
fi/nan/cier
fi/nanc/ing
finch
find
finder
find/ing
find/ings
fine
fined
finely
finer
fin/ery
fines
fine/spun
fi/nesse
fin/est
fin/ger
fin/gers
fin/ger/tips
fini/cal
finis
fin/ish
fin/ished
fin/ish/ers
fin/ishes
fin/ish/ing
fi/nite
fir
fire
fire/bug
fired
fire/fly
fire/man
fire/men
fire/place
fire/proof

fire/proof/ing
fires
fire/side
fire/trap
fire/works
fir/kin
firm
fir/ma/ment
firmer
firmly
firm/ness
first
first aid
first class
first/hand
firstly
firth
fis/cal
fish
fisher
fish/er/man
fish/hook
fish/ing
fis/sion
fis/sure
fist
fistic
fis/tula
fit
fit/ful
fits
fit/ted
fit/ting
five
fix
fix/ate
fixa/tion

fixa/tive	flat
fixed	flats
fixes	flat/ten
fix/ture	flat/tened
fix/tures	flat/ter
fizz	flat/tery
fiz/zle	flatu/lent
flabby	flaunt
flac/cid	fla/vor
flag	fla/vors
flag/el/late	flaw
flag/el/la/tion	flaw/less
flagged	flaw/lessly
flag/ging	flax
flagon	flay
flag/pole	flea
fla/grant	fleck
flags	fled
flag/ship	fledg/ling
flag/staff	flee
flail	fleece
flair	fleecy
flake	fleet
flam/beau	Flemish
flam/boy/ant	flesh
flame	fleshi/ness
fla/mingo	fleshy
flam/ma/ble	flew
flange	flexi/bil/ity
flank	flexi/ble
flan/nel	flexi/bly
flap	flick
flap/per	flicker
flare	flier
flash	flies
flash/light	flight
flashy	flighti/ness

flus/ter

flights	flo/rist
flim/si/ness	floss
flimsy	flo/tilla
flinch	flot/sam
fling	flounce
flint	floun/der
flip	flour
flip/pancy	flour/ish
flip/pant	floury
flirt	flout
flir/ta/tion	flow
flir/ta/tious	flowed
flit	flower
float	flow/er/pot
floater	flow/ers
float/ing	flown
floats	fluc/tu/ate
floc/cu/lent	fluc/tu/ated
flock	fluc/tu/ates
flocks	fluc/tu/a/tion
floe	fluc/tu/a/tions
flog	flue
flood	flu/ent
flood/ing	fluff
flood/light	fluffy
flood/lights	fluid
floods	flu/ids
floor	fluke
floor/ing	flunk
floors	fluo/res/cence
floor/walker	fluo/res/cent
flop	fluo/ri/da/tion
floppy	fluo/ride
flo/ral	fluo/ro/scope
flo/res/cent	flurry
florid	flush
florin	flus/ter

124

flute	folly
flut/ter	fo/ment
flux	fond
fly	fon/dant
flyer	fon/dle
fly/ing	font
fly/leaf	food
fly/wheel	foods
foal	fool
foam	fool/ery
fob	fool/hardy
focal	fool/ish
focus	fools/cap
fod/der	foot
foe	foot/age
fog	foot/ball
fogy	foot/hill
foi/ble	foot/hold
foi/bles	foot/ing
foil	foot/lights
foist	foot/note
fold	foot/path
folded	foot/print
folder	foot/sore
fold/ers	foot/step
folds	foot/stool
fo/liage	foot/wear
folio	foot/work
folk	fop
folks	for
folk song	for/age
fol/li/cle	foray
fol/low	for/bade
fol/lowed	for/bear
fol/lower	for/bid
fol/low/ing	for/bid/den
fol/lows	for/bore

for/mula

force	for/ests
forced	fore/tell
force/ful	fore/thought
for/ceps	fore/told
ford	for/ever
fore	fore/warn
fore/arm	fore/word
fore/cast	for/feit
fore/cast/ing	for/feited
for/close	for/fei/ture
fore/clo/sure	forge
fore/fa/ther	forger
fore/fin/ger	forges
fore/front	for/get
forego	for/get/ful
fore/go/ing	for/get/ful/ness
fore/gone	for/get/ting
fore/ground	for/give
fore/hand	for/give/ness
fore/head	for/got
for/eign	for/got/ten
for/eigner	fork
fore/knowl/edge	for/lorn
fore/lock	form
fore/man	for/mal
fore/men	for/mali/ties
fore/most	for/mal/ity
fore/noon	for/mally
for/ren/sic	for/mat
fore/see	for/ma/tion
fore/see/able	for/ma/tive
fore/shadow	former
fore/sight	for/merly
for/est	for/mi/da/ble
fore/stall	form/ing
for/ester	form/less
for/estry	for/mula

for/mu/late
for/mu/lat/ing
for/mu/la/tion
for/ni/ca/tion
for/sake
for/sooth
for/swear
for/sythia
fort
forth
forth/com/ing
forth/right
forth/with
for/ti/fi/ca/tion
for/tify
for/tis/simo
for/ti/tude
fort/night
for/tress
for/tu/itous
for/tu/nate
for/tu/nately
for/tune
forum
for/ward
for/warded
for/ward/ers
for/ward/ing
for/wards
fos/sil
fos/ter
fought
foul
fouled
foul/ness
found
foun/da/tion

foun/da/tional
foun/da/tions
foun/der
foun/ders
foun/ding
found/ling
foundry
fount
foun/tain
four
four/fold
four/teenth
fourth
fowl
fox
foyer
fra/cas
frac/tion
frac/tious
frac/ture
frag/ile
frag/ment
frag/ments
fra/grance
fra/grances
fra/grant
frail
frai/lty
frame
framed
frames
frame/work
fram/ing
franc
fran/chise
fran/chised
fran/chis/ers

127

frisk

fran/chises
fran/chis/ing
frank
frank/in/cense
frankly
fran/tic
frat
fra/ter/nal
fra/ter/nally
fra/ter/nity
frat/ri/cide
fraud
frauds
fraudu/lence
fraudu/lent
fraught
fray
frayed
freak
freckle
free
free/dom
free/doms
free/hand
free/hold
free/ing
freely
free/load/ers
free/way
free/wheel/ing
freeze
freezer
freezes
freez/ing
freight
freighter
freight/ers

French
fre/netic
frenzy
fre/quen/cies
fre/quency
fre/quent
fre/quently
fresco
fres/coes
fresh
fresher
freshly
fresh/man
fret
fret/work
fria/ble
friar
fric/as/see
fric/tion
Friday
friend
friend/less
friend/li/ness
friendly
friends
friend/ship
frig/ate
fright
frighten
fright/ened
fright/en/ing
fright/ful
frigid
fri/gid/ity
frill
fringe
frisk

frit/ter
frit/ters
fri/vol/ity
frivo/lous
frizz
fro
frock
frog
frolic
frol/ic/some
from
frond
front
fron/tier
fron/tiers
fron/tis/piece
frost
frost/bite
frosted
frost/ing
frost/proof
frosty
froth
frown
frowzy
froze
fro/zen
fru/gal
fru/gal/ity
fruit
fruit/ful
fru/ition
fruit/less
fruits
frus/trate
frus/tra/tion
fry

fryer
fuch/sia
fudge
fuel
fu/gi/tive
fugue
ful/crum
ful/fill
ful/fill/ing
ful/fill/ment
ful/filled
ful/fills
full
fuller
full/est
full/ness
fully
ful/mi/nate
ful/some
fum/ble
fume
fu/mi/gate
fu/mi/ga/tion
fun
func/tion
func/tional
func/tion/ary
func/tioned
func/tion/ing
func/tions
fund
fun/da/men/tal
fun/da/men/tally
fun/da/men/tals
funded
fu/neral
fu/ne/real

fuzz

fun/gi/cide
fun/gus
fu/nicu/lar
funk
fun/nel
funny
fur
fur/be/low
fur/bish
fu/ri/ous
furl
fur/long
fur/lough
fur/nace
fur/nish
fur/nished
fur/nish/ing
fur/nish/ings
fur/ni/ture
furor
fu/rore
fur/ri/er
fur/row
furry
fur/ther
fur/ther/ance
fur/ther/ing
fur/ther/more
fur/ther/most
fur/thest
fur/tive
fury
furze
fuse
fused
fu/se/lage
fus/ible

fu/sil/lade
fu/sion
fuss
fussy
fu/tile
fu/til/ity
fu/ture
fu/tur/is/tic
fu/tu/rity
fuzz

G

gab	gb
gab/ar/dine	gbdn
gab/ble	gb
gable	gb
gad	gd
gad/fly	gdfi
gad/get	ggt
gaff	gf
gag	gg
gage	gaj
gai/ety	ga)
gaily	gal
gain	gn
gained	gn̄
gain/ful	gnf
gain/ing	gn̄
gains	gns
gait	ga
gai/ter	ga
gala	gla
gal/axy	glxe
gale	gal
gall	gal
gal/lant	gl-
gal/lantry	gl-re
gal/ler/ies	glys
gal/lery	gly
gal/ley	gl
gal/leys	gls
Gallic	glc
gal/li/vant	glv-
gal/lon	gln (gal)
gal/lons	glns
gal/lop	glp
gal/lows	gloo
gall/stone	glsn
ga/lore	glo
gal/vanic	glvnc
gal/va/nize	glvnz
gal/va/nized	glvnz̄
gal/va/niz/ing	glvnz
gam/bit	grbl
gam/ble	grb
gam/bler	grb

gear

game		gar/ni/ture	
games		gar/ret	
game/ster		gar/ri/son	
gamin		gar/ru/lity	
gamut		gar/ru/lous	
gang		gar/ter	
ganged		gas	
gan/glion		gas/eous	
gang/plank		gases	
gan/grene		gash	
gang/ster		gashes	
gang/way		gas/ket	
gant/let		gas/light	
gan/try		gaso/line	
gaol		gasp	
gap		gasps	
gape		gas/tric	
gaps		gas/tron/omy	
ga/rage		gate	
garb		gate/way	
gar/bage		gather	
gar/ble		gath/ered	
gar/den		gath/er/ing	
gar/dener		gaudy	
gar/de/nia		gauge	
gar/dens		gaug/ing	
gar/gle		gaunt	
gar/goyle		gaunt/let	
gar/ish		gauze	
gar/land		gave	
gar/lic		gavel	
gar/ment		gay	
gar/ments		gaze	
gar/ner		ga/zelle	
gar/net		ga/zette	
gar/nish		gaz/et/teer	
gar/nishee		gear	

geared
gears
geese
gela/tin
ge/lat/i/nous
gelid
gem
gem/stone
gen/darme
gen/der
gene
ge/ne/al/ogy
gen/eral
gen/er/a/lis/simo
gen/er/al/i/ties
gen/er/al/ity
gen/er/al/iza/tion
gen/er/al/ize
gen/er/ally
gen/er/ate
gen/er/ates
gen/er/at/ing
gen/era/tion
gen/era/tions
gen/era/tor
gen/era/tors
ge/neric
gen/er/os/ity
gen/er/ous
gen/er/ously
gene/sis
ge/netic
ge/net/ics
ge/nial
ge/nial/ity
genie
geni/tal

geni/tive
ge/nius
geno/cide
gen/teel
gen/tile
gen/til/ity
gen/tle
gen/tle/man
gen/tle/men
gently
gen/try
genu/flect
genu/ine
genu/inely
genus
geo/detic
ge/og/ra/pher
geo/graphic
geo/graphi/cally
ge/og/ra/phy
ge/ol/o/gist
ge/ol/o/gists
ge/ol/ogy
geo/met/ric
ge/om/e/try
geo/physi/cal
geo/physi/cist
ge/ra/nium
geri/at/ric
germ
German
ger/mane
ger/mi/cide
ger/mi/nate
ger/mi/na/tion
ger/und
ge/stapo

glassy

Word	Shorthand	Word	Shorthand
ges/tate	jsa	gird	gd
ges/ta/tion	jsj	girder	gd
ges/ticu/late	jscla	gir/dle	gdl
ges/ticu/la/tion	jsc jscj	girl	ge
ges/ture	jsc	girls	gls
get	ge	girl/hood	gehd
gets	gls	girl/ish	ges
gey/ser	gz	girth	gt
ghastly	gsl	gist	j,
gher/kin	gcn	give	gv
ghetto	gto	give/aways	gv gvaivas
ghet/tos	gtos	given	gv
ghost	go,	giver	gv
ghostly	gsl	gives	gvs
ghoul	gul	giv/ing	gv̄
giant	ji-	giz/zard	gzd
gi/ants	ji--	gla/cial	gx
gib/ber/ish	jbs	gla/cier	gs
gibe	jb	glad	gd
gib/let	jbl	glade	gd
gid/di/ness	gde'	gladi/ator	gde
giddy	gde	gladi/ators	gde//
gift	gf	gla/dio/lus	gdelx
gifts	gfs	gladly	gdl
gi/gan/tic	jg-c	glam/or/ous	gx
gig/gle	ggl	glam/our	g
gild	ged	glance	g/
gill	gl (jl)	gland	g—
gilt	gll	glands	g— —
gim/let	grll	glan/du/lar	g—l
gim/mick	grc	glare	ga
gin	jn	glar/ing	ga
gin/ger	jj	glass	g'
gin/ger/bread	jjBd	glasses	g"
gin/gerly	jjl	glass/ful	gsf
ging/ham	gg	glass/ware	gsva
gi/raffe	jf	glassy	gse

god/son

glaze	
gla/zier	
glaz/ing	
gleam	
glean	
gleaned	
glee	
glee/ful	
glen	
glide	
glider	
glim/mer	
glimpse	
glint	
glis/ten	
glit/ter	
glit/ter/ing	
gloam/ing	
gloat	
glob	
global	
globe	
globu/lar	
gloom	
gloom/ily	
gloomy	
glo/rify	
glo/ri/ous	
glory	
gloss	
glos/sary	
glossi/ness	
glossy	
glove	
gloves	
glow	
glower	
glow/ing	
glow/worm	
glu/cose	
glue	
glum	
glum/ness	
glut	
glu/ten	
glu/ti/nous	
glut/ton	
glut/ton/ous	
glut/tony	
glyc/erin	
gnarl	
gnash	
gnat	
gnaw	
gnome	
gnos/ti/cism	
go	
goad	
goal	
goals	
goat	
gob/ble	
gob/bler	
gob/let	
God	
god/child	
god/dess	
god/fa/ther	
god/less	
god/like	
god/mother	
god/par/ent	
god/send	
god/son	

135

gram

goes		gour/met	
gog/gle		gout	
going		gov/ern	
goi/ter		gov/erned	
gold		gov/ern/ess	
golden		gov/ern/ing	
gold/smith		gov/ern/ment	
golf		gov/ern/mental	
gon/dola		gov/ern/ments	
gon/do/las		gov/er/nor	
gon/do/lier		gov/er/nors	
gone		gov/er/nor/ship	
gong		gov/erns	
good		gown	
good-bye		grab	
goodly		grab bag	
good-natured		grace	
good/ness		grace/ful	
goods		gra/cious	
goofy		gra/ciously	
goose		gra/da/tion	
goose/neck		grade	
go/pher		graded	
gore		grades	
gorge		gra/di/ent	
gor/geous		grad/ing	
go/rilla		grad/ual	
gory		gradu/ally	
gos/pel		gradu/ate	
gos/sa/mer		gradu/ated	
gos/sip		gradu/at/ing	
got		gradu/ation	
got/ten		graft	
gouge		grafter	
gou/lash		grain	
gourd		grained	
gour/mand		gram	

Grecian

gram/mar		grass	
gram/mar/ian		grasses	
gram/mati/cal		grassy	
grams		grate	
gra/nary		grate/ful	
grand		grate/fully	
grand/child		grati/fi/ca/tion	
grand/chil/dren		grati/fied	
grand/daugh/ter		grati/fier	
gran/deur		grat/ify	
grand/fa/ther		grati/fy/ing	
gran/dilo/quent		gra/tis	
gran/di/ose		grati/tude	
grand/mother		gra/tu/ities	
grand/par/ent		gra/tu/itous	
grand/son		gra/tu/ity	
grand/stand		grave	
grange		grave/dig/ger	
gran/ite		gravel	
grant		graver	
granted		grav/est	
grantee		grave/stone	
grant/ing		gravi/tate	
grantor		gravi/ta/tion	
granu/lar		grav/ity	
granu/late		gravy	
granu/la/tion		gray	
gran/ule		grayer	
grape		graze	
grape/vine		grease	
graph		greasy	
graphic		great	
graph/ics		greater	
graph/ite		great/est	
gra/phol/ogy		greatly	
grap/ple		great/ness	
grasp		Grecian	

137

grow

greed	gd	grip	gp
greed/ily	gdl	gripe	gp
greedi/ness	gde'	grisly	gzl
greedy	gde	grist	g,
green	gn	gris/tle	gsl
green/gage	gngg	grit	gt
green/gro/cer	gngs	grit/ting	gt—
green/horn	gnh	griz/zly	gzl
green/house	gnh—	groan	gn
greet	ge	gro/cer	gs
greeted	ge—	gro/cers	gs//
greet/ing	ge—	gro/cery	gsy
gre/gari/ous	ggyx	grog	gg
grem/lin	gln	groggy	gge
gre/nade	gnd	groin	gyn
grena/dier	gnde	grom/met	gl
grew	gu	groom	gu
grey	ga	groove	gu
grey/hound	gahn—	grope	gop
grid	gd	gross	go'
grid/dle	gdl	grossly	gsl
grief	gef	gro/tesque	gtsc
griev/ance	ge/	grouch	gc
griev/ances	ge//	ground	gu—
griev/ant	ge—	grounded	gu——
grieve	ge	ground/ing	gu——
griev/ous	gex	ground/less	gu——l'
grif/fon	gfn	ground/man	gu——n—
grill	gl	grounds	gu———
grim	g	ground/work	gu——uc
gri/mace	gs	group	gup
grimly	gl	grouped	gup—
grin	gn	group/ing	gup—
grind	gu—	grouse	gus
grinder	gu—/	grove	go
grind/ing	gu——	grovel	gvl
grind/stone	gu—sn	grow	go

gusto

grower
grow/ing
growl
growl/ing
grown
growth
grub
grudge
gruel
gru/el/ing
grue/some
gruff
grum/ble
grumpy
grunt
guar/an/tee
guar/an/teed
guar/an/tees
guar/an/tor
guar/anty
guard
guard/house
guard/ian
guard/ian/ship
guard/room
guards
guards/man
gu/ber/na/to/rial
guer/rilla
guess
guessed
guess/ing
guess/work
guest
guests
guf/faw
guid/ance

guide
guided
guide/line
guides
guild
guile
guil/lo/tine
guilt
guilti/ness
guilt/less
guinea
guise
gui/tar
gulf
gull
gull/ible
gully
gulp
gum
gummed
gummy
gump/tion
gun
gun/boat
gun/fire
gun/ner
gun/ning
gun/pow/der
gun/run/ner
gun/shot
gun/smith
gun/wale
gur/gle
gush
gus/set
gust
gusto

139

gy/ro/scope

gut
gut/ter
gut/tural
guy
guys
guz/zle
gym
gym/na/sium
gym/nast
gym/nas/tic
gyp
gyp/sum
Gypsy
gy/rate
gy/ra/tion
gy/ro/scope

ha/beas cor/pus	hbes Cpr
hab/er/dasher	hBdS
hab/er/dash/ery	hBdSy
ha/bili/ment	hbl-
ha/bili/tate	hblla
habit	hbl
hab/it/able	hblb
ha/bi/tant	hbl-
habi/tat	hbtt
habi/ta/tion	hbly
hab/its	hbls
ha/bit/ual	hbCul
ha/bitu/ate	hbCa
ha/ci/enda	hse—a
hack	hc
hack/ney	hcne
had	h
had/dock	hdc
hadn't	h-
hag	hg
hag/gard	hgd
hag/gle	hgl

hail	hal
hail/storm	hlS
hair	ha
hair/dresser	haDs
hairy	hy
hal/cyon	hlsen
hale	hal
half	hf
half/back	hfbc
half/penny	hfpne
half/tone	hftn
half/way	hfwa
hali/but	hlbl
hall	hal
hall/mark	hlrc
hal/low	hlo
Halloween	hlwn
hal/lu/ci/nate	hlsna
hal/lu/ci/na/tion	hlsny
hall/way	hlwa
halo	hlo
halt	hll

141

har/di/ness

hal/ter	hl	hand/saw	h — sa
halve	hv	hand/some	h — s
halves	hvs	hand/somely	h — srl
hal/yard	hlyd	hand/som/est	h — s,
ham	h	hand/work	h — Uc
ham/burger	hBg	hand/writ/ing	h — rc
ham/let	hll	handy	h — e
ham/mer	hv	hang	hg
ham/mered	hv	han/gar	hg
ham/mock	hmc	hanger	hg
ham/per	hp	hang/ing	hg
ham/ster	hS	hang/man	hg —
ham/string	hSg	hang up (verb)	hgp
hand	h —	hang-up (noun)	hgp
hand/bag	h — bg	hank	hg
hand/ball	h — bal	han/ker	hg
hand/bill	h — bl	han/som	hl
hand/book	h — bc	hap/haz/ard	hphzd
hand brakes	h — Bcs	hap/less	hpl'
hand/cuff	h — cf	hap/pen	hpn
hand-feed	h — fd	hap/pened	hpn
hand-feeding	h — fd	hap/pen/ing	hpn
handed	h —	hap/pen/ings	hpn
hand/ful	h — f	hap/pi/est	hpe,
handi/cap	h — cp	hap/pily	hpl
handi/capped	h — cp	hap/pi/ness	hpe'
handi/craft	h — Cf	happy	hpe
handi/work	h — Uc	ha/rangue	Hg
hand/ker/chief	hgCf	ha/rass	H'
han/dle	h — l	ha/rass/ment	Ho —
han/dled	h — l̄	har/bin/ger	Hbg
han/dles	h — ls	har/bor	Hb
han/dling	h — l	hard	Hd
hand/made	h — rd	harder	Hd
hand/out	h — ou	hard/head	Hdhd
hand/rail	h — rl	hard/hearted	HdHt
hands	h — —	har/di/ness	Hde'

haz/ards

hardly *Hdl*	has/sock *hsc*
hard/ship *HdS*	haste *ha,*
hard/tack *Hdlc*	has/ten *hsn*
hard/ware *Hdwa*	hasty *hs)*
hard/wood *Hdwd*	hat *hl*
hardy *Hde*	hat/box *hlbx*
hare *ha*	hatch *hC*
hare/lip *halp*	hatch/ery *hCy*
harem *H*	hatchet *hCl*
hark *Hc*	hatch/way *hCwa*
har/le/quin *Hlqn*	hate *ha*
har/lot *Hll*	hate/ful *haf*
harm *H*	hates *has*
harm/ful *Hrf*	hat rack *hlrc*
harm/less *Hrl'*	ha/tred *hTd*
har/mon/ica *Hmca*	hat/stand *hls—*
har/mo/ni/ous *Hmx*	hat/ter *h'*
har/mo/nize *Hmz*	haughty *h)*
har/mo/nizes *Hmzs*	haul *hal*
har/ness *H'*	hauled *hal*
harp *Hp*	haul/ing *hal_*
harp/ist *Hp,*	haunch *hC*
har/poon *Hpn*	haunt *h—*
harp/si/chord *HpsCd*	have *v*
harpy *Hpe*	haven *hvn*
har/ri/dan *Hdn*	haven't *v—*
har/row *Ho*	hav/er/sack *hvsc*
harry *hy*	hav/ing *v*
harsh *HS*	havoc *hvc*
hart *Hl*	Hawaiian *hwn*
har/vest *Hv,*	hawk *hc*
har/vester *HvS*	haw/ser *hz/*
har/vest/ers *HvSs*	haw/thorn *hTn*
has *as*	hay *ha*
hash *hS*	haz/ard *hZd*
hasn't *as—*	haz/ard/ous *hZdx*
hasp *hs*	haz/ards *hZds*

143

haze *hz*	heart/ache *Hac*
hazel *hzl*	heart/break *HBc*
hazi/ness *hze'*	heart/en/ing *Hn*
hazy *hze*	heart/felt *Hfl*
he *h*	hearth *Hl*
head *hd*	hearth/stone *Hlsn*
head/ache *hdac*	hearti/est *Hle,*
head/band *hdb—*	heart/ily *Hll*
head count *hdkt*	hearti/ness *Hle'*
headed *hd*	heart/less *Hll'*
head/first *hdf,*	heart/rend/ing *Hr—*
head/ing *hd*	hearts *Hls*
head/land *hdl—*	heart/sick *Hlsc*
head/light *hdlt*	heart/string *HlSq*
head/liner *hdlr*	heat *he*
head/long *hdlg*	heated *hē*
head/quar/ters *hdQ*	heater *he'*
head/quar/tered *hdQ*	heat/ers *he''*
head/room *hdrn*	heath *hel*
head start *hdSt*	hea/then *hln*
head/stone *hdsn*	heather *hT*
head/strong *hdSg*	heat/ing *he*
head/way *hdwa*	heave *he*
heal *hel*	heaven *hvn*
health *hll*	heav/en/ward *hvnl rd*
health/ful *hlf*	heavier *hve'*
health/ily *hlll*	heavi/est *hve,*
healthi/ness *hlle'*	heavily *hvl*
healthy *hlle*	heavi/ness *hve'*
heap *hep*	heavy *hve*
hear *he'*	heavy/set *hvest*
heard *Hd*	heavy/weight *hvel a*
hear/ing *he*	Hebrew *hBu*
hear/ken *Hcn*	heckle *hcl*
hear/say *hesa*	hect/are *hc*
hearse *Hs*	hec/tic *hcc*
heart *Hl*	hec/to/graph *hcgf*

he/red/ity

hec/tor	help/less/ness
hedge	help/mate
hedge/hog	hem
he/do/nist	hemi/sphere
heed	hemi/sphe/ric
heed/less	hem/lock
heel	he/mo/glo/bin
heels	he/mo/philia
heft	hem/or/rhage
he/ge/mony	hem/or/rhoid
he/gira	hemp
heifer	hem/stitch
height	hen
heighten	hence
heights	hence/forth
hei/nous	hench/man
heir	henna
heir/ess	hens
heir/loom	hep
heirs	hep/ta/gon
held	her
he/li/cal	her/ald
he/li/cop/ter	her/alded
he/lio/graph	her/aldry
he/lium	herb
hell	her/ba/ceous
he'll	her/bi/cides
hel/lion	her/bivo/rous
hello	herd
helm	herder
hel/met	herds
help	here
helped	here/about
helper	here/af/ter
help/ful	hereby
help/ing	he/redi/tary
help/less	he/red/ity

145

hill/side

herein	hen	hia/tus	hitx
here/in/af/ter	henaf	hi/ber/nate	hBna
hereof	hev	hi/ber/na/tion	hBny
her/esy	Hse	hi/bis/cus	hbscx
here/tic	Htc	hic/cup	hcp
hereto	hel	hick	hc
here/to/fore	helf	hick/ory	hcy
here/un/der	hell	hid	hd
here/upon	hepn	hid/den	hdn
here/with	hew	hide	hd
heri/tage	Hly	hide/ous	hdx
her/metic	Hrtc	hie	he
her/mit	Hrl	hi/er/ar/chal	Hrcl
her/mit/age	Hrly	hi/er/ar/chy	Hrce
her/nia	Hna	hi/ero/glyphic	Hgfc
her/nias	Hnas	high	he
hero	Ho	higher	he
he/roes	Hos	high/est	he,
he/roic	Hoc	high-handed	hch—
heroin	Hon	high/land	hil—
hero/ine	Hon	high/light	hile
hero/ism	Hoz	high/light/ing	hile
heron	Hn	highly	hil
her/ring	Hg	high/ness	hi'
hers	h//	high/road	hird
her/self	Hs/	high/tail	hill
hesi/tancy	hzt/	high/way	hiwa
hesi/tant	hzt-	high/way/man	hiwan-
hesi/tate	hzla	hi/jack	hjc
hesi/tates	hzlas	hike	hic
hesi/ta/tion	hzly	hi/lari/ous	hlyx
het/ero/dox	htdx	hi/lar/ity	h2)
het/ero/ge/neous	htgnx	hill	hl
hew	hu	hilli/ness	hl'
hex	hx	hill/ock	hlc
hexa/gon	hegn	hills	hls
hey/day	hd	hill/side	hlsd

hill/top	hit
hilly	hitch
hilt	hither
him	hive
him/self	hoard
hind	hoarse
hin/der	hoary
hin/der/ing	hoax
hin/drance	hob/bies
hind/sight	hob/ble
hinge	hobby
hinged	hob/gob/lin
hint	hob/nail
hin/ter/land	hobo
hints	hock
hip	hockey
hip/bone	hod
hip/po/drome	hoe
hip/po/pota/mus	hog
hip/ster	hogs/head
hire	hoi pol/loi
hired	hoist
hire/ling	hoists
hires	hokum
hir/ing	hold
hir/sute	holder
his	hold/ing
hiss	hold out
his/ta/mine	hold/over
his/tol/ogy	holdup
his/to/rian	hole
his/to/ri/ans	holes
his/toric	holey
his/tori/cal	holi/day
his/to/ries	holi/days
his/tory	ho/li/ness
his/tri/onic	Hollander

hol/low
hol/low/ness
holly
ho/lo/caust
ho/lo/graph
hol/ster
holy
hom/age
home
home/com/ing
home/less
home/like
home/li/ness
homely
home/made
home/maker
home/mak/ing
ho/meo/path
home/owner
home/sick
home/spun
home/stead
home/ward
home/work
ho/mi/cide
hom/ily
hom/iny
ho/mo/ge/ne/ity
ho/mo/ge/neous
ho/moge/nous
ho/molo/gous
hom/onym
hone
hon/est
hon/estly
hon/esty
honey
honk
hon/ey/comb
hon/ey/dew
hon/ey/moon
hon/ey/suckle
honor
hon/or/able
hono/rar/ium
hon/or/ary
hon/ored
hon/or/ing
hood
hood/lum
hoods
hoo/doo
hood/wink
hood
hook
hooks
hoop
hoot
hop
hope
hoped
hope/ful
hope/fully
hope/less
hope/lessly
hope/less/ness
hopes
hop/ing
hop/per
horde
hore/hound
ho/ri/zon
ho/ri/zons
ho/ri/zon/tal

hor/mone	hos/tile
horn	hos/til/ity
hor/net	hos/tler
horn/pipe	hot
horo/scope	hotel
hor/ri/ble	hot/head
hor/rid	hot/house
hor/rific	hotly
hor/rify	hot/ness
hor/ror	hound
hors d'oeuvre	hour
horse	hourly
horse/back	hours
horse/flesh	house
horse/hair	house/coat
horse/hide	housed
horse/man	house/ful
horse/men	house/hold
horse/play	house/keeper
horse/power	house/keep/ing
horse/shoe	house/maid
horse/whip	house/owner
horse/woman	houses
hors/ing	house/warm/ing
hor/ti/cul/ture	house/wife
hose	house/wives
ho/siery	house/work
hos/pi/ta/ble	hous/ing
hos/pi/tal	hovel
hos/pi/tal/ity	hover
hos/pi/tal/iza/tion	how
hos/pi/tal/ized	how/ever
host	howl
hos/tage	howler
hos/tel	hoy/den
hos/telry	hub
host/ess	hub/bub

149

huck/le/berry
huck/ster
hud/dle
hue
huff
huff/ily
huffy
hug
huge
Huguenot
hulk
hull
hul/la/ba/loo
hum
human
hu/mane
hu/man/ist
hu/mani/tar/ian
hu/mani/ties
hu/man/ity
hu/man/kind
hu/manly
hum/ble
hum/ble/ness
hum/bly
hum/bug
hum/dinger
hum/drum
humid
hu/mid/ify
hu/mid/ity
hu/mi/dor
hu/mili/ate
hu/mili/a/tion
hu/mil/ity
hum/mock
humor
hu/mor/ist
hu/mor/ous
hu/mor/ously
hump
humus
hunch
hun/dred
hun/dredth
hun/dred/weight
hung
Hungarian
hun/ger
hun/grier
hun/grily
hun/gry
hunk
hunt
hunter
hunts
hunts/man
hur/dle
hurdy-gurdy
hurl
hurly-burly
hur/rah
hur/ri/cane
hur/ried
hurry
hurt
hurt/ful
hur/tle
hus/band
hus/bands
hus/bandry
husk
husk/ily
huski/ness

husky
hus/sar
hussy
hus/tle
hut
hutch
hya/cinth
hy/bird
Hydra-Matic
hy/dran/gea
hy/drant
hy/drate
hy/drau/lic
hy/drau/li/cally
hy/dro/chlo/ride
hy/dro/elec/tric
hy/dro/gen
hy/dro/ge/nated
hy/droly/sis
hy/drome/ter
hy/dro/pho/bia
hy/dro/plane
hy/dro/scope
hy/dro/static
hy/drous
hy/drox/ide
hyena
hy/giene
hy/gienic
hymen
hy/me/neal
hymn
hy/per/bola
hy/per/bole
hy/per/sen/si/tive
hy/per/ten/sion
hy/per/ten/sive

hy/phen
hy/phen/ate
hyp/no/sis
hyp/notic
hyp/no/tist
hy/po/chon/dria
hy/po/chon/driac
hy/poc/risy
hypo/crite
hy/po/der/mic
hy/pote/nuse
hy/pothe/cate
hy/pothe/ses
hy/pothe/sis
hy/po/theti/cal
hys/sop
hys/te/ria
hys/teri/cal
hys/ter/ics

word	shorthand	word	shorthand
I	ι	ide/al/is/tic	ιdlsc
iam/bic	ιbc	ide/al/ize	ιdlz
ibex	ιbx	ide/ally	ιdl
ibis	ιbs	ide/als	ιdls
ice	ιs	iden/ti/cal	ιd-cl
ice/berg	ιsbg	iden/ti/fi/ca/tion	ιd-fc̄
ice/boat	ιsbo	iden/ti/fied	ιd-f̄
ice/bound	ιsbr—	iden/ti/fies	ιd-fs
ice/box	ιsbx	iden/tify	ιd-f
ice/man	ιsɱ-	iden/ti/fy/ing	ιd-f̧
ici/cle	ιscl	iden/tity	ιd-)
icily	ιsl	ideo/gram	ιdeg
ice/ness	ιse'	idi/ocy	ιdese
icon	ιk	idiom	ιdeɱ
icono/clast	ιkc,	idi/om/atic	ιdeɱc
icono/scope	ιkscp	idi/oms	ιdeɱs
icy	ιse	id/io/syn/crasy	ιdesɱcse
I'd	ιd	idiot	ιdel
idea	ιd	idi/otic	ιdelc
ideal	ιdl	idle	ιdl
ide/al/ism	ιdlz̧	idle/ness	ιdl'
ide/al/ist	ιdl,	idling	ιdl̲

idly	*idl*	il/lu/mine	
idol	*idl*	il/lu/sion	
idola/trous	*idl*	il/lu/sions	
idola/try	*idl*	il/lu/sive	
idol/ize	*idlz*	il/lu/sory	
idyll	*idl*	il/lus/trate	
idyl/lic	*idlc*	il/lus/trated	
if		il/lus/trates	
igloo	*iglu*	il/lus/trat/ing	
ig/ne/ous		il/lus/tra/tion	
ig/nite		il/lus/tra/tions	
ig/ni/tion		il/lus/tra/tor	
ig/no/ble		il/lus/tri/ous	
ig/no/mini/ous		I'm	
ig/no/miny		image	
ig/no/ra/mus		imag/ery	
ig/no/rance		imag/in/able	
ig/no/rant		imagi/nary	
ig/nore		imagi/na/tion	
ig/nored		imagi/na/tive	
ilk		imag/ine	
ill		im/bal/ance	
I'll		im/be/cile	
il/le/gal		imbed	
il/le/gally		im/bed/ded	
il/legi/ble		im/bibe	
il/le/giti/macy		im/bri/cate	
il/le/giti/mate		im/bro/glio	
il/licit		imbue	
il/lit/er/ate		imi/tate	
ill/ness		imi/ta/tion	
ill/nesses		imi/ta/tor	
il/logi/cal		im/macu/late	
ill-tempered		im/ma/nent	
il/lu/mi/nate		im/ma/te/rial	
il/lu/mi/nat/ing		im/ma/ture	
il/lu/mi/na/tion		im/mea/sur/able	

im/mea/sur/ably
im/me/di/acy
im/me/di/ate
im/me/di/ately
im/me/mo/rial
im/mense
im/merse
im/mi/grant
im/mi/grants
im/mi/grate
im/mi/gra/tion
im/mi/nence
im/mi/nent
im/mo/bile
im/mo/bi/lize
im/mod/er/ate
im/mod/est
im/mo/late
im/moral
im/mor/tal
im/mor/tal/ity
im/mov/able
im/mune
im/mu/ni/ties
im/mu/nity
im/mu/nize
im/mure
im/mu/ta/ble
imp
im/pact
im/pair
im/pairs
im/pale
im/pal/pa/ble
im/panel
im/part
im/par/tial

im/passe
im/pas/si/ble
im/pas/sion
im/pas/sive
im/pa/tience
im/pa/tient
im/peach
im/pec/ca/ble
im/pe/cu/nious
im/ped/ance
im/pede
im/pedi/ment
im/pedi/menta
impel
im/pend
im/pene/tra/ble
im/peni/tent
im/pera/tive
im/per/cep/ti/ble
im/per/fect
im/per/fec/tions
im/per/fo/rate
im/pe/rial
im/pe/ri/al/ism
im/peril
im/pe/ri/ous
im/per/ish/able
im/per/me/able
im/per/sonal
im/per/son/ate
im/per/ti/nence
im/per/ti/nent
im/per/turb/able
im/per/vi/ous
im/petu/ous
im/pe/tus
im/pi/ety

155

in/ac/ces/si/ble

im/pinge
im/pi/ous
imp/ish
im/pla/ca/ble
im/plant
im/ple/ment
im/ple/men/ta/tion
im/ple/mented
im/ple/ment/ing
im/pli/cate
im/pli/ca/tion
im/pli/ca/tions
im/plicit
im/plic/it/ness
im/plied
im/plore
imply
im/ply/ing
im/po/lite
im/poli/tic
im/pon/dera/ble
im/port
im/por/tance
im/por/tant
im/por/ta/tions
im/ported
im/porter
im/port/ing
im/por/tune
im/pose
im/posed
im/pos/si/bil/ity
im/pos/si/ble
im/pos/tor
im/po/tent
im/pound
im/pov/er/ish

im/prac/ti/cal
im/pre/ca/tion
im/preg/na/ble
im/preg/nated
im/pre/sa/rio
im/press
im/pressed
im/pres/sion
im/pres/sions
im/pres/sive
im/pri/ma/tur
im/print
im/printed
im/print/ing
im/prison
im/proba/ble
im/promptu
im/proper
im/pro/pri/ety
im/prove
im/proved
im/prove/ment
im/prove/ments
im/provi/dent
im/prov/ing
im/pro/vise
im/pru/dent
im/pu/dent
im/pugn
im/pulse
im/pu/nity
im/pure
im/pu/ta/tion
im/pute
in
in/abil/ity
in/ac/ces/si/ble

in/ac/cu/rate
in/ac/tion
in/ac/tive
in/ade/qua/cies
in/ade/quate
in/ad/mis/si/ble
in/ad/ver/tently
in/ad/vis/able
in/alien/able
inane
in/ani/mate
inan/ity
in/ap/pli/ca/ble
in/ap/pro/pri/ate
in/ap/ti/tude
in/ar/ticu/late
in/as/much as
in/at/ten/tion
in/at/ten/tive
in/au/di/ble
in/au/gu/ral
in/au/gu/rate
in/au/gu/rated
in/au/gu/ra/tion
in/aus/pi/cious
in-between
in/bound
in/bred
in/cal/cu/la/ble
in/ca/les/cent
in/can/des/cent
in/can/ta/tion
in/ca/pa/ble
in/ca/paci/tated
in/car/cer/ate
in/car/cer/ated
in/car/na/tion

in/cau/tious
in/cen/di/ary
in/cense
in/cen/tive
in/cep/tion
in/ces/sant
in/cest
inch
inches
in/cho/ate
in/ci/dence
in/ci/den/tal
in/ci/den/tally
in/ci/den/tals
in/ci/dents
in/cin/er/ate
in/cin/era/tor
in/cipi/ent
in/cise
in/ci/sor
in/cite
in/ci/vility
in/clem/ent
in/cli/na/tion
in/cline
in/clined
in/clude
in/cluded
in/cludes
in/clud/ing
in/clu/sion
in/clu/sive
in/cog/nito
in/cog/ni/zant
in/co/her/ent
in/come
in/comes

in/deli/cate

in/com/ing
in/com/men/su/rate
in/com/mode
in/com/mu/ni/ca/ble
in/com/mu/ni/cado
in/com/pa/ra/ble
in/com/pati/ble
in/com/pe/tence
in/com/pe/tent
in/com/plete
in/com/pre/hen/si/ble
in/con/clu/sive
in/con/gru/ous
in/con/se/quen/tial
in/con/sid/er/ate
in/con/sis/tent
in/con/sis/tently
in/con/sol/able
in/con/spicu/ous
in/con/stant
in/con/test/able
in/con/ti/nent
in/con/tro/vert/ible
in/con/ve/nience
in/con/ve/nienced
in/con/ve/nient
in/cor/po/rate
in/cor/po/rated
in/cor/po/rates
in/cor/po/rat/ing
in/cor/po/ra/tion
in/cor/po/real
in/cor/rect
in/cor/rectly
in/cor/ri/gi/ble
in/cor/rupt/ible
in/crease

in/creased
in/creases
in/creas/ing
in/creas/ingly
in/credi/ble
in/credu/lous
in/cre/ment
in/cre/ments
in/crimi/nate
incrust
in/crus/ta/tion
in/cu/bate
in/cu/ba/tor
in/cu/bus
in/cul/cate
in/cul/pate
in/cum/bent
incur
in/cur/able
in/cu/ri/ous
in/curred
in/cur/sion
in/debted
in/debt/ed/ness
in/de/cency
in/de/cent
in/de/ci/sion
in/de/ci/sive
in/de/co/rous
in/deed
in/de/fati/ga/ble
in/de/fea/si/ble
in/de/fin/able
in/defi/nite
in/defi/nitely
in/del/ible
in/deli/cate

158

in/dem/ni/fi/ca/tion
in/dem/nify
in/dem/nity
in/dent
in/den/ture
in/de/pen/dence
in/de/pen/dent
in/de/pen/dently
in/de/scrib/able
in/de/struc/ti/ble
in/de/ter/mi/nate
index
in/dexes
Indian
Indians
in/di/cate
in/di/cated
in/di/cates
in/di/cat/ing
in/di/ca/tion
in/dica/tive
in/dict
in/dicted
in/dif/fer/ence
in/dif/fer/ent
in/dige/nous
in/di/gent
in/di/gest/ible
in/di/ges/tion
in/dig/nant
in/dig/na/tion
in/dig/nity
in/digo
in/di/rect
in/di/rectly
in/dis/creet
in/dis/cre/tion
in/dis/crimi/nate
in/dis/pens/able
in/dis/posed
in/dis/pu/ta/ble
in/dis/solu/ble
in/dis/tinct
in/dite
in/di/vid/ual
in/di/vidu/al/ist
in/di/vidu/al/ity
in/di/vidu/ally
in/di/visi/ble
in/doc/tri/nate
in/doc/tri/nated
in/doc/tri/na/tion
in/do/lent
in/domi/ta/ble
Indonesian
in/doors
in/du/bi/ta/ble
in/duce
in/duce/ment
in/duc/ing
in/duct
in/duct/ees
in/duc/tion
in/dulge
in/dul/gence
in/dulg/ing
in/du/rate
in/dus/trial
in/dus/tri/al/ist
in/dus/tri/al/ists
in/dus/tries
in/dus/tri/ous
in/dus/try
ine/bri/ate

in/for/mal/ity

in/ef/fa/ble
in/ef/face/able
in/ef/fec/tive
in/ef/fec/tual
in/ef/fi/cient
in/ele/gant
in/eli/gi/ble
in/eluc/ta/ble
inept
in/equal/ity
in/eq/ui/ties
in/eq/uity
in/eradi/ca/ble
inert
in/er/tia
in/es/cap/able
in/es/ti/ma/ble
in/evi/ta/ble
in/evi/ta/bly
in/ex/act
in/ex/cus/able
in/ex/haust/ible
in/exo/ra/ble
in/ex/pen/sive
in/ex/pe/ri/ence
in/ex/pert
in/ex/pli/ca/ble
in/ex/press/ible
in/ex/tri/ca/ble
in/fal/li/ble
in/fa/mous
in/fancy
in/fant
in/fan/tile
in/fan/try
in/fatu/ate
in/fect

in/fec/tion
in/fec/tious
infer
in/fer/ence
in/fer/ences
in/fe/rior
in/fe/ri/or/ity
in/fer/nal
in/ferno
in/fest
in/fi/del
in/fi/del/ity
in/field
in/fil/trate
in/fil/tra/tion
in/fi/nite
in/fini/tesi/mal
in/fini/tive
in/fin/ity
in/fir/mi/ties
in/flame
in/flam/ma/tion
in/flate
in/fla/tion
in/fla/tion/ary
in/flect
in/flexi/ble
in/flict
in/flow
in/flu/ence
in/flu/ences
in/flu/en/tial
in/flu/enza
in/flux
in/form
in/for/mal
in/for/mal/ity

in/for/mally
in/for/mant
in/for/mants
in/for/ma/tion
in/for/ma/tional
in/for/ma/tive
in/formed
in/form/ing
in/frac/tion
in/fran/gi/ble
in/fra/red
in/fre/quent
in/fre/quently
in/fringe
in/fu/ri/ate
in/fuse
in/fu/sion
in/ge/nious
in/ge/nue
in/ge/nu/ity
in/genu/ous
in/ges/tion
in/glo/ri/ous
ingot
in/grain
in/grate
in/gra/ti/ate
in/grati/tude
in/gre/di/ent
in/gre/di/ents
in/gress
in/grown
in/hab/it
in/hab/it/ant
in/ha/la/tion
in/hale
in/her/ently

in/herit
in/heri/tance
in/hibi/tors
in/hos/pi/ta/ble
in/hu/man
in/imi/cal
in/imi/ta/ble
in/iq/ui/tous
ini/tial
ini/tialed
ini/tially
ini/ti/ate
ini/ti/at/ing
ini/tia/tion
ini/tia/tive
in/ject
in/ject/able
in/jec/tion
in/junc/tion
in/jure
in/jured
in/ju/ries
in/ju/ri/ous
in/jury
in/jus/tice
ink
ink/ling
ink stain
ink/stand
ink/well
in/laid
in/land
inlay
inlet
in/mate
in/mates
in/most

in/solu/ble

inn
in/nate
inner
in/ner/most
inn/keeper
in/no/cence
in/no/cent
in/no/cently
in/nocu/ous
in/no/vate
in/no/vat/ing
in/no/va/tion
in/no/va/tive
in/nu/endo
in/nu/mera/ble
in/ocu/late
in/of/fen/sive
in/op/era/ble
in/op/por/tune
in/or/di/nate
in/or/ganic
input
in/quest
in/qui/etude
in/quire
in/quired
in/quires
in/quir/ing
in/quiry
in/qui/si/tion
in/quisi/tive
in/quisi/tor
in/road
in/rush
in/sa/lu/bri/ous
in/sane
in/sani/tary

in/san/ity
in/sa/tia/ble
in/scribe
in/scribed
in/scrip/tion
in/scru/ta/ble
in/sect
in/sec/ti/cide
in/sec/ti/cides
in/se/cure
in/se/cu/rity
in/sen/sate
in/sen/si/ble
in/sen/si/tive
in/sen/tient
in/sepa/ra/ble
in/sert
in/serted
in/sert/ing
in/ser/tion
in/serts
in/side
in/sidi/ous
in/sight
in/sights
in/sig/nia
in/sig/nifi/cant
in/sin/cere
in/sinu/ate
in/sipid
in/sist
in/sist/ence
in/sists
in/so/far
in/sole
in/so/lent
in/solu/ble

in/sol/vent
in/som/nia
in/so/much
in/sou/ci/ance
in/spect
in/spected
in/spec/tion
in/spec/tor
in/spi/ra/tion
in/spi/ra/tional
inspire
in/spir/ing
in/sta/bil/ity
in/stall
in/stal/la/tion
in/stal/la/tions
in/stalled
in/stall/ing
in/stance
in/stances
in/stant
in/stan/ta/neous
in/stantly
in/stead
in/step
in/sti/gate
in/still
in/stinct
in/stinc/tive
in/sti/tute
in/sti/tuted
in/sti/tu/tion
in/sti/tu/tional
in/struct
in/structed
in/struc/tion
in/struc/tional

in/struc/tive
in/struc/tor
in/stru/ment
in/stru/men/tal
in/stru/men/ta/tion
in/sub/or/di/nate
in/suf/fer/able
in/suf/fer/ably
in/suf/fi/cient
in/su/lar
in/su/late
in/su/lated
in/su/lat/ing
in/su/la/tor
in/su/lin
in/sult
in/su/pera/ble
in/sup/port/able
in/sup/port/abil/ity
in/sura/ble
in/sur/ance
in/sure
in/sured
in/sures
in/sur/gent
in/surg/ing
in/sur/mount/able
in/suror
in/sur/rec/tion
in/tact
in/ta/glio
in/take
in/tan/gi/ble
in/te/ger
in/te/gral
in/te/grant
in/te/grate

in/ter/ro/gate

in/te/grated
in/te/grat/ing
in/te/gra/tion
in/teg/rity
in/tegu/ment
in/tel/lect
in/tel/lec/tual
in/tel/lec/tu/al/ize
in/tel/li/gence
in/tel/li/gent
in/tel/li/gently
in/tem/per/ate
in/tend
in/tended
in/tend/ers
in/tense
in/ten/si/fies
in/ten/sify
in/ten/sity
in/ten/sive
in/tent
in/ten/tion
in/ten/tional
in/ten/tion/ally
inter
in/ter/act
in/ter/ac/tion
in/ter/cede
in/ter/cept
in/ter/ces/sion
in/ter/change
in/ter/change/abil/ity
in/ter/change/able
in/ter/col/le/giate
in/ter/com
in/ter/course
in/ter/dict

in/ter/est
in/ter/ested
in/ter/est/ing
in/ter/est/ingly
in/ter/fere
in/ter/fer/ence
in/terim
in/te/rior
in/ter/ject
in/ter/line
in/ter/locu/tor
in/ter/loper
in/ter/lude
in/ter/mar/riage
in/ter/marry
in/ter/me/di/ate
in/ter/ment
in/ter/mi/na/ble
in/ter/mis/sion
in/ter/mit/tent
in/ter/mix
in/ter/mixed
in/tern
in/ter/nal
in/ter/na/tional
in/ter/na/tion/ally
in/ter/ne/cine
in/ter/po/late
in/ter/pose
in/ter/pret
in/ter/pre/ta/tion
in/ter/pre/ta/tions
in/ter/preted
in/ter/pret/ing
in/ter/pre/tive
in/ter/reg/num
in/ter/ro/gate

164

in/ter/ro/ga/tion
in/ter/rupt
in/ter/rupted
in/ter/rup/tion
in/ter/rup/tions
in/ter/sect
in/ter/sec/tion
in/ter/sec/tions
in/ter/sperse
in/ter/state
in/ter/stice
in/ter/twine
in/ter/ur/ban
in/ter/val
in/ter/vals
in/ter/vene
in/ter/ven/ing
in/ter/ven/tion
in/ter/view
in/ter/viewed
in/ter/view/ing
in/ter/weave
in/ter/wo/ven
in/tes/tate
in/tes/ti/nal
in/tes/tine
in/ti/macy
in/ti/mate
in/ti/ma/tion
in/timi/date
into
in/tol/era/ble
in/tol/er/ant
in/to/na/tion
in/toxi/cant
in/toxi/cate
in/trac/ta/ble

in/tran/si/gent
in/tran/si/tive
in/tra/state
in/tra/ve/nous
in/trepid
in/tri/cate
in/trigue
in/trigued
in/trigu/ing
in/trin/sic
in/tro/duce
in/tro/duced
in/tro/duces
in/tro/duc/ing
in/tro/duc/tion
in/tro/duc/tions
in/tro/duc/tory
in/tro/spec/tion
in/tro/vert
in/trude
in/tru/sion
in/tu/ition
in/tu/itive
in/un/date
inure
in/vade
in/valid
in/valu/able
in/valu/ably
in/vari/able
in/va/sion
in/vec/tive
in/veigh
in/vei/gle
in/vent
in/ven/tion
in/ven/tive

165

ir/re/triev/able

in/ven/tor
in/ven/to/ries
in/ven/tory
in/ven/to/ry/ing
in/vert
in/verted
in/vest
in/ves/ti/gate
in/ves/ti/gated
in/ves/ti/gat/ing
in/ves/ti/ga/tion
in/ves/ti/ga/tions
in/ves/ti/ga/tive
in/ves/ti/ga/tor
in/ves/ti/ture
in/vest/ment
in/vest/ments
in/vet/er/ate
in/vidi/ous
in/vigo/rate
in/vin/ci/ble
in/vio/late
in/visi/ble
in/vi/ta/tion
in/vi/ta/tions
in/vite
in/vited
in/vit/ing
in/voice
in/voke
in/voked
in/vol/un/tary
in/volve
in/volved
in/volve/ment
in/volv/ing
in/vul/nera/ble

in/ward
io/dine
ion
iota
ipso facto
Iranian
iras/ci/ble
irate
ire
iri/des/cent
irid/ium
Irish
irk
iron
ironi/cal
ironi/cally
ir/ra/di/ate
ir/ra/tio/nal
ir/rec/on/cil/able
ir/re/deem/able
ir/re/duc/ible
ir/ref/ra/ga/ble
ir/re/fut/able
ir/regu/lar
ir/regu/lari/ties
ir/regu/lar/ity
ir/rele/vant
ir/re/li/gious
ir/re/me/dia/ble
ir/repa/ra/ble
ir/re/press/ible
ir/re/proach/able
ir/re/sist/ible
ir/reso/lute
ir/re/spec/tive
ir/re/spon/si/ble
ir/re/triev/able

ir/rev/er/ent
ir/re/vers/ible
ir/re/vo/ca/ble
ir/ri/gate
ir/ri/gated
ir/ri/ga/tion
ir/ri/ta/ble
ir/ri/tant
ir/ri/tate
ir/ri/tated
ir/ri/ta/tion
is
isin/glass
is/land
isle
isn't
iso/late
iso/lated
iso/la/tion
isos/ce/les
iso/tope
iso/topes
Israel
is/su/ance
issue
is/sued
is/sues
is/su/ing
isth/mus
it
Italian
italic
itch
item
item/ize
item/ized
item/iz/ing

it/er/ate
itin/er/ant
itin/er/aries
itin/er/ary
its
it/self
I've
ivory
ivy

J

jab
jabot
jack
jackal
jacket
jack/eted
jack/knife
jac/quard
jade
jag
jag/uar
jail
ja/lopy
jal/ou/sie
jam
jamb
jam/bo/ree
jam/ming
jan/gle
jani/tor
jani/to/rial

jani/tress
January
Japanese
jar
jar/di/niere
jar/gon
jars
jas/mine
jas/per
jaun/dice
jaunt
jaunty
jave/lin
jaw
jay
jazz
jeal/ous
jeans
jeer
Jehovah
je/june

joy/ous

jell	jo/cose
jelly	jocu/lar
jeop/ar/dize	jo/cund
jeop/ar/dized	jog
jeop/ar/diz/ing	join
jeop/ardy	joined
jere/miad	join/ing
jerk	joins
jerky	joint
jer/kin	jointly
jer/sey	joints
jest	joint venture
Jesuit	joist
jet	joisted
jets	joke
jet/sam	joker
jet/ti/son	jokes
jetty	jol/lity
jewel	jolly
jew/eler	jolt
jew/elry	jon/quil
jib	josh
jibe	jos/tle
jibes	jot
jiffy	jot/ting
jig	jounce
jigs	jour/nal
jilt	jour/nal/ism
jin/gle	jour/nal/ist
jingo	jour/nals
jinx	jour/ney
jit/ter	jour/ney/man
job	jo/vial
job/ber	jowl
job/bers	joy
jobs	joy/ful
jockey	joy/ous

170

ju/bi/lant
ju/bi/la/tion
ju/bi/lee
Judaic
Judaism
judge
judges
judg/ment
judg/ments
ju/di/ca/ture
ju/di/cial
ju/di/ciary
ju/di/cious
judo
jug
jug/ger/naut
jug/gle
jugu/lar
juice
juici/ness
juicy
ju/jitsu
ju/jube
juke
juke/box
julep
July
jum/ble
jump
jumped
junc/tion
junc/ture
June
jun/gle
ju/nior
ju/ni/per
junk

junta
ju/ris/dic/tion
ju/ris/dic/tional
ju/ris/dic/tions
ju/ris/pru/dence
ju/rist
juror
jury
just
jus/tice
jus/ti/fi/ca/tion
jus/ti/fied
jus/ti/fies
jus/tify
justly
just/ness
just so
jut
jute
ju/ve/nile
ju/ve/niles
jux/ta/po/si/tion

K

kabob *cbb*
kai/ser *cz*
ka/lei/do/scope *cldscp*
kan/ga/roo *cgu*
ka/olin *caln*
kapok *cpc*
kaput *cpt*
ka/rate *(c.)*
karma *cra*
kayak *cic*
kedge *cj*
keel *cel*
keen *cn*
keen/ness *cn'*
keep *cp*
keep/ing *cp*
keeps *cps*
keep/sake *cpsc*
keg *cg*
kelp *clp*
ken/nel *cnl*

ken/nels *cnls*
kept *cp*
ker/nel *cnl*
kero/sene *csn*
ketch *cc*
ketch/up *ccp*
ket/tle *cll*
ket/tle/drum *clld*
key *ce*
key/board *cebd*
key/boards *cebds*
keyed *ce*
key line *celi*
key/note *cenl*
key/not/ing *cenl*
key punch (noun) *cepc*
key/punch (verb) *cepc*
key/punch/ing *cepc*
keys *ces*
key/stone *cesn*
key/ston/ing *cesn*

knob

khaki *cce*	ki/netic *cnlc*
khan *cn*	king *cg*
khe/dive *cde*	king/dom *cgd*
kick *cc*	kings *cgs*
kick/off *ccof*	kink *cq*
kid *cd*	kin/ship *cnS*
kid/nap *cdnp*	kins/man *cnz-*
kid/ney *cdne*	kiosk *cesc*
kids *cds*	kip/per *cp*
kill *cl*	kis/met *czt*
killed *cl̄*	kiss *c'*
killer *cl*	kit *ct*
kill/ers *cll*	kitchen *ccn*
kill/ing *cl̲*	kitch/en/ette *ccnt*
kiln *cln*	kitch/ens *ccns*
kilo *clo*	kitch/en/ware *ccnwa*
kilo/cy/cle *clscl (kc)*	kite *ct*
kilo/gram *clg (kg)*	kith *ct*
ki/lo/me/ter *clv (km)*	kits *cts*
kilo/volt *clvll (kv)*	kit/ten *ctn*
kilo/watt *clvt (kw)*	klep/to/ma/niac *cp-mec*
kilowatt hour *clvt r*	knack *nc*
kilowatt hours *clvt rs*	knap/sack *npsc*
kilo/watts *clvts (kws)*	knave *na*
kilt *cll*	knead *nd*
ki/mono *c-ma*	knee *ne*
kin *cn*	kneel *nel*
kind *cu*	knell *nl*
kin/der/gar/ten *c-rgtn*	knew *nu*
kind/est *cc,*	knick/knack *ncnc*
kind/hearted *ciht̄*	knife *nf*
kin/dle *c-l*	knife-like *nflc*
kind/li/ness *cil'*	knight *nt*
kindly *cil*	knit *nt*
kind/ness *ci'*	knit/ting *nt̲*
kinds *cis*	knives *nwz*
kin/dred *c-rd*	knob *nb*

knock *nc*
knock out *ncou*
knocks *ncs*
knoll *nol*
knot *n*
know *no*
know-how *nohw*
know/ing *no̱*
know/ingly *noḻ*
knowl/edge *nlj*
knowl/edge/able *nljb*
known *no*
knows *nos*
knuckle *ncl*
Kodak *cdc*
Korean *cen*
ko/sher *cs*

L

lab
la/bel
la/beled
la/bel/ing
la/bels
la/bor
labo/ra/to/ries
labo/ra/tory
la/bored
la/borer
la/bo/ri/ous
la/bors
la/bur/num
laby/rinth
lac
lace
lac/er/ate
lac/era/tion
lach/ry/mal
lach/ry/mose
lack
lacka/dai/si/cal
lacked
lackey
lack/ing
la/conic
lac/quer
la/crosse
lac/ta/tion
lac/teal
lac/tic
la/cuna
lad
lad/der
lad/ders
lade
la/dies
lad/ing
ladle
lady
lag
lager

lag/gard
la/goon
laid
lain
lair
laird
laity
lake
lakes
lamb
lam/baste
lam/bastes
lam/bency
lam/bent
lamb/skin
lame
la/ment
lam/en/ta/tion
lami/nate
lamp
lam/poon
lamp/post
lam/prey
lamps
lance
lan/cet
land
lan/dau
land/holder
land/lady
land/lord
land/mark
land/marked
land/marks
land/owner
land/own/ers
lands

land/scape
land/scap/ing
land/slide
lane
lanes
lan/guage
lan/guages
lan/guid
lan/guish
lan/guor
lank
lano/lin
lan/tern
lan/yard
Laotian
lap
lapel
lapi/dary
lapse
lapsed
lapses
lar/ce/nous
lar/ceny
lard
large
largely
large/ness
larger
lar/gess
larg/est
lar/iat
lark
lark/spur
larva
lar/vae
lar/yn/gi/tis
lar/ynx

las/civi/ous
lash
lass
las/si/tude
lasted
last/ing
lastly
latch
late
lately
late/ness
la/tent
later
lat/eral
lat/est
lath
lathe
lather
lati/tude
lat/ter
lat/tice
Latvian
laud
laud/able
lau/da/num
laugh
laugh/able
laugh/ter
launch
launched
launch/ing
laun/der
laun/der/ing
laun/dress
laun/dries
laun/dry
lau/re/ate

lau/rel
lava
lava/tory
lave
lav/en/der
lav/ish
law
law/ful
law/less
law/maker
lawn
law/suit
law/yer
lax
laxa/tive
lax/ity
lay
layer
lay/ette
lay/ettes
lay/ing
lay/man
lay/men
lay off (verb)
lay/off (noun)
lay out (verb)
lay/out (noun)
lays
lazy
leach
leach/ing
lead
leaden
leader
lead/er/ship
lead/ing
leaf

length

leaf/let	leg
leaf/lets	leg/acy
league	le/gal
leak	le/gal/ity
leak/age	le/gal/ize
leak/ing	le/gally
lean	leg/ate (noun)
leaner	le/gate (verb)
leans	lega/tee
leap	le/ga/tion
learn	le/gato
learned	leg/end
learner	leg/end/ary
learn/ing	leg/er/de/main
lease	leg/horn
leased	legi/bility
lease/hold	legi/ble
leash	legi/bly
leas/ing	le/gion
least	le/gions
leather	leg/is/late
leave	leg/is/lated
leaven	leg/is/la/tion
leaves	leg/is/la/tive
leav/ing	leg/is/la/tor
lech/er/ous	leg/is/la/ture
lec/tern	leg/is/la/tures
lec/ture	le/giti/macy
lec/turer	le/giti/mate
lec/tures	lei/sure
led	lei/surely
ledge	lemon
led/ger	lem/on/ade
leech	lend
leer	lender
lee/way	lend/ing
left	length

lengthen
length/ier
lengths
length/wise
lengthy
le/nience
le/niency
le/nient
lens
lent
len/til
leo/nine
leop/ard
leo/tard
lep/rosy
le/sion
less
les/see
lessen
less/ens
lesser
les/son
les/sons
lest
let
le/thal
le/thar/gic
leth/argy
lets
let/ter
let/ter/head
let/ter/heads
let/ter/ing
let/ter/press
let/ters
let/ting
let/tuce

levee
level
lev/el/ing
lev/els
lever
le/ver/age
le/via/than
le/vied
levi/ta/tion
lev/ity
levy
lewd
lexi/cog/ra/pher
lexi/cog/ra/phy
lexi/con
lia/bil/ity
lia/ble
li/ai/son
liar
li/ba/tion
libel
li/bel/ous
lib/eral
lib/er/ality
lib/er/al/ize
lib/er/als
lib/er/ate
lib/era/tion
lib/era/tor
lib/er/tine
lib/erty
li/bidi/nous
li/bido
li/brar/ian
li/brari/ans
li/braries
li/brary

li/bretto
lice
li/cense
li/censed
li/censee
li/censes
li/cens/ing
li/cen/tious
li/chen
licit
lick
lico/rice
lid
lie
liege
lien
lies
lieu/ten/ant
life
life/boat
life/less
life/like
life/line
life/long
life/saver
life/sav/ing
life/time
lift
lifted
lift/ing
lift-off
lifts
liga/ment
liga/ture
light
lighted
lighten

light/ened
lighter
light/house
light/ing
lightly
light/ning
light/ship
light/weight
lig/ne/ous
lig/nite
like
like/able
liked
like/li/hood
likely
like/ness
likes
like/wise
lik/ing
lilac
lit
lily
limb
lim/ber
lime
lime/light
lim/er/ick
lime/stone
lime/wa/ter
li/mi/nal
limit
limi/ta/tion
limi/ta/tions
lim/ited
lim/it/ing
lim/it/less
lim/its

li/thog/ra/phy

limn
lim/ou/sine
limp
lim/pet
lim/pid
linch/pin
line
line/age
lineal
linea/ment
linear
lined
line/man
line/men
linen
lin/ens
liner
lin/ers
lines
lin/ger
lin/ge/rie
lingo
lin/guist
lin/guis/tics
lin/guists
lini/ment
lin/ing
link
linked
link/ing
links
li/no/leum
lin/seed
lint
lin/tel
lion
li/on/ess

lip
liq/ue/fac/tion
liq/ue/fied
liq/uefy
li/queur
liq/uid
liq/ui/date
liq/ui/da/tion
liq/uor
lisle
lisp
lis/some
list
listed
lis/ten
lis/tened
lis/tener
lis/ten/ers
lis/ten/ing
list/less
lit
lit/any
liter
lit/er/acy
lit/eral
lit/er/ally
lit/er/ary
lit/er/ate
li/te/rati
lit/era/ture
lithe
lithe/some
lith/ium
litho/graph
litho/graphed
li/thog/ra/pher
li/thog/ra/phy

183

loge

Lithuanian	*lthnen*	lob/ster	*lbS*
liti/gant	*llg-*	local	*lcl*
liti/gate	*llga*	lo/cale	*lcl*
liti/ga/tion	*llgj*	lo/cali/ties	*lcl))*
li/ti/gious	*llyx*	lo/cal/ity	*lcl)*
lit/mus	*llnx*	lo/cal/ize	*lclz*
lit/ter	*l*	lo/cally	*lcl*
lit/tle	*ll*	lo/cate	*lca*
lit/urgy	*ltje*	lo/cated	*lcā*
liv/able	*lvb*	lo/cates	*lcas*
live	*lv (li)*	lo/cat/ing	*lca_*
lived	*lv̄*	lo/ca/tion	*lcj*
lives	*lvs*	lo/ca/tions	*lcjs*
live/li/hood	*lvlhd*	lock	*lc*
live/long	*lvlg*	locked	*lc̄*
lively	*lvl*	locker	*lc'*
liver	*lv*	lock/ing	*lc_*
live/stock	*lvsc*	lock/jaw	*lcja*
livid	*lvd*	lock out (verb)	*lcou*
liv/ing	*lv_*	lock/out (noun)	*lcou*
liz/ard	*lzd*	lock/smith	*lcsl*
load	*ld*	lo/co/mo/tion	*lcj*
loaded	*ld̄*	lo/co/mo/tive	*lcv*
loader	*ld'*	lo/co/mo/tives	*lcvs*
load/ing	*ld_*	locus	*lcx*
loaf	*lof*	lo/cust	*lc,*
loam	*lo*	lo/cu/tion	*lcj*
loan	*ln*	lode	*ld*
loan/able	*lnb*	lode/stone	*ldsn*
loaned	*ln̄*	lodge	*lj*
loathe	*lol*	lodges	*ljs*
loath/some	*llsn*	lodg/ing	*lj_*
loaves	*lovz*	loft	*lf*
lobby	*lbe*	lofty	*lf)*
lob/by/ing	*lbe_*	log	*lg*
lob/by/ists	*lbē,,*	loga/rithm	*lgl*
lobe	*lob*	loge	*loz*

log/gia	
logic	
logi/cal	
logi/cally	
lo/gi/cian	
logo	
logo/pedic	
logo/type	
logy	
loin	
loin/cloth	
loi/ter	
loll	
lol/li/pop	
lone	
lone/li/est	
lone/li/ness	
lonely	
lone/some	
long	
long/boat	
long distance	
longer	
long/est	
lon/gev/ity	
long/hand	
long/ing	
lon/gi/tude	
long-range	
long/shore/man	
long/shore/men	
look	
looked	
look/ing	
look/out	
loom	
loon	
loop	
loop/hole	
loose	
loosely	
loosen	
lo/qua/cious	
lord	
lore	
lor/gnette	
lorry	
lose	
loses	
los/ing	
loss	
losses	
lost	
lot	
lo/tion	
lots	
lot/tery	
loud	
loud/speaker	
lounge	
louse	
lout	
lou/ver	
lov/able	
love	
loved	
love/li/ness	
lovely	
lov/ers	
love-sick	
low	
low-born	
low/brow	
low-cost	

lyri/cal

lower	
low/ered	
low/er/ing	
low/est	
low/land	
lox	
loyal	
loy/alty	
loz/enge	
lub/ber	
lu/bri/cant	
lu/bri/cate	
lu/bri/cat/ing	
lu/bri/ca/tion	
lu/bri/cious	
lucid	
lu/cid/ity	
luck	
luck/ier	
lucky	
lu/cra/tive	
lucre	
lu/cu/bra/tion	
lu/di/crous	
lug	
lug/gage	
lu/gu/bri/ous	
luke/warm	
lull	
lul/laby	
lum/bago	
lum/ber	
lu/mi/nary	
lu/mi/nous	
lump	
lumps	
lu/nacy	
lunar	
lu/na/tic	
lunch	
lun/cheon	
lunch/room	
lu/nette	
lung	
lunge	
lunges	
lurch	
lure	
lured	
lurid	
lurk	
lurk/ing	
lus/cious	
lush	
lust	
lus/ter	
lus/trous	
lusty	
lute	
Lutheran	
luxu/ri/ant	
luxu/ri/ate	
luxu/ries	
luxu/ri/ous	
lux/ury	
ly/ceum	
lye	
lymph	
lym/phatic	
lynch	
lynx	
lyre	
ly/on/naise	
lyric	
lyri/cal	

186

ma/ca/bre
mac/adam
maca/roni
maca/roon
mace
mac/er/ate
mac/era/tion
mach
ma/chete
machi/na/tion
ma/chine
ma/chinery
ma/chin/ist
ma/chin/ists
mack/erel
macki/naw
mac/ro/cosm
ma/cron
mad
madam
made

ma/de/moi/selle
ma/dras
mad/ri/gal
mael/strom
mae/stro
maga/zine
maga/zines
ma/genta
mag/got
magic
ma/gi/cian
mag/is/te/rial
mag/is/trate
mag/na/nim/ity
mag/nani/mous
mag/nani/mously
mag/nate
mag/ne/sia
mag/ne/sium
mag/net
mag/netic

mag/ne/tism
mag/ne/tize
mag/neto
mag/ni/fi/ca/tion
mag/nifi/cence
mag/nifi/cent
mag/nify
mag/ni/tude
mag/no/lia
mag/num
mag/pie
ma/ha/raja
ma/hog/any
maid
maiden
maid/en/hair
maid/ser/vant
mail
mail/able
mail/bag
mail/box
mailer
mail/ing
mail/ings
mail/man
maim
main
main/land
main/liner
mainly
main/stay
main/tain
main/tained
main/tain/ing
main/te/nance
maize
ma/jes/tic

maj/esty
ma/jol/ica
major
ma/jor/domo
ma/jority
make
mak/ers
make/shift
make up (verb)
make/up (noun)
mak/ing
mala/chite
mal/ad/just/ment
mal/ad/min/is/ter
mal/adroit
mal/ady
mal/aise
ma/laria
mal/con/tent
male
male/dic/tion
male/faction
male/fac/tor
ma/lefic
ma/levo/lent
mal/fea/sance
mal/for/ma/tion
mal/formed
mal/func/tion
mal/ice
ma/li/cious
ma/lign
ma/lig/nancy
ma/lig/nant
ma/ligner
mall
mal/lard

mal/lea/ble
mal/let
mal/low
mal/nu/tri/tion
mal/oc/clu/sion
mal/odor/ous
mal/prac/tice
malt
malt/ose
mal/treat
mama
mam/mal
mam/mon
mam/moth
man
mana/cle
man/age
man/age/able
man/aged
man/age/ment
man/ager
mana/ge/rial
man/ag/ers
man/ag/ing
man/ci/ple
man/da/mus
man/da/rin
man/date
man/da/tory
man/di/ble
man/do/lin
man/drel
mane
ma/neu/ver
ma/neu/ver/abil/ity
man/ga/nese
mange

man/ger
man/gle
mango
man/grove
man/han/dle
man/hole
man/hood
mania
ma/niac
mani/cure
mani/fest
mani/fes/ta/tion
mani/festo
mani/fold
mani/kin
ma/nipu/late
ma/nipu/la/tion
ma/nipu/la/tor
man/kind
manly
manna
man/ne/quin
man/ner
man/ner/ism
man/nish
manor
ma/no/rial
man power
manse
man/ser/vant
man/sion
man/slaugh/ter
man/teau
man/tel
man/tilla
man/tle
man/ual

mar/vel/ous

manu/ally	
manu/fac/ture	
manu/fac/turer	
manu/fac/tur/ing	
manu/mis/sion	
ma/nure	
manu/script	
many	
Maori	
map	
maple	
mar	
mara/schino	
mara/thon	
ma/raud	
mar/ble	
mar/ble/ize	
mar/ca/site	
March	
marches	
mar/chesa	
mar/chese	
mar/chio/ness	
mare	
mar/ga/rine	
mar/gin	
mar/ginal	
mar/gi/na/lia	
mar/grave	
mari/gold	
ma/rina	
mari/nade	
mari/nate	
ma/rine	
mari/ner	
mari/onette	
mari/tal	

mari/time	
mar/jo/ram	
mark	
marker	
mar/ket	
mar/ket/able	
mar/keted	
mar/ket/ing	
mar/ket/place	
mark/ing	
marl	
mar/lin	
mar/ma/lade	
mar/mo/set	
mar/mot	
ma/roon	
mar/quee	
mar/que/try	
mar/quis	
mar/quise	
mar/riage	
mar/riage/able	
mar/row	
marry	
marsh	
mar/shal	
marsh/mal/low	
mart	
mar/ten	
mar/tial	
mar/tially	
mar/ti/net	
mar/tini	
mar/tyr	
mar/tyr/dom	
mar/vel	
mar/vel/ous	

mas/cara
mas/cot
mas/cu/line
mas/cu/linity
mash
mask
mask/ing
mas/och/ism
mas/och/ist
mason
ma/sonry
mas/quer/ade
mass
mas/sa/cre
mas/sage
mas/seur
mas/seuse
mas/sif
mas/sive
mast
mas/ter
mas/ter/ful
mas/ter/piece
mas/ter/works
mas/tery
mast/head
mas/ti/cate
mas/ti/ca/tion
mas/tiff
mast/odon
mas/toid
mat
mata/dor
match
match/book
match/ing
match/less

match/maker
mate
ma/te/rial
ma/te/ri/al/ism
ma/te/ri/al/ist
ma/te/ri/al/ize
ma/te/ri/ally
ma/ter/nal
ma/ter/nity
mathe/mati/cal
mathe/ma/ti/cian
mathe/mat/ics
mati/nee
ma/tri/arch
ma/tri/ar/chy
matri/ces
ma/tricu/late
ma/tricu/la/tion
mat/ri/mo/nial
mat/ri/mony
ma/trix
ma/tron
ma/tronly
mat/ter
mat/ters
mat/tock
mat/tress
mat/tresses
matu/rate
matu/ra/tion
ma/ture
ma/tu/rity
ma/tu/ti/nal
matzo
maud/lin
maul
maun/der

mau/so/leum
mauve
mav/er/ick
maw
mawk/ish
max/illa
max/il/lary
maxim
maxi/mum
may
maya
maybe
Mayday
may/hem
may/on/naise
mayor
may/or/alty
maze
ma/zurka
me
mead
meadow
mea/ger
meal
mean
me/an/der
me/an/der/ing
mean/ing
mean/ing/ful
mean/ness
meant
mean/time
mean/while
mea/sles
mea/sly
meas/ur/able
mea/sure

mea/sure/ment
mea/surer
mea/sur/ing
meat
me/atus
mecca
me/chanic
me/chani/cal
me/chani/cally
mecha/nism
mecha/ni/za/tion
mecha/nized
medal
me/dal/lion
med/dle
med/dle/some
media
me/dial
me/dian
me/di/ate
me/dia/tion
me/dia/tor
medi/ca/ble
medi/cal
me/di/ca/ment
medi/care
medi/cate
medi/ca/tion
me/dici/nal
medi/cine
me/di/eval
me/dio/cre
me/di/oc/rity
medi/tate
medi/ta/tion
me/dium
med/ley

meek
meer/schaum
meet
meet/ing
mega/cy/cle
mega/phone
mega/ton
mel/an/cho/lia
mel/an/choly
Melanesian
me/lange
mela/noid
meld
melee
me/lio/rate
me/lio/ra/tion
mel/lif/lu/ous
mel/low
me/lo/deon
me/lo/di/ous
melo/drama
mel/ody
melon
melt
melt/ing
mem/ber
mem/ber/ship
mem/brane
mem/bra/nous
me/mento
memo
mem/oir
memo/ra/bi/lia
memo/ra/ble
memo/randa
memo/ran/dum
me/mo/rial
me/mo/ri/al/ize
memo/ries
memo/rize
mem/ory
men
men/ace
men/ac/ing
me/nage
me/nag/erie
mend
mcn/da/cious
men/di/cant
me/nial
me/nin/ges
men/in/gi/tis
meno/pause
men's
men/ses
men/strual
men/stru/ate
men/strua/tion
men/sura/ble
men/su/ra/tion
men/tal
men/tal/ity
men/tally
men/thol
men/tion
men/tioned
men/tion/ing
men/tor
menu
me/phitic
mer/can/tile
mer/ce/nary
mer/cer/ize
mer/chan/dise

met/tle/some

mer/chan/dis/ers
mer/chan/dis/ing
mer/chant
mer/chant/man
mer/ci/ful
mer/ci/less
mer/cu/rial
mer/cury
mercy
mere
merely
mere/tri/cious
merge
merger
me/rid/ian
me/ringue
me/rino
merit
meri/to/ri/ous
mer/maid
mer/man
mer/rily
mer/ri/ment
merry
mesa
mes/al/liance
mesh
me/sial
mes/mer/ism
mes/mer/ize
mess
mes/sage
mes/sen/ger
mes/siah
messieurs
messy
mes/tizo

met
me/tabo/lism
metal
me/tal/lic
met/al/loid
met/al/lurgy
meta/mor/phic
meta/mor/pho/ses
meta/mor/pho/sis
meta/phor
meta/phori/cal
meta/physi/cal
meta/phys/ics
me/tas/ta/sis
meta/tar/sal
mete
me/teor
me/te/or/ite
me/teo/rolo/gist
me/teo/rology
meter
method
me/thodi/cal
Methodist
meth/od/ize
meth/od/ology
meth/yl/ate
me/ticu/lous
me/tier
met/ric
met/ri/cal
met/ro/nome
me/tropo/lis
met/ro/poli/tan
me/tropoly
met/tle
met/tle/some

194

mil/lionth

Mexican
mez/za/nine
mezzo-soprano
mi/asma
mica
mice
mi/crobe
mi/cro/bial
mi/cro/cosm
mi/cro/film
mi/cro/or/ga/nism
mi/cro/phone
mi/cro/scope
mic/ro/scopic
mi/cro/sec/ond
mi/cro/wave
mid
mid/after/noon
mid/course
mid/day
mid/den
mid/dle
midget
mid/land
mid/night
mid/ship/man
midst
mid/sum/mer
mid/way
mid/week
mid/west
mid/western
mid/wife
mid/year
mien
miff
might

mighti/ness
mighty
mi/gnon/ette
mi/graine
mi/grate
mi/gra/tion
mi/kado
milch
mild
mil/dew
mildly
mild/ness
mile
mile/age
mile/post
mile/stone
mi/lieu
mili/tant
mili/ta/rist
mili/tary
mili/tate
mi/li/tia
milk
milk/ing
milk/sop
mill
mil/len/nium
miller
mil/let
mil/li/gram
mil/li/me/ter
mil/li/ner
mil/li/nery
mill/ing
mil/lion
mil/lion/aire
mil/lionth

195

mil/li/sec/ond
mill/stone
mill/work
mim/eo/graph
mim/eo/graph/ing
mimic
mim/icry
mi/mosa
mina/ret
mi/na/tory
mince
mind
mind/ful
mind/ing
mind/less
mine
miner
min/eral
min/er/alogy
min/gle
minia/ture
mini/mal
mini/mize
mini/mum
min/ing
min/ion
min/is/cule
min/is/ter
min/is/tered
min/is/trant
min/is/try
mini/track
mink
min/now
minor
mi/nor/ity
min/ster

min/strel
mint
minu/end
minuet
minus
min/ute
min/utely
mi/nu/tiae
mira/cle
mi/racu/lous
mi/rage
mire
mir/ror
mirth
mis/ad/ven/ture
mis/an/thrope
mis/ap/pli/ca/tion
mis/ap/pre/hen/sion
mis/ap/pro/pri/ate
mis/be/got/ten
mis/be/have
mis/be/lief
mis/cal/cu/late
mis/car/ry/ing
mis/ce/ge/na/tion
mis/cel/la/neous
mis/cel/lany
mis/chance
mis/chief
mis/chie/vous
mis/ci/ble
mis/con/cep/tion
mis/con/duct
mis/con/struc/tion
mis/con/strue
mis/cre/ant
mis/cue

mis/deal
mis/deed
mis/de/meanor
mis/di/rect
miser
mis/era/ble
mis/ery
mis/fea/sance
mis/fire
mis/fit
mis/for/tune
mis/giv/ing
mis/gov/ern
mis/guide
mis/hap
mis/in/form
mis/in/for/ma/tion
mis/in/ter/pret
mis/judge
mis/lay
mis/lead
mis/man/age
mis/no/mer
mi/sogy/nous
mis/place
mis/print
mis/pro/nounce
mis/quo/ta/tion
mis/read
mis/reckon
mis/rep/re/sent
mis/rule
miss
missed
misses
mis/shapen
mis/sile

mis/sile/man
miss/ing
mis/sion
mis/sion/ary
mis/sive
mis/spell
mis/state
mis/stated
mis/step
mist
mis/take
mis/taken
mis/tle/toe
mis/took
mis/tral
mis/treat
mis/tress
mis/trial
mis/trust
misty
mis/un/der/stand
mis/un/der/stand/ing
mis/un/der/stood
mis/use
mite
miter
miti/gate
miti/ga/tor
mitt
mit/ten
mit/ti/mus
mix
mixer
mix/ing
mix/ture
mix-up
miz/zen

miz/zle
mne/monic
moan
moat
mob
mo/bile
mo/bility
mo/bi/lize
mo/bi/liz/ing
mob/ster
moc/ca/sin
mocha
mock
mock/ery
mode
model
mod/er/ate
mod/er/ately
mod/era/tion
mod/era/tor
mod/ern
mod/er/nity
mod/ern/iza/tion
mod/ern/ize
mod/est
mod/esty
modi/cum
modi/fi/able
modi/fi/ca/tion
modi/fier
modify
mod/ish
mo/diste
modu/lar
modu/late
modu/la/tion
mod/ule

modu/lus
modus vi/vendi
mogul
mo/hair
Mohammedan
moi/ety
moil
moist
moist/en
mois/ture
molar
mo/las/ses
mold
molder
mold/ing
moldy
mole
mo/lecu/lar
mole/cule
mo/lest
mo/les/ta/tion
mol/li/fi/ca/tion
mol/lify
mol/lusk
mol/ly/cod/dle
molt
mol/ten
mo/lyb/de/num
mo/ment
mo/men/tary
mo/men/tous
mo/men/tum
mon/arch
mon/ar/chism
mon/ar/chy
mon/as/tery
mo/nas/tic

mon/au/ral
Monday
mone/tary
money
Mongolian
mon/grel
moni/tor
moni/tored
moni/tress
monk
mon/key
mon/key/shine
mono/chrome
mono/cle
mo/noga/mous
mo/nog/amy
mono/gram
mono/graph
mo/nogyny
mo/no/lith
mono/logue
mono/ma/nia
mono/plane
mo/nopo/list
mo/nopo/lize
mo/nopoly
mono/syl/la/ble
mono/tone
mo/noto/nous
mo/notony
mon/ox/ide
mon/sieur
mon/si/gnor
mon/soon
mon/ster
mon/strosity
mon/strous

mon/tage
month
monthly
monu/ment
monu/men/tal
mood
moodi/ness
moody
moon
moon/beam
moon/light
moon/lighter
moon/lit
moon/rise
moon/scape
moon/shine
moon/stone
moor
moor/age
Moorish
moose
moot
mop
mope
mop/pet
mo/raine
moral
mo/rale
mor/al/ist
mo/ral/ity
mor/al/ize
mor/ally
mo/rass
mora/to/rium
mor/bid
mor/bidity
mor/dant

more
more/over
mores
morgue
mori/bund
Mormon
morn
morn/ing
mo/rocco
moron
mo/rose
mor/phia
mor/phine
mor/row
mor/sel
mor/tal
mor/tal/ity
mor/tar
mor/tar/board
mort/gage
mort/gagee
mort/ga/gor
mor/ti/cian
mor/ti/fi/ca/tion
mor/tify
mor/tise
mor/tu/ary
mo/saic
mosey
Moslem
mosque
mos/quito
moss
moss/back
most
mote
motel

moth
mother
moth/er/hood
mother-in-law
mother/land
moth/erly
moth/proof
motif
mo/tile
mo/tion
mo/tion/less
mo/ti/vate
mo/ti/vat/ing
mo/ti/va/tion
mo/tive
mot/ley
motor
mo/tor/boat
mo/tor/cade
mo/tor/car
mo/tor/cy/cle
mo/tor/ist
mo/tor/ize
mo/tor/man
mot/tle
motto
mound
mount
moun/tain
moun/tain/eer
moun/tain/ous
moun/te/bank
mounted
mount/ing
mourn
mourn/ful
mouse

mousse
mousy
mouth
mouth/ful
mouth/piece
mov/able
move
mover
move/ment
movie
mov/ing
mow
mower
mown
Mr.
Mrs.
much
mu/ci/lage
mu/ci/lagi/nous
muck
muck/raker
mu/cous
mucus
mud
mud/di/ness
mud/dle
muddy
mud/guard
mud/slinger
mu/ez/zin
muff
muf/fin
muf/fle
muf/fler
mufti
mug
mug/ger

mug/wump
mu/latto
mul/berry
mulch
mulct
mule
mull
mul/lion
mul/ti/fari/ous
mul/ti/form
Multigraph
mul/ti/lat/eral
Multimeter
mul/ti/mil/lion/aire
mul/ti/ped
mul/ti/ple
mul/ti/plex
mul/ti/pli/able
mul/ti/pli/cand
mul/ti/pli/ca/tion
mul/ti/plic/ity
mul/ti/plier
mul/ti/ply
mul/ti/stage
mul/ti/tude
mul/ti/tu/di/nous
mum
mum/ble
mum/mify
mummy
mumps
munch
mun/dane
mu/nici/pal
mu/nici/pali/ties
mu/nici/pality
mu/nifi/cence

201

my/thology

mu/nifi/cent	musti/ness
mu/ni/tion	musty
mural	mu/ta/ble
mur/der	mu/tate
mur/derer	mu/ta/tion
mur/der/ous	mute
murk	mu/ti/late
mur/mur	mu/ti/lated
mur/mur/ous	mu/ti/la/tion
mur/rain	mu/ti/nous
mus/ca/tel	mu/tiny
mus/cle	mut/ter
mus/cu/lar	mut/ton
mus/cu/larity	mu/tual
mus/cu/la/ture	mu/tu/ally
muse	muz/zle
mu/sette	my
mu/seum	myo/pia
mush	myo/pic
mush/room	myr/iad
mushy	myr/mi/don
music	myrrh
mu/si/cal	my/self
mu/si/cian	mys/te/ri/ous
musk	mys/tery
mus/ket	mys/tic
mus/ke/teer	mys/ti/cal
musk/rat	mys/ti/cism
Muslim	mys/ti/fi/ca/tion
mus/lin	mys/tify
muss	mys/tique
mus/sel	myth
must	mythi/cal
mustache	my/thology
mus/tang	
mus/tard	
mus/ter	

N

nab	nape
nabob	na/pery
na/celle	naph/tha
nacre	nap/kin
na/cre/ous	na/po/leon
nadir	Napoleonic
nag	nar/cis/sist
nag/ger	nar/cis/sus
nail	nar/cotic
nails	nar/coti/cism
naive	nar/co/tism
na/iveté	nar/rate
naked	nar/rated
namby-pamby	nar/ra/tion
name	nar/ra/tive
named	nar/ra/tor
name/less	nar/row
namely	nar/rower
name/sake	nar/rowly
nam/ing	nar/row/ness
nap	nasal

ne/cropo/lis

na/sality
na/sal/ize
na/scent
nas/tily
nas/ti/ness
nas/tur/tium
nasty
natal
na/tant
na/ta/to/rial
na/ta/to/rium
na/tion
na/tional
na/tion/al/ist
na/tion/ality
na/tion/al/ize
na/tion/ally
na/tion/als
na/tive
na/tively
na/tivity
natty
natu/ral
natu/ral/ism
natu/ral/ist
natu/ral/iza/tion
natu/rally
natu/ral/ness
na/ture
naught
naugh/ti/ness
naughty
nau/sea
nau/se/ate
nau/seous
nau/ti/cal
nau/ti/lus

Navaho
naval
nave
navi/gate
navi/ga/tion
navi/ga/tor
navy
nay
Nazi
Neanderthal
near
nearby
nearer
near/est
near/ing
nearly
near/ness
near/sighted
neat
neater
neat/est
neat/ness
nebula
nebu/lae
nebu/lar
nebu/lous
nec/es/sarily
nec/es/sary
ne/ces/si/tate
ne/ces/si/tates
ne/ces/si/tat/ing
ne/ces/si/tous
ne/ces/sity
neck
neck/lace
neck/tie
ne/cropo/lis

ne/cro/sis
nec/tar
nec/tar/ine
nee
need
needed
need/ful
needi/est
needi/ness
need/ing
nee/dle
need/less
need/lessly
needn't
needy
ne/fari/ous
ne/gate
ne/gates
ne/ga/tion
nega/tive
nega/tives
nega/tiv/ism
ne/glect
ne/glected
ne/glect/ful
neg/li/gee
neg/li/gence
neg/li/gent
ne/li/gi/ble
ne/go/tia/bility
ne/go/tia/ble
ne/go/ti/ate
ne/go/ti/ated
ne/go/ti/at/ing
ne/go/tia/tion
ne/go/tia/tor
Negro

neigh
neigh/bor
neigh/bor/hood
neigh/bor/hoods
neigh/borly
neigh/bors
nei/ther
neme/sis
neon
neo/lithic
neo/phyte
neo/plasm
neo/teric
nephew
ne/phri/tis
nepo/tism
nerve
nerve/less
ner/vous
ner/vous/ness
nervy
nest
nest/ing
nes/tle
net
nether
neth/er/most
nets
net/ting
net/tle
net/work
neu/ral
neu/ral/gia
neur/as/the/nia
neu/ri/tis
neu/rolo/gist
neu/rology

neu/ron
neu/ro/sis
neu/rotic
neu/ter
neu/tral
neu/trality
neu/tral/lize
neu/tron
never
nev/er/the/less
new
new/comer
newel
newer
new/est
newly
new/ness
news
news/cast/ter
news/let/ter
news/pa/per
news/pa/per/man
news/pa/per/men
news/print
news/stand
news/wor/thy
next
nib
nib/ble
nib/lick
nice
nicely
nicer
nicety
niche
nick
nickel

nick/el/odeon
nicker
nick/name
nico/tine
nifty
Nigerian
niece
nig/gard
nig/gardly
nig/gle
nigh
night
night/cap
night/fall
night/gown
night/in/gale
nightly
night/mare
nights
night/time
ni/hil/ist
ni/hil/is/tic
nil
nim/ble
nim/bus
nin/com/poop
nine
ninety
ninth
nip
nip/ple
nir/vana
nisei
niter
ni/trate
ni/tric
ni/tride

ni/trify
ni/trite
ni/tro/gen
ni/tro/glyc/erin
ni/trous
nit/wit
no
no/bil/ity
nobile
no/ble/man
no/ble/wom/an
nobly
no/body
noc/tur/nal
noc/turne
nod
nodu/lar
node
nod/ule
nod/ules
noise
noise/less
noisily
noi/some
noisy
nomad
no/madic
no/men/cla/ture
nomi/nal
nomi/nally
nomi/nate
nomi/nated
nomi/nat/ing
nomi/na/tion
nomi/na/tions
nomi/na/tor
nomi/nee

nomi/nees
nonce
non/cha/lance
non/cha/lant
non/com/ba/tant
non/com/mit/tal
non com/pos men/tis
non/con/duc/tor
non/con/form/ist
non/de/script
none
non/en/tity
non/es/sen/tial
non/ex/ist/ent
non/fea/sance
non/in/ter/ven/tion
non/join/der
non/pa/reil
non/par/ti/san
non/plus
non/pro/fes/sional
non/pro/fit
non/sense
non/stop
non/sup/port
non/union
noo/dle
nook
noon
noon/day
noon/time
noose
nor
Nordic
norm
nor/mal
nor/mality

nude

nor/mally
Norse
north
north/east
north/east/er
north/east/ern
north/erly
north/ern
Northerner
north/ward
north/west
north/west/ern
Norwegian
nose
nose/bleed
nose/gay
nose/piece
nos/tal/gia
nos/tril
nos/trum
not
no/ta/bil/ity
no/ta/ble
no/ta/bly
no/tar/ial
no/ta/rize
no/tary
no/ta/tion
no/ta/tions
notch
note
note/book
note/books
note/wor/thy
noth/ing
no/tice
no/tice/able

no/ticed
no/tices
no/ti/fi/ca/tion
no/ti/fied
no/ti/fies
no/tify
not/ing
no/tion
no/tional
no/to/ri/ety
no/to/ri/ous
not/with/stand/ing
noun
nour/ish
nova
novel
nov/el/ette
nov/el/ist
nov/elty
November
no/vena
nov/ice
no/vi/tiate
Novocain
now
nowa/days
no/where
nox/ious
noz/zle
nu/ance
nub
nub/bin
nu/bile
nu/clear
nu/clea/tion
nu/cleus
nude

nudge
nu/dity
nug/get
nui/sance
null
nul/li/fi/ca/tion
nul/li/fied
nul/li/fier
nul/lify
nul/li/fy/ing
numb
num/ber
num/bered
num/ber/less
num/bers
numb/ness
numb/skull
nu/meral
nu/mer/ate
nu/mera/tor
nu/meri/cal
nu/mer/ous
nu/mis/mat/ics
nu/mis/ma/tist
Nun
nun/cio
nun/cu/pa/tive
nun/nery
nup/tial
nurse
nur/sery
nurses
nurs/ing
nurs/ling
nur/ture
nut
nut/meg

nu/tri/ent
nu/tri/tion
nu/tri/tious
nu/tri/tive
nut/shell
nuz/zle
nylon
nymph

oaf *of*
oak *oc*
oakum *ok*
oar *o*
oar/lock *olc*
oasis *oss*
oat *ot*
oat/cake *otcc*
oat/meal *otl*
ob/bli/gato *obglo*
ob/du/racy *obDse*
ob/du/rate *obDt*
obe/di/ence *obde/*
obe/di/ent *obde—*
obei/sance *obs/*
obe/lisk *oblsc*
obese *obs*
obe/sity *obs)*
obey *oba*
ob/fus/cate *obfsca*
ob/fus/ca/tion *obfscy*

obi *obe*
obit *obt*
obituary *obCy*
ob/ject *ob*
ob/jec/tion *oby*
ob/jec/tion/able *obyb*
ob/jec/tive *obv*
ob/jec/tively *obvl*
ob/jec/tivity *obv)*
ob/jec/tor *ob*
ob/jur/gate *ob Jga*
ob/jur/ga/tion *ob Jg1*
oblate *oba*
ob/li/gate *obga*
ob/li/gat/ing *obga—*
ob/li/ga/tion *obg1*
obliga/tory *obgly*
oblige *oby*
obliger *oby*
oblique *obc*
oblit/er/ate *obta*

211

oblit/era/tion
oblivion
oblivi/ous
ob/long
ob/lo/quy
ob/nox/ious
oboe
obo/ist
ob/scene
ob/scenity
ob/scu/ra/tion
ob/scure
ob/scu/rity
ob/se/qui/ous
ob/seq/uity
ob/se/quy
ob/ser/vance
ob/ser/vant
ob/ser/va/tion
ob/ser/va/tory
observe
ob/server
ob/serv/ing
ob/sess
ob/ses/sion
ob/so/les/cence
ob/so/lete
ob/sta/cle
ob/stet/ri/cal
ob/ste/tri/cian
ob/sti/nacy
ob/sti/nate
ob/strep/er/ous
ob/struct
ob/struc/tion
ob/tain
ob/tain/able
ob/tain/ing
ob/trude
ob/tru/sion
ob/tru/sive
ob/tuse
ob/verse
ob/ver/sion
ob/vi/ate
ob/vi/ous
ob/vi/ously
oc/ca/sion
oc/ca/sional
oc/ca/sion/ally
oc/ci/dent
oc/ci/den/tal
oc/cipi/tal
oc/ci/put
oc/clude
oc/clu/sion
oc/cult
oc/cult/ism
oc/cu/pan/cy
oc/cu/pant
oc/cu/pa/tional
oc/cu/pies
oc/cupy
oc/cu/py/ing
oc/cur
oc/cur/rence
oc/cur/ring
ocean
ocean/front
ocean/go/ing
oce/lot
ocher
o'clock
oc/ta/gon

oc/ta/go/nal
oc/tane
oc/tan/gu/lar
oc/tant
oc/ta/vo
October
oc/to/ge/nar/ian
oc/to/pus
oc/u/lar
oc/u/list
odd
odd/ball
oddi/ties
oddity
oddly
ode
odi/ous
odium
odome/ter
odor
odor/if/er/ous
odor/less
odor/ous
od/ys/sey
of
off
offal
off/beat
off/cast
of/fend
of/fender
of/fense
of/fen/sive
offer
of/fer/ing
of/fer/tory
off/hand

of/fice
of/fi/cer
of/fi/cial
of/fi/cially
of/fi/ci/ate
of/fi/cia/tor
of/fi/cious
off/set
off/shoot
off/shore
off/spring
often
of/ten/times
ogle
ogre
ohm
oil
oil/cloth
oili/ness
oil/skin
oily
oint/ment
okay
okay/ing
old
older
old/ness
old/ster
ole/agi/nous
ole/og/ra/phy
oleo/mar/ga/rine
ol/fac/tory
oli/gar/chy
olive
Olympic
omega
om/elet

213

op/ti/mism

omen
omi/nous
omis/sion
omit
omit/ting
om/ni/bus
om/ni/fari/ous
om/nipo/tence
om/nipo/tent
om/ni/science
om/ni/scient
om/nivo/rous
on
once
on/com/ing
one
one/ness
oner/ous
one/self
onion
on/ion/skin
on/looker
only
on/rush
onset
on/slaught
onto
onus
on/ward
onyx
oo/dles
ooze
opacity
opal
opal/es/cent
opaque
open

opener
open/ing
openly
opera
op/era/ble
op/er/ate
op/er/at/ing
op/era/tion
op/era/tional
op/era/tor
op/er/etta
oph/thal/mo/scope
opi/ate
opine
opin/ion
opin/ion/ated
opium
op/po/nent
op/por/tune
op/por/tu/ni/ties
op/por/tu/nity
op/pos/able
op/pose
op/pos/ing
op/po/site
op/po/si/tion
op/press
op/pres/sion
op/pres/sive
op/pres/sor
op/pro/bri/ous
op/pro/brium
opt
optic
op/ti/cal
op/ti/cian
op/ti/mism

op/ti/mist
op/ti/mis/tic
op/ti/mum
op/tion
op/tional
op/tome/trist
op/tome/try
opu/lence
opu/lent
opus
or
ora/cle
oracu/lar
oral
or/ange
or/ange/ade
ora/tion
ora/tor
ora/tori/cal
ora/to/rio
orb
or/bicu/lar
orbit
or/bital
or/chard
or/ches/tra
or/ches/tral
or/ches/trate
or/ches/tra/tion
or/chid
or/dain
or/deal
order
or/der/ing
or/der/li/ness
or/derly
or/di/nal
or/di/nance
or/di/nar/ily
or/di/nary
or/di/nate
ord/nance
ore
organ
or/ganic
or/ga/nism
organ/ist
or/ga/ni/za/tion
or/ga/ni/za/tional
or/ga/nize
or/ga/nizer
or/ga/niz/ing
or/gies
orgy
ori/ent
ori/en/tal
ori/en/tate
ori/en/ta/tion
ori/fice
ori/gin
origi/nal
origi/nality
origi/nally
origi/nate
origi/nat/ing
origi/na/tion
origi/na/tor
ori/ole
ori/son
or/molu
or/na/ment
or/na/men/tal
or/nate
or/nery

out/pour

or/ni/thology	*onllje*	ought	*al*
oro/tund	*ol —*	ounce	*oz*
or/phan	*ofn*	our	*r*
or/phan/age	*ofnj*	our/selves	*rsl*
ortho/don/tia	*oldca*	oust	*ou,*
or/tho/dox	*oldx*	ouster	*ouS*
or/thog/ra/pher	*olgf*	out	*ou*
or/tho/graphic	*olgfc*	out/bid	*oubd*
or/thog/ra/phy	*olgfe*	out/board	*ouBd*
or/tho/pe/dic	*olpdc*	out/break	*ouBc*
os/cil/late	*osla*	out/burst	*ouB,*
os/cil/lat/ing	*osla*	out/cast	*ouc,*
os/cil/la/tion	*oslj*	out/class	*ouc'*
os/cil/la/tor	*osla*	out/come	*ouk*
os/cil/lo/scope	*oslscp*	out/cry	*ouci*
os/cu/late	*oscla*	out/dated	*oudā*
os/cu/la/tion	*osclj*	outdo	*oudu*
os/mium	*oz (@s)*	out/door	*oudo*
os/mo/sis	*oss*	outer	*ou*
os/prey	*ospe*	out/field	*oufld*
os/se/ous	*osx*	out/fit	*oufl*
os/si/fi/ca/tion	*osfcj*	out/go/ing	*oug*
os/sify	*osf*	out/grow	*ougo*
os/ten/si/ble	*oo/b*	out/growth	*ougl*
os/ten/ta/tion	*oo-j*	out/ing	*ou*
os/ten/ta/tious	*oo-x*	out/land/ish	*oul— s*
os/teo/my/eli/tis	*osenlls*	out/last	*oul,*
os/teo/path	*osepl*	out/law	*oula*
os/teo/pathic	*oseplc*	out/lay	*oula*
os/te/opa/thist	*osepl,*	out/let	*oull*
os/te/opa/thy	*oseple*	out/line	*ouli*
os/tra/cism	*oSsj*	out/lin/ing	*oulc*
os/tra/cize	*oSsz*	out/live	*oulv*
os/trich	*oSc*	out/look	*oulc*
other	*J*	out/ly/ing	*ouli*
oth/er/wise	*Jwz*	out/post	*oupo,*
ouch	*ouc*	out/pour	*oupo*

over/tone

out/put	oup	over/come	Ok
out/rage	oury	over/crowd	OCrd
out/ra/geous	ouryx	overdo	Odu
out/rank	ourq	over/draft	ODf
out/right	owt	over/draw	ODa
out/sell	ousl	over/due	Odu
out/set	ousl	over/flow	Ofo
out/side	ousd	over/hand	Oh—
out/sider	ousd	over/hang	Ohg
out/skirts	ousCls	over/haul	Ohal
out/smart	ous t	over/head	Ohd
out/spo/ken	ouscn	over/hear	Ohe
out/spo/kenly	ouScnl	over/lap	Olp
out/stand/ing	ous——	over/look	Olc
out/stay	ousa	over/ly/ing	Oli
out/ward	out d	over/night	Oni
out/wear	ou a	over/paid	Opd
out/weigh	ou a	over/power	Opr
out/wit	ou t	over/pro/duc/tion	Opdcj
out/worn	out m	over/reach	Orc
oval	ovl	over/ride	Ord
ovally	ovl	over/rule	Orl
ovary	ovy	over/run	Orn
ova/tion	ovj	over/seas	Oses
oven	ovn	over/see	Ose
over	O	over/shadow	OSdo
over/age	Oj	over/shoe	OSu
over/all	Oal	over/sight	Osi
over/awe	Oa	over/sleep	Osp
over/bal/ance	Obl/	over/stay	Osa
over/bear	Oba	over/step	Osp
over/board	OBd	overt	ovt
over/build	Obld	over/take	Otc
over/came	Ok	over/threw	Otu
over/cast	Oc,	over/throw	Oto
over/charge	OCg	over/time	Oti
over/coat	Oco	over/tone	Otn

over/ture　Oc
over/turn　Otn
over/view　Ovu
over/weight　Ova
over/whelm　Owl
over/work　Ork
over/wrought　Ort
ovoid　ovyd
ovule　ovl
ovum　ov
owe　o
owing　o̲
owl　o̅ul
own　on
owner　on
own/er/ship　ons
own/ing　on̲
ox　ox
ox/alic　xlc
ox/ford　xfd
oxi/da/tion　xdj
oxide　xd
oxi/dize　xdz
oxi/diz/ing　xdz
oxy/gen　xjn (O)
oxy/gen/ate　xjna
oys/ter　ys
ozone　ozn

P

pabu/lum
pace
pace/maker
pacer
pa/cific
paci/fier
paci/fism
paci/fist
pacify
pack
pack/age
pack/ag/ers
pack/ag/ing
packer
packet
pack/ing
pact
pad
pad/ding
pad/dle
pad/dock
paddy

pad/lock
padre
pagan
pa/gan/ism
page
pag/eant
pag/eantry
pagi/na/tion
pag/ing
pa/goda
paid
pail
pain
pain/ful
pain/less
pains/tak/ing
paint
painter
paint/ing
pair
pais/ley
pa/jama

para/dise

Pakistani	pan/chro/matic
pal	pan/creas
pal/ace	pan/creatic
pal/at/able	pan/demic
pal/atal	pan/de/mo/nium
pal/ate	pan/der
pa/la/tial	pane
pala/tine	panel
pa/la/ver	pan/el/ists
pale	pang
pale/ness	panic
pal/ette	pan/oply
pali/sade	pano/rama
pall	pano/ramic
pall/bearer	pansy
pal/li/ate	pant
pal/lia/tive	pan/the/ism
pal/lid	pan/theon
pal/lor	pan/ther
palm	pan/to/mime
pal/mate	pan/try
pal/metto	pa/pacy
palm/istry	papal
palo/mino	paper
pal/pa/ble	pa/per/back
pal/pate	paper work
pal/pi/tate	papier-mâché
pal/pi/ta/tion	pa/poose
palsy	pa/prika
pal/try	pa/py/rus
pam/per	par
pam/phlet	par/able
pan	pa/rabola
pana/cea	para/bolic
pan/ama	para/chute
Pan-American	pa/rade
pan/cake	para/dise

para/dox
para/doxi/cal
par/af/fin
para/gon
para/graph
par/al/lel
par/al/lelo/gram
pa/raly/sis
para/lytic
para/lyze
pa/rame/ter
para/mount
par/amour
para/noia
para/pet
para/pher/na/lia
para/phrase
para/ple/gic
para/site
para/sitic
para/sol
para/trooper
par/boil
par/cel
par/cel post
parch
parch/ment
par/don
par/don/able
pare
pare/go/ric
par/ent
pa/ren/tal
pa/ren/the/ses
pa/ren/the/sis
par/en/theti/cal
pa/re/sis

par/fait
pa/riah
par/ish
pa/rish/io/ner
Parisian
parity
park
parka
park/ing
park/way
par/lance
par/lay
par/ley
par/lia/ment
par/lia/men/tary
par/lor
par/lous
pa/ro/chial
parody
pa/role
par/ox/ysm
par/quet
par/ri/cide
par/rot
parry
parse
par/si/mo/ni/ous
par/si/mony
pars/ley
pars/nip
par/son
part
par/take
par/tial
par/tiality
par/tially
par/tici/pant

pat/en/tee

par/tici/pate
par/tici/pat/ing
par/tici/pa/tion
par/tici/pa/tor
par/ti/cip/ial
par/ti/ci/ple
par/ti/cle
par/ticu/lar
par/ticu/larity
par/ticu/lar/ize
par/ticu/larly
par/ties
part/ing
par/ti/san
par/ti/san/ship
par/ti/tion
partly
part/ner
part/ner/ship
par/took
par/tridge
party
par/venu
pas/chal
pasha
pass
pass/able
pas/sage
pas/sage/way
pass/book
passé
passed
pas/sel
pas/sen/ger
passer
pass/ing
pas/sion

pas/sion/ate
pas/sion/less
pas/sive
pass/key
Passover
pass/port
pass/word
past
paste
pas/tel
pas/tern
pas/teur/iza/tion
pas/teur/ize
pas/tiche
pas/tille
pas/time
pas/tor
pas/to/ral
pas/to/rally
pas/tor/ate
pas/tor/ship
pastry
pas/tur/age
pas/ture
pasty
pat
patch
patch/ing
patch/work
patchy
pate
pa/tella
paten
pa/tent
pat/ent/able
pa/tented
pat/en/tee

pearl

pa/ter/nal
pa/ter/nal/ism
pa/ter/nally
pa/ter/nity
path
pa/thetic
path/finder
path/less
patho/genic
patho/logic
patho/logi/cal
pa/tholo/gist
pa/thology
pa/thos
path/way
pa/tience
pa/tient
pa/tina
patio
pa/tois
pa/tri/arch
pa/tri/ar/chal
pa/tri/ar/chy
pa/tri/cian
pat/ri/cide
pat/ri/mony
pa/triot
pa/tri/otic
pa/trio/tism
pa/trol
pa/trol/man
pa/tron
pa/tron/age
pa/tron/ize
pa/troon
patsy
pat/ter

pat/tern
patty
pau/city
paunch
pau/per
pau/per/ism
pau/per/ize
pauses
pave
pave/ment
pa/vil/ion
pav/ing
paw
pawn
pawn/bro/ker
pawn/shop
pay
pay/able
payee
payer
pay/ing
pay/mas/ter
pay/ment
pay/roll
pea
peace
peace/able
peace/ful
peace/maker
peach
pea/cock
pea/hen
peak
peal
pea/nut
pear
pearl

223

pen/du/lum

pearl/ite *plu*	pedi/gree *pdge*
pearly *pl*	pedi/ment *pd-*
peas/ant *pz-*	pe/dome/ter *pdv*
peas/antry *pz-re*	peek *pec*
peat *pe*	peel *pel*
peb/ble *pb*	peel/ing *pel_*
pecan *pcn*	peen *pn*
pec/ca/ble *pcb*	peep *pep*
pec/ca/dillo *pcdlo*	peer *pe*
pec/cancy *pc/*	peer/age *pej*
pec/cant *pc-*	peer/ess *pe'*
peck *pc*	peer/less *pel'*
pec/tin *pcn*	peeve *pe*
pec/to/ral *pctl*	pee/vish *pes*
pecu/late *pcla*	peg *pg*
pecu/la/tion *pcly*	pei/gnoir *pnur*
pecu/la/tor *pcla'*	pekoe *pco*
pe/cu/liar *pcl*	peli/can *plcn*
pe/cu/liari/ties *pcl'))*	pel/let *pll*
pe/cu/liarity *pcl')*	pel/lu/cid *plsd*
pe/cu/liarly *pcdl*	pelt *pll*
pe/cu/ni/ary *pcny*	pelt/ing *pll_*
peda/gogic *pdgjc*	pel/vis *plvs*
peda/gogi/cal *pdgjcl*	pen *pn*
peda/gog/ics *pdgjcs*	penal *pnl*
peda/gogue *pdgg*	pe/nal/iza/tion *pnlzj*
peda/gogy *pdgje*	pe/nal/ize *pnlz*
pedal *pdl*	pen/al/ties *pnl'))*
ped/ant *pd-*	pen/alty *pnl)*
pe/dan/tic *pd-c*	pen/ance *pn/*
ped/antry *pd-re*	pence *p/*
ped/dle *pdl*	pen/chant *pC-*
ped/dler *pdl'*	pen/cil *pl'l*
ped/es/tal *pdsl*	pen/dant *p— -*
pe/des/trian *pdSen*	pend/ing *p—_*
pe/di/at/ric *pderc*	pen/du/lous *p— ls*
pe/dia/tri/cian *pdeTj*	pen/du/lum *p— ln*

224

pene/tra/bil/ity
pene/tra/ble
pene/trate
pene/tra/tion
pene/tra/tive
pen/guin
peni/cil/lin
pen/in/sula
pen/in/su/lar
peni/tence
peni/tent
peni/ten/tiary
pen/man/ship
pen/nant
pen/ni/less
penny
pen/ny/weight
penny-wise
pe/no/logi/cal
pe/nolo/gist
pe/nology
pen/sion
pen/sion/ary
pen/sioner
pen/sive
pent
pen/ta/gon
pen/tago/nal
pent/house
pen/tode
pe/nu/ri/ous
pen/ury
peon
pe/on/age
peony
peo/ple
pep

pep/per
pep/per/mint
pep/pery
pep/sin
pep/tic
per
per/am/bu/late
per/am/bu/la/tion
per/am/bu/la/tor
per/am/bu/la/tory
per annum
per/cale
per capita
per/ceiv/able
per/ceive
per/cent
per/cent/age
per/cen/tile
per/cept
per/cep/ti/ble
per/cep/tion
per/cep/tive
per/cep/tual
perch
per/chance
per/cipi/ence
per/cipi/ency
per/cipi/ent
per/co/late
per/co/la/tion
per/co/la/tor
per/cus/sion
per/cus/sive
per diem
per/di/tion
pere/gri/nate
pere/gri/na/tion

per/petu/ally

pe/remp/to/rily
pe/remp/to/ri/ness
pe/remp/tory
pe/ren/nial
per/fect
per/fect/ible
per/fec/tion
per/fec/tion/ism
per/fectly
per/fecto
per/fidi/ous
per/fidy
per/fo/rate
per/fo/ra/tion
per/fo/ra/tor
per/force
per/form
per/for/mance
per/former
per/form/ing
per/fume
per/fumer
per/fum/ery
per/func/tory
per/haps
peri/car/dium
peril
per/il/ous
pe/rime/ter
peri/neal
peri/neum
pe/riod
pe/ri/odic
pe/ri/odi/cal
pe/ri/odi/cally
peri/pa/tetic
pe/riph/eral

pe/riph/ery
peri/scope
peri/scopic
per/ish
per/ish/able
peri/win/kle
per/jure
per/jurer
per/jury
perk
perky
per/ma/nence
per/ma/nency
per/ma/nent
per/ma/nently
per/man/ga/nate
per/me/ability
per/me/able
per/me/ate
per/me/ation
per/me/ative
per/mis/si/ble
per/mis/sion
per/mis/sive
per/mit
per/mit/ting
per/mu/ta/tion
per/ni/cious
per/orate
per/ora/tion
per/ox/ide
per/pen/dicu/lar
per/pe/trate
per/pe/tra/tion
per/pe/tra/tor
per/petual
per/petu/ally

226

per/petu/ate
per/petu/ation
per/petu/ator
per/pe/tuity
per/plex
per/plexity
per/qui/site
per se
per/se/cute
per/se/cu/tion
per/se/cu/tor
per/se/ver/ance
per/se/vere
Persian
per/si/flage
per/sim/mon
per/sist
per/sis/tence
per/sis/tent
per/snickety
per/son
per/son/able
per/son/age
per/sonal
per/son/ali/ties
per/son/ality
per/son/al/ize
per/son/ally
per/soni/fi/ca/tion
per/sonify
per/son/nel
per/spec/tive
per/spi/ca/cious
per/spi/cacity
per/spi/cuity
per/spicu/ous
per/spi/ra/tion
per/spira/tory
per/spire
per/suade
per/sua/si/ble
per/sua/sion
per/sua/sive
pert
per/tain
per/tain/ing
per/ti/na/cious
per/ti/nacity
per/ti/nence
per/ti/nent
per/turb
per/turb/able
per/tur/ba/tion
pe/rusal
pe/ruse
pe/ruser
per/vade
per/va/sion
per/va/sive
per/verse
per/ver/sion
per/ver/sity
per/ver/sive
per/vert
per/vert/ible
per/vi/ous
pesky
pes/si/mism
pes/si/mist
pes/si/mis/tic
pest
pes/ter
pes/ti/cide
pes/tif/er/ous

pes/ti/lence
pes/ti/lent
pes/ti/len/tial
pes/tle
pet
petal
petit
pe/tite
pe/ti/tion
pe/ti/tion/ary
pe/ti/tioner
pet/ri/fac/tion
pet/ri/fac/tive
pet/ri/fi/ca/tion
pet/rify
pet/rol
pet/ro/la/tum
pe/tro/leum
pet/ro/logic
pe/trology
pet/ti/coat
pet/ti/fog
pet/ti/fog/ger
pet/tily
pet/ti/ness
petty
petu/lance
petu/lant
pew
pew/ter
pfen/nig
pha/langes
pha/lanx
phan/tasm
phan/tas/ma/go/ria
phan/tom
pha/roah

phar/ma/ceu/tic
phar/ma/ceu/ti/cal
phar/ma/cist
phar/ma/cology
phar/macy
phase
pheas/ant
phe/nomena
phe/nome/nal
phe/nome/non
phial
phi/lan/der
phi/lan/derer
phil/an/thropic
phi/lan/thro/pist
phi/lan/thropy
phi/lat/ely
phil/har/monic
phi/lip/pic
Philippine
phi/lis/tine
phi/lis/tin/ism
phi/lolo/gist
phi/lology
phi/loso/pher
philo/sophic
philo/sophi/cal
phi/loso/phies
phi/loso/phy
phil/ter
phlegm
phleg/matic
pho/bia
phoe/nix
phone
pho/netic
pho/ne/ti/cian

pie crust

phon/ing
pho/no/graph
pho/no/graphic
phony
phos/phate
phos/pho/resce
phos/pho/res/cence
phos/pho/res/cent
phos/pho/ric
phos/pho/rus
photo
pho/to/copy
pho/to/elec/tric
pho/to/ge/nic
pho/to/graph
pho/tog/ra/pher
pho/tog/ra/phy
pho/to/gra/vure
pho/tome/ter
pho/to/play
pho/to/stat
pho/to/static
pho/to/syn/the/sis
phrase
phrase/ology
phre/netic
phre/nolo/gist
phre/nology
phy/lum
physic
physi/cal
physi/cally
phy/si/cian
physi/cist
phys/ics
physi/og/nomy
physi/og/ra/phy

phys/io/graphi/cally
physi/olo/gist
physi/ology
phys/io/therapy
phy/sique
pia/nis/simo
pia/nist
piano
pi/as/ter
pi/azza
pica
pica/dor
pi/ca/resque
pica/yune
pic/colo
pick
pickax
picker
pick/erel
picket
pick/et/ing
pick/ing
pickle
pic/nic
picot
pic/to/graph
pic/tog/ra/phy
pic/to/rial
pic/ture
pic/tur/esque
pid/dle
pid/gin
pie
piece
piece/meal
piece/work
pie/crust

229

pie pan
pier
pierce
piety
pif/fle
pig
pi/geon
pigeon/hole
pig/gy/back
pig/ment
pig/men/tary
pig/men/ta/tion
pigmy
pig/pen
pig/skin
pike
piker
pi/las/ter
pile
pil/fer
pil/grim
pil/grim/age
pill
pil/lage
pil/lar
pill/box
pil/lion
pil/lory
pil/low
pil/low/case
pilot
pim/ple
pin
pince-nez
pin/cer
pinch
pincher

pinch/ing
pine
pine/ap/ple
pin/feather
pin/head
pin/hole
pin/ion
pink
pin/na/cle
pi/nochle
pin/point
pint
pinup
pio/neer
pio/neered
pious
pip
pipe
pipe/line
pip/ing
pi/quancy
pi/quant
pique
pi/racy
pi/rate
pi/rati/cal
pi/rat/ing
pir/ou/ette
pis/ca/to/rial
pis/ta/chio
pis/til
pis/tol
pis/ton
pit
pitch
pitcher
pite/ous

Word	Shorthand	Word	Shorthand
pit/fall	plfal	plan	pn
pith	pl	plane	pn
pithi/ness	ple'	planet	pnl
pithy	ple	plane/tarium	pnly
piti/able	pleb	plane/tary	pnly
piti/ful	plf	plan/gent	pj-
piti/less	pll'	plank	pg
pit/tance	pl/	plan/ner	pn
pi/tu/itary	pluly	plan/ning	pn-
pity	p)	plant	p-
pivot	pvl	plan/ta/tion	p-j
piv/otal	pvll	planter	p-j
pixie	pxe	plant/ing	p=
pla/ca/bility	pcb)	plaque	pc
pla/ca/ble	pcb	plasma	pzma
plac/ard	pcd	plas/ter	ps
pla/cate	pca	plas/terer	ps/
pla/ca/tory	pcly	plas/ter/ing	ps-
place	pl	plas/tic	psc
place/ment	pl-	plas/ticity	pss)
placid	psd	plate	pa
pla/cidity	psd)	pla/teau	plo
plac/ing	pl-	platen	pln
placket	pcl	plat/form	plf
pla/gia/rism	pjz	plat/ing	pl-
pla/gia/rist	pj)	plati/num	pln (Pl)
pla/gia/rize	pjz	plati/tude	pttd
plague	pag	plati/tu/di/nous	pttdnx
plaid	pd	pla/tonic	plnc
plain	pn	pla/toon	pln
plainly	pnl	plat/ter	p
plain/ness	pn'	plau/dit	pdl
plains/man	pnsn-	plau/si/bility	pzb)
plaint	pa-	plau/si/ble	pzb
plain/tiff	pa-f	play	pa
plain/tive	pa-v	play/bill	pabl
plait	pa	play/boy	paby

plu/ral/ize

player	pa
play/fel/low	paflo
play/ful	paf
play/ground	paGr
play/house	pah
play/ing	pa
play/mate	para
play/room	par
play/thing	pa
play/time	pali
play/wright	pari
plaza	pza
plea	pe
plead	pd
pleader	pd
plead/ingly	pdl
pleas/ant	pz-
pleas/antry	pz-re
please	p
pleas/ing	p-
plea/sur/able	pzb
pleas/ure	pz
pleat	pe
plebe	peb
ple/be/ian	pben
plebi/scite	pbsc
pledge	pj
ple/nary	pny
pleni/po/ten/tiary	pnplCy
pleni/tude	pntd
plen/te/ous	p-x
plen/ti/ful	p-f
plenty	p-e
pleth/ora	pa
pleura	pa
pleu/risy	pse
plexus	pee

pli/ability	pib)
pli/able	pib
pli/ancy	pi/
pli/ant	pi-
pli/ers	pi//
plight	pi
plod	pd
plod/der	pd
plop	pp
plot	pl
plot/ter	p
plot/ting	pl
plow	pi
plower	pi
pluck	pc
plug	pg
plugged	pḡ
plum	pr
plum/age	puj
plumb	p
plumber	pv
plumb/ing	p-
plume	pu
plum/met	pml
plump	pmp
plumper	pmp
plump/ness	pmp'
plun/der	p
plun/derer	p-r
plunge	pj
plunger	pj
plunk	pg
plu/per/fect	pl pfc
plu/ral	pl
plu/ral/ism	plz
plu/rality	pl)
plu/ral/ize	plz

232

plus	po/lar/ize
plush	pole
plu/toc/racy	po/lemic
plu/to/crat	po/lice
plu/to/cratic	po/lice/man
ply	poli/cies
pneu/matic	policy
pneu/mo/nia	poli/cy/holder
pneu/monic	polio
poach	po/lio/my/eli/tis
pock	pol/ish
pocket	po/lite
pock/et/book	po/litely
pock/mark	po/lite/ness
pod	poli/tic
po/dia/try	po/liti/cal
podium	po/liti/cally
poem	poli/ti/cian
poet	poli/tics
po/etic	polka
po/eti/cal	poll
po/etry	pol/len
po/grom	pol/len/ate
poi/gnancy	poll/ster
poi/gnant	pol/lute
poin/set/tia	pol/lu/tion
point	polo
pointed	po/lo/naise
pointer	poly/an/dry
point/less	poly/an/thus
poise	poly/chro/matic
poi/son	poly/clinic
poi/son/ous	poly/es/ter
poke	po/lyga/mist
polar	po/lyga/mous
po/larity	po/lygamy
po/lar/iza/tion	poly/glot

233

poly/gon	pop/gun
poly/graph	pop/in/jay
poly/mer	pop/lar
Polynesian	poppy
polyp	pop/py/cock
poly/phonic	popu/lace
poly/syl/labic	popu/lar
poly/tech/nic	popu/larity
po/made	popu/lar/ize
pom/mel	popu/larly
pomp	popu/late
pom/pa/dour	popu/la/tion
pom/pano	popu/lous
pom/posity	por/ce/lain
pomp/ous	porch
pon/cho	por/cine
pond	por/cu/pine
pon/der	pore
pon/der/able	pork
pon/der/ing	por/nog/ra/phy
pon/der/ous	po/rous
pone	por/poise
pon/iard	por/ridge
pon/tiff	port
pon/tifi/cal	por/ta/ble
pon/tifi/cate	por/tage
pon/toon	por/tal
pony	por/tend
poo/dle	por/tent
pool/ing	por/ten/tous
poor	por/ter
poorer	port/fo/lio
poorly	port/hole
pop	por/tico
pop/corn	por/tiere
Pope	por/tion
pop/ery	port/li/ness

portly
port/man/teau
por/trait
por/trai/ture
por/tray
por/trayal
Portuguese
pose
po/seur
posh
po/si/tion
posi/tive
posi/tron
posse
pos/sess
pos/sessed
pos/ses/sing
pos/ses/sion
pos/ses/sive
pos/ses/sor
pos/si/bili/ties
pos/si/bility
pos/si/ble
pos/si/bly
post
post/age
postal
postal card
post/card
post/date
post/di/lu/vian
poster
pos/te/rior
pos/terity
pos/tern
post/gradu/ate
post/haste

post/hu/mous
post/ing
post/man
post/mark
post/mas/ter
post/me/ridian
post/mor/tem
post office
post/paid
post/pone
post/pone/ment
post/pon/ing
post/script
pos/tu/lant
pos/tu/late
pos/tu/la/tion
pos/ture
post/war
posy
pot
po/ta/ble
pot/ash
po/tas/sium
po/ta/tion
po/tato
po/tency
po/tent
po/ten/tate
po/ten/tial
po/ten/ti/ality
po/ten/tially
po/tently
pother
pot/holes
po/tion
pot/luck
pot/pourri

pre/clude

pot/tage
pot/ter
pot/tery
pouches
poul/tice
poul/try
pounce
pound
pound/age
pour
pour/ing
pout
pov/erty
pow/der
pow/dered
pow/dery
power
pow/er/ful
pow/er/house
pow/er/less
prac/ti/ca/bility
prac/ti/ca/ble
prac/ti/cal
prac/ti/cality
prac/ti/cally
prac/tice
prac/tic/ing
prac/ti/tioner
prag/matic
prag/mati/cal
prag/ma/tism
prag/ma/tist
prai/rie
praise
pra/line
prance
prank

prank/ish
prate
prat/tle
prawn
pray
prayer
prayer/ful
pray/ing
preach
preacher
pre/am/ble
pre/ar/ranged
pre/cari/ous
pre/cau/tion
pre/cau/tion/ary
pre/cau/tious
pre/cede
pre/ce/dence
pre/ce/dent
pre/ced/ing
pre/cept
pre/cep/tive
pre/cep/tor
pre/cep/tory
pre/cinct
pre/cious
preci/pice
pre/cipi/tance
pre/cipi/tant
pre/cipi/tate
pre/cipi/ta/tion
pre/cipi/ta/tor
pre/cipi/tous
pré/cis
pre/cise
pre/ci/sion
pre/clude

pre/clu/sion	pre/fer
pre/clu/sive	pref/era/ble
pre/co/cious	pre/fera/bly
pre/cocity	pref/er/ence
pre/con/ceive	pref/er/en/tial
pre/con/cep/tion	pre/ferred
pre/cur/sor	pre/fix
pre/cur/sory	preg/na/ble
preda/tor	preg/nancy
preda/tory	preg/nant
pre/de/cease	pre/hen/sile
prede/ces/sor	pre/his/toric
pre/des/tine	preju/dice
pre/de/ter/mine	preju/di/cial
pre/dica/ment	prel/ate
predi/cate	pre/limi/nary
predi/ca/tion	pre/lude
pre/dict	pre/ma/ture
pre/dict/able	pre/ma/tu/rity
pre/dic/tion	pre/medi/tate
pre/dic/tor	pre/medi/ta/tion
pre/di/lec/tion	pre/mier
pre/dis/pose	prem/ise
pre/dis/po/si/tion	pre/mium
pre/domi/nance	pre/mo/ni/tion
pre/domi/nant	pre/moni/tory
pre/domi/nate	pre/na/tal
pre/emi/nence	pre/oc/cu/pa/tion
pre/emi/nent	pre/oc/cupy
pre/empt	pre/or/dain
pre/emp/tory	pre/paid
preen	prepa/ra/tion
pre/fab/ri/cate	pre/para/tive
pref/ace	pre/para/tory
prefa/tory	pre/pare
pre/fect	pre/pared
pre/fec/ture	pre/pared/ness

pre/pared/ness

pre/par/ing
pre/pay
pre/pay/ment
pre/pon/der/ance
pre/pon/der/ant
pre/pon/der/ate
prepo/si/tion
prepo/si/tional
pre/pos/sess
pre/pos/ses/sion
pre/pos/ter/ous
pre/req/ui/site
pre/roga/tive
pre/sage
Presbyterian
pre/scient
pre/scribe
pre/scrib/ing
pre/scrip/tion
pres/ence
pres/ent
pre/sent/able
pre/sen/ta/tion
pre/sen/ti/ment
pre/sent/ing
pres/ently
pres/er/va/tion
pre/ser/va/tive
pre/serve
pre/serv/ing
pre/side
presi/dency
presi/dent
presi/den/tial
pre/sid/ing
pre/sidium
press

pressed
presser
press/ing
press/man
press/room
pres/sure
pres/sur/iza/tion
pres/tige
pre/sum/able
pre/sum/ably
pre/sume
pre/sum/edly
pre/sump/tion
pre/sump/tive
pre/sump/tu/ous
pre/sup/pose
pre/sup/po/si/tion
pre/tend
pre/tender
pre/tense
pre/ten/sion
pre/ten/tious
pre/text
pret/tily
pret/ti/ness
pretty
pret/zel
pre/vail
pre/vail/ing
preva/lence
preva/lent
pre/vari/cate
pre/vari/ca/tion
pre/vari/ca/tor
pre/vent
pre/vent/able
pre/vent/ing

pre/ven/tion
pre/ven/tive
pre/view
pre/vi/ous
pre/vi/ously
pre/vi/sion
prey
price
price/less
pric/ing
prick
prickle
prickly
pride
priest
priest/ess
priest/hood
priestly
prig
prim
pri/macy
prima donna
prima facie
pri/mal
pri/marily
pri/mary
prime
primer
pri/me/val
primi/tive
primp
prim/rose
prince
princely
prin/cess
prin/ci/pal
prin/ci/pality

prin/ci/pally
prin/ci/pal/ship
prin/ci/ple
print
print/able
printer
print/ing
prior
pri/or/ess
pri/ori/ties
pri/ority
prism
pris/matic
prison
pris/oner
pris/tine
pri/vacy
pri/vate
pri/va/teer
pri/vately
pri/va/tion
privi/lege
privi/leged
privi/leges
privy
prize
proba/bility
proba/ble
proba/bly
pro/bate
pro/ba/tion
pro/ba/tional
pro/ba/tion/ary
pro/ba/tioner
probe
prob/ity
prob/lem

prob/lem/atic
prob/lem/ati/cal
pro/bos/cis
pro/ce/dural
pro/ce/dure
pro/ceed
pro/ceed/ings
pro/cess
pro/cess/ing
pro/cessor
pro/ces/sion
pro/ces/sional
pro/claim
proc/la/ma/tion
pro/clivity
pro/cras/ti/nate
pro/cras/ti/na/tion
pro/cras/ti/na/tor
pro/cre/ate
pro/cre/ation
pro/cre/ative
proc/tor
proc/to/rial
pro/cur/able
procu/ra/tion
procu/ra/tor
procu/ra/tory
pro/cure
pro/cure/ment
pro/curer
pro/cur/ess
pro/cur/ing
prodi/gal
prodi/gality
pro/di/gious
prodigy
pro/duce

pro/ducer
pro/duc/ible
pro/duc/ing
prod/uct
pro/duc/tion
pro/duc/tive
pro/duc/tively
pro/duc/tivity
pro/fa/na/tory
pro/fane
pro/fanity
pro/fess
pro/fes/sion
pro/fes/sional
pro/fes/sion/al/ism
pro/fes/sion/ally
pro/fes/sor
pro/fes/so/rial
pro/fes/sor/ship
prof/fer
pro/fi/ciency
pro/fi/cient
pro/file
profit
prof/it/ability
prof/it/able
prof/it/ably
profi/teer
prof/li/gacy
prof/li/gate
pro/found
pro/foundly
pro/fun/dity
pro/fuse
pro/fusely
pro/fu/sion
pro/geni/tor

proof/reader

progeny	pjne
prog/no/sis	pgnss
prog/nos/tic	pgnsc
prog/nos/ti/cate	pgnsca
prog/nos/ti/ca/tion	pgnscj
pro/gram	pg
pro/gram/ming	pg—
pro/gram/mer	pgr
prog/ress (noun)	pg'
pro/gress (verb)	pg'
pro/gressed	pg,
pro/gress/ing	pg—'
pro/gres/sional	pgjl
pro/gres/sive	pgsv
pro/hibit	phbt
pro/hi/bi/tion	pbj
pro/hi/bi/tion/ist	pbj,
pro/hibi/tive	phbv
pro/hibi/tively	phbvl
proj/ect (noun)	pjc
pro/ject (verb)	pjc
pro/jected	pjc—
pro/jec/tile	pjcl
pro/jec/tion	pjcj
pro/jec/tor	pjc
pro/late	pla
pro/le/tar/ian	pllyn
pro/le/tariat	pllyt
pro/lif/era/tion	plfj
pro/lific	plfc
pro/lix	plx
pro/lixity	plx)
pro/logue	plg
pro/long	plg
pro/lon/gate	plga
pro/lon/ga/tion	plgj
prom	p—
prome/nade	pmd
prome/nader	pmd/
promi/nence	pm/
promi/nent	pm—
promi/nently	pm—l
pro/mis/cu/ity	pscu)
pro/mis/cu/ous	pscx
prom/ise	pms
prom/ised	pms,
prom/is/ing	pms—
prom/is/sory	psy
prom/on/tory	p—-y
pro/mot/able	prob
pro/mote	pro
pro/moter	pro
pro/mot/ing	pro—
pro/mo/tion	pmj
pro/mo/tional	pmjl
pro/mo/tive	pmv
prompt	p—
prompter	pr
prompt/ing	p——
promp/ti/tude	p—td
promptly	pml
prompt/ness	p—'
pro/mul/gate	pmlga
pro/mul/ga/tion	pmlgj
prone	pn
prong	pg
pro/noun	pnen
pro/nounce	pner/
pro/nounce/able	pner/b
pro/nounce/ment	pner/—
pro/nun/cia/tion	pnn/j
proof	puf
proof/ing	puf—
proof/reader	pfrd

241

pro/tec/tor

prop	
pro/pa/ganda	
pro/pa/gan/dist	
propa/gate	
propa/ga/tion	
propa/ga/tor	
pro/pel	
pro/pel/lant	
pro/pel/ler	
pro/pense	
pro/pen/sity	
proper	
prop/erly	
prop/er/ties	
prop/erty	
prophecy	
prophe/sier	
proph/esy	
prophet	
pro/phetic	
pro/phy/lac/tic	
pro/pin/quity	
pro/pi/ti/ate	
pro/pi/tia/tor	
pro/pi/tia/tory	
pro/pi/tious	
pro/po/nent	
pro/por/tion	
pro/por/tional	
pro/por/tion/ate	
pro/por/tion/ately	
pro/posal	
pro/pose	
pro/pos/ing	
propo/si/tion	
propo/si/tional	
pro/pound	
pro/pri/etary	
pro/pri/etor	
pro/pri/ety	
pro/pul/sion	
pro/pul/sive	
pro rata	
pro/rate	
pro/rat/ing	
pro/ra/tion	
pro/saic	
pro/sce/nium	
pro/scribe	
pro/scrip/tion	
prose	
prose/cute	
prose/cu/tion	
prose/cu/tor	
prose/lyte	
pros/pect	
pro/spec/tive	
pro/spec/tus	
pros/per	
pros/per/ing	
pros/perity	
pros/per/ous	
pros/tate	
pros/ti/tute	
pros/ti/tu/tion	
pros/trate	
pros/tra/tion	
prosy	
pro/tago/nist	
pro/tect	
pro/tect/ing	
pro/tec/tion	
pro/tec/tive	
pro/tec/tor	

pro/tec/tor/ate
pro/tege
pro/tein
pro tem
pro/test
Protestant
Protestantism
pro/tes/ta/tion
pro/to/col
pro/ton
pro/to/plasm
pro/to/plast
pro/to/type
pro/tract
pro/trac/tile
pro/trac/tion
pro/trac/tor
pro/trude
pro/tru/sion
pro/tru/sive
pro/tu/ber/ance
pro/tu/ber/ant
proud
prov/able
prove
proven
prov/en/der
prover
prov/erb
pro/ver/bial
pro/vide
provi/dence
provi/dent
provi/den/tial
pro/vid/ing
prov/ince
pro/vin/cial

pro/vin/cial/ism
pro/vin/cially
pro/vi/sion
pro/vi/sion/ally
pro/vi/sion/ary
pro/viso
pro/vi/sory
provo/ca/tion
pro/voca/tive
pro/voke
pro/vost
prow
prow/ess
prowl
prox/ies
proxi/mal
proxi/mate
prox/imity
proximo
proxy
prude
pru/dence
pru/dent
pru/den/tial
prud/ish
prud/ishly
prune
pru/ri/ence
pru/ri/ent
pry
psalm
pseudo
pseud/onym
psy/che
psy/chi/at/ric
psy/chia/trist
psy/chia/try

psy/chic
psy/cho/analy/sis
psy/cho/ana/lyze
psy/cho/logi/cal
psy/cholo/gist
psy/cholo/gize
psy/chology
psy/cho/path
psy/cho/sis
psy/cho/so/matic
pu/berty
pub/lic
pub/li/ca/tion
pub/li/cist
pub/licity
pub/li/cize
pub/li/ciz/ing
pub/licly
pub/lish
pub/lisher
pub/lish/ing
pucker
pucker/ing
pud/ding
pud/dle
pudgy
Pueblo
pu/er/ile
puff
pug
pu/gi/lism
pu/gi/list
pu/gi/lis/tic
pug/na/cious
pug/nacity
pull
pul/let

pul/ley
pul/ling
Pullman
pul/mo/nary
pul/mo/tor
pulp
pulpi/ness
pul/pit
pulpy
pul/sate
pul/sa/tion
pul/sa/tor
pulse
pul/ver/ize
pul/ver/izer
pum/ice
pum/mel
pump
pum/per/nickel
pumping
pump/kin
pun
punch
punch/ing
punch line
punc/tilio
punc/tili/ous
punc/tual
punc/tu/ality
punc/tu/ally
punc/tu/ate
punc/tua/tion
punc/ture
pun/dit
pun/gency
pun/gent
pun/ish

pun/ish/able
pun/ish/ment
pu/ni/tive
pu/ni/tory
punk
pun/ster
punt
puny
pup
pupil
pup/pet
pup/petry
puppy
pur/chas/able
pur/chase
pur/chased
pur/chaser
pur/chas/ing
pure
puree
purely
pure/ness
pur/ga/tive
pur/ga/tory
purge
purg/ing
pu/ri/fi/ca/tion
pu/ri/fier
pu/rify
pur/ism
pur/ist
pu/ri/tan
pu/ri/tani/cal
pu/rity
purl
pur/lieu
pur/loin

pur/ple
pur/plish
pur/port
pur/port/ing
pur/pose
pur/posely
purr
purse
purser
pur/sual
pur/su/ant
pur/sue
pur/suit
pur/vey
pur/veyor
pur/view
pus
push
pusil/lani/mous
pus/tu/lant
pus/tu/lar
pus/tule
put
pu/ta/tive
pu/tre/fac/tion
pu/trefy
pu/tres/cence
pu/tres/cent
pu/trid
putt
put/tee
put/ter
putt/ing
putty
puz/zle
pygmy
pylon

pyr/rhic

py/or/rhea
pyra/mid
pyre
py/rite
py/ro/ma/niac
py/rome/ter
py/ro/tech/nic
pyr/rhic

quack
quack/ery
quad
quad/ran/gle
qua/dran/gu/lar
quad/rant
qua/dren/nial
qua/dren/nium
quad/ri/lat/eral
qua/drille
qua/dril/lion
qua/droon
quad/ru/ped
qua/dru/ple
qua/dru/plet
qua/dru/pli/cate
quaff
quag/mire
quaint
quake
Quaker
quali/fi/ca/tion

quali/fi/ca/tions
quali/fied
quali/fies
qualify
quali/fy/ing
quality
quality-controlled
qualm
quan/dary
quan/ti/ta/tive
quan/ti/ta/tively
quan/ti/ties
quan/tity
quar/an/tine
quar/rel
quar/rel/some
quarry
quart
quar/ter
quar/terly
quar/ters
quar/tet

quarto
quarts
quartz
quash
quasi
qua/train
quaver
quay
queen
queer
quell
quench
queru/lous
query
quest
ques/tion
ques/tion/able
question-and-answer
ques/tioner
ques/tion/ing
ques/tion/ingly
ques/tion/naire
ques/tions
queue
quib/ble
quick
quick-change
quicken
quick/est
quickly
quick/ness
quick/sand
quick/sil/ver
qui/es/cence
qui/es/cent
quiet
qui/etly

qui/et/ness
qui/etude
qui/etus
quill
quilt
quilted
quilt/ing
qui/nine
quin/tes/sence
quin/tet
quin/tu/plet
quin/tu/pli/cate
quip
quire
quirk
quis/ling
quit
quit/claim
quite
quit/tance
quiver
qui vive
quix/otic
quiz
quiz/zi/cal
quo/rum
quota
quot/able
quo/tas
quo/ta/tion
quo/ta/tions
quote
quoted
quo/tient
quot/ing

R

rabbi	rbi	radi/antly	rde-l
rab/bit	rbt	radi/ate	rda
rab/bitry	rbtre	radia/tion	rdy
rab/ble	rb-	radia/tor	rda
rabid	rbd	radi/cal	rdcl
rabies	rbz	radi/cal/ism	rdclz
rac/coon	rcn	radi/cally	rdcl
race	ras	radii	rdi
racer	rs	radio	rdo
racial	rx	radio/ac/tive	rdeacv
rac/ing	ras_	radio/gram	rdeg
rac/ism	rsz	radio/graph	rdegf
rac/ist	rs,	radio/graphers	rdegfs
rack	rc	radio/graphic	rdegfc
racket	rct	radi/ology	rdelj
racke/teer	rcte	radio/tele/gram	rdellg
rac/on/teur	rktu	radio/tele/graph	rdellgf
radar	rdr	radio/tele/phone	rdelel
radar/scope	rDscp	rad/ish	rd8
radial	rdel	radium	rde (Ra)
radi/ance	rdel	radius	rdx
radi/ant	rde-	raf/fia	rfa

rarity

- raf/fle
- raft
- rafter
- rag
- raga/muf/fin
- rage
- ragout
- raid
- rail
- rail/ing
- rail/lery
- rail/road
- rail/way
- rai/ment
- rain
- rain/bow
- rain/coat
- rain/drop
- rain/fall
- rainy
- raise
- rai/sin
- rais/ing
- rake
- rak/ish
- rally
- ram
- ram/ble
- rame/kin
- rami/fi/ca/tion
- ramify
- ramp
- ramp/age
- ramp/ant
- ram/part
- ram/rod
- ram/shackle

- ran
- ranch
- ranchers
- ran/cid
- ran/cor
- ran/cor/ous
- ran/dom
- rang
- range
- rang/ing
- rangy
- rank
- rank/ing
- ran/kle
- ran/sack
- ran/som
- rant
- rap
- rapa/cious
- rapac/ity
- rape
- rapid
- rapidity
- rapidly
- rapier
- rap/ine
- rap/port
- rap/proche/ment
- rapt
- rap/ture
- rap/tur/ous
- rare
- rare/fac/tion
- rar/efy
- rarely
- rare/ness
- rarity

ras/cal	rscl	reach	reC
rascality	rscl)	reaches	reCs
rash	rʃ	reach/ing	reC̱
rasher	rʃ/	react	rac
rashly	rʃl	reac/tion	racj
rasp	rs	reac/tion/ary	racjy
rasp/berry	rzby	reac/ti/vated	racv̱a
rat	rt	reac/tor	rac/
rat/able	rab	read	rd
ratchet	rCl	read/able	rdb
rate	ra	reader	rd/
rather	r⌐	readily	rdl
rati/fi/ca/tion	rtfcj	readi/ness	rde'
ratify	rtf	read/ing	rḏ
rat/ing	ra̱	read/out	rdou
ratio	rSo	read/just/ment	rajs–
rati/oci/na/tion	rtesnj	ready	rde
ration	rj	reaf/firm	ra≠
rational	rjl	real	rl
rationale	rjl	realign/ment	rali–
ration/al/ize	rjlz	real/ism	rlz⌐
rat/tan	rtn	real/ist	rl,
rat/tle	rtl	real/is/tic	rlsc
rau/cous	rcx	real/is/tic/ally	rlscl
rau/cously	rcx/	reali/ties	rl))
rav/age	ruj	reality	rl)
rave	ra	reali/za/tion	rlzj
raven	rvn	real/ize	rlz
raven/ous	rvnx	real/iz/ing	rlẕ
ravine	rvn	reallo/ca/tion	ralcj
rav/ing	ra̱	really	rl
rav/ish	rvʃ	realm	rl⌐
raw	ra	real/tor	rl/
ray	ra	realty	rl)
rayon	ran	ream	re
raze	rz	reamer	re/
razor	rz/	reani/mate	rama

reap
reap/point
reap/praisal
rear
rear/range
rear/range/ment
rea/son
rea/son/able
rea/son/ably
rea/son/ing
reas/sign/ment
reas/sur/ance
reas/sure
rebate
rebel
rebel/lion
rebel/lious
rebirth
rebound
rebuff
rebuilt
rebuke
rebut
rebut/tal
recal/ci/trant
recall
recant
reca/pitu/late
reca/pitu/la/tion
recap/ture
recede
receipt
receiv/able
receive
receiver
receiv/er/ship
receiv/ing

recent
recently
recep/ta/cle
recep/tion
recep/tion/ist
recep/tive
recess
reces/sional
reces/sive
recharge
recheck
recipe
recipi/ent
recip/ro/cal
recip/ro/cate
recip/ro/ca/tion
reci/procity
recital
reci/ta/tion
recite
reck/less
reckon
reclaim
rec/la/ma/tion
recline
re/clin/ing
recluse
rec/og/ni/tion
rec/og/niz/able
recog/ni/zance
rec/og/nize
rec/og/niz/ing
recoil
rec/ol/lect
rec/ol/lec/tion
recom/mence
rec/om/mend

rec/om/men/da/tion		rec/ti/tude	
rec/om/men/ding		rec/tor	
recom/mit		rec/tory	
rec/om/pense		rec/tum	
rec/on/cile		recum/bent	
rec/on/cili/a/tion		recu/per/ate	
rec/on/cil/ing		recu/pera/tion	
rec/on/dite		recur	
recon/nais/sance		recur/rence	
rec/on/noi/ter		recur/rent	
recon/quer		recur/ring	
recon/sider		red	
recon/sti/tute		redeem	
recon/struct		redeem/able	
recon/struc/tion		redeemer	
rec/ord		redemp/tion	
recorder		redi/rect	
record/ing		redis/trib/ute	
recoup		redo/lence	
recourse		redo/lent	
recover		redoubt/able	
recov/er/ing		redress	
recov/ery		reduce	
re/cre/ate		reduced	
rec/rea/tion		reduc/tion	
rec/rea/tional		redun/dancy	
recrimi/na/tion		redun/dant	
recruit		reed	
recruit/ing		reef	
recruit/ment		reefer	
rec/tangle		reek	
rec/tan/gu/lar		reel	
rec/ti/fi/ca/tion		ree/lect	
rec/ti/fier		ree/lec/tion	
rec/tify		reen/act	
rec/tify/ing		reen/force	
rec/ti/linear		reen/list	

regret

reen/ter	refund
rees/tab/lish	refund/able
rees/tab/lish/ment	refund/ing
reex/ami/na/tion	refur/bish
refer	refusal
ref/eree	refuse
ref/er/ence	refu/ta/ble
ref/er/en/dum	refu/ta/tion
ref/er/ral	refute
ref/er/ring	regain
refine	regal
refine/ment	regale
refiner	rega/lia
refin/ery	regard
refit	regard/ing
reflect	regard/less
reflect/ing	regatta
reflec/tion	regency
reflec/tor	regen/er/ate
reflex	regen/era/tive
reflex/ive	regent
reform	regi/cide
ref/or/ma/tion	regime
reforma/tory	regi/men
refract	regi/ment
refrac/tion	regi/men/ta/tion
refrac/tory	region
refrain	regional
refresh	reg/is/ter
refresh/ing	reg/is/ter/ing
refresh/ment	reg/is/trar
refrig/er/ant	reg/is/tra/tion
refrig/er/ate	reg/is/try
refrig/era/tion	regress
refrig/era/tor	regressed
ref/uge	regres/sion
refu/gee	regret

regret/ful	reju/ve/nate
regret/fully	relapse
regret/ta/ble	relate
regret/ta/bly	rela/tion
regu/lar	rela/tion/ship
regu/larity	rela/tive
regu/larly	rela/tively
regu/late	relax
regu/la/tion	relaxa/tion
regu/la/tory	relay
regur/gi/tate	release
reha/bili/tate	released
reha/bili/ta/tion	releas/ing
rehash	rele/gate
rehearsal	relent
rehearse	relent/less
reign	rele/vance
reim/burse	rele/vancy
reim/burse/ment	rele/vant
rein	reli/able
rein/car/na/tion	reli/ably
rein/deer	reli/ance
rein/force	relic
rein/force/ment	relief
rein/forc/ing	relieve
rein/sert	reli/gion
rein/state	reli/gious
rein/stat/ing	relin/quish
rein/sure	rel/ish
reit/er/ate	rel/ishes
reit/era/tion	reluc/tance
reject	reluc/tant
rejec/tion	rely
rejoice	remain
rejoin	remain/der
rejoin/ing	remain/ing
rejoin/der	remand

remand

255

repeat/ing

remark
remark/able
remark/ably
reme/dial
reme/died
remedy
remem/ber
remem/bering
remem/brance
remind
reminder
remind/ing
remi/nis/cence
remi/nis/cent
remiss
remis/sion
remit
remit/tance
remit/tent
remit/ting
rem/nant
remodel
remodel/ing
remon/strance
remon/strate
remon/stra/tion
remorse
remorse/less
remote
remov/able
removal
remove
remover
remov/ing
remu/ner/ate
remu/nera/tion
remu/nera/tive

renais/sance
renal
rend
ren/der
ren/der/ing
ren/dez/vous
ren/di/tion
rene/gade
renege
renew
renew/able
renewal
renew/ing
ren/net
renomi/nate
renounce
reno/vate
reno/vat/ing
reno/va/tion
reoc/cupy
reo/pen
reor/gani/za/tion
reor/gan/ize
repair
repair/man
repair/men
repa/ra/tion
rep/ar/tee
repast
repay
repay/ment
repeal
repeat
repeated
repeat/edly
repeater
repeat/ing

repel
repel/lent
repent
repen/tance
repen/tant
reper/cus/sion
rep/er/toire
rep/er/tory
repe/ti/tion
repe/ti/tious
repe/ti/tive
repine
replace
replace/able
replace/ment
replac/ing
replen/ish
replen/ish/ment
replete
replevin
rep/lica
reply
reply/ing
report
reporter
report/ing
repose
reposi/tory
repos/sess
repos/sessed
rep/re/hend
rep/re/hen/sible
rep/re/sent
rep/re/sen/ta/tion
rep/re/senta/tive
rep/re/sent/ing
repress
repressed
repres/sion
reprieve
rep/ri/mand
reprint
reprinted
reprint/ing
reprisal
reproach
rep/ro/bate
repro/duce
repro/duc/tion
reproof
reprove
rep/tile
rep/til/ian
repub/lic
repub/li/can
repu/di/ate
repu/dia/tion
repug/nance
repug/nant
repulse
repul/sion
repul/sive
repu/table
repu/ta/tion
repute
request
request/ing
requiem
require
require/ment
requir/ing
req/ui/site
req/ui/si/tion
req/ui/si/tioned

rest

requital	res/in/ous
requite	resist
rerun	resist/ance
resale	resist/ant
rescind	resist/ing
rescind/ing	resis/tor
rescis/sion	reso/lute
res/cue	reso/lu/tion
research	resolve
researcher	resolv/ing
research/ing	reso/nance
resem/blance	reso/nant
resem/ble	reso/na/tor
resent	resort
resent/ful	resound
resent/ment	resound/ing
res/er/va/tion	resource
res/er/va/tionist	resource/ful
reserve	respect
reserved	respect/ability
reserv/ing	respect/able
res/er/voir	respect/ful
reset	respect/fully
reside	respect/ive
resi/dence	respect/ively
resi/dent	res/pi/ra/tion
resi/den/tial	res/pi/ra/tor
resid/ing	respira/tory
residual	res/pite
residu/ary	resplend/ent
resi/due	respond
residuum	respond/ent
resign	response
res/ig/na/tion	respon/si/bility
resili/ence	respon/sible
resil/ient	respon/sive
resin	rest

revenge

res/tau/rant	
res/tau/ra/teur	
res/ti/tu/tion	
res/tive	
rest/less	
res/to/ra/tion	
restora/tive	
restore	
restrain	
restraint	
restrict	
restric/tion	
restric/tive	
result	
result/ant	
result/ing	
resume	
résumé	
resump/tion	
resur/gence	
res/ur/rect	
res/ur/rec/tion	
resus/ci/tate	
resus/ci/ta/tion	
retail	
retailer	
retail/ing	
retain	
retainer	
retali/ate	
retal/ia/tory	
retard	
retar/da/tion	
retarded	
retch	
reten/tion	
reten/tive	
reti/cence	
reti/cent	
reti/cule	
ret/ina	
reti/nue	
retire	
retire/ment	
retir/ing	
retort	
retouch	
retract	
retract/able	
retrac/tion	
retreat	
retrench	
ret/ri/bu/tion	
retrieve	
ret/ro/ac/tive	
ret/ro/ac/tively	
ret/ro/cede	
ret/ro/ces/sion	
ret/ro/grade	
ret/ro/gres/sion	
ret/ro/spect	
ret/ro/spec/tive	
return	
return/able	
return/ing	
reun/ion	
reu/nite	
rev	
reveal	
reveal/ing	
reveille	
revel	
reve/la/tion	
revenge	

259

rift

reve/nue
rever/ber/ate
rever/bera/tion
revere
rev/er/ence
rev/er/end
rev/er/ent
rev/er/en/tial
rev/erie
reverse
revers/ible
rever/sion
revert
review
reviewer
review/ing
revile
revise
revi/sion
revi/sory
revi/tal/ize
revival
revive
revivify
revo/cable
revo/ca/tion
revoke
revok/ing
revolt
revo/lu/tion
revo/lu/tion/ary
revo/lu/tion/ize
revolve
revolved
revolver
revolv/ing
revue

revul/sion
reward
rhap/sody
rheo/stat
rheto/ric
rhe/tori/cal
rheu/matic
rheu/ma/tism
rhine/stone
rhom/boid
rhom/bus
rhu/barb
rhyme
rhythm
rhyth/mic
rib
rib/ald
rib/bon
rice
rich
richer
rich/est
rick
rickets
rico/chet
rid
rid/dle
ride
rider
ridge
ridi/cule
ridicu/lous
ridicu/lously
rife
riff/raff
rifle
rift

Word	Shorthand	Word	Shorthand
rig	rg	riveted	rvt̄
right	rt	rivu/let	rvlt
right/eous	rtx	roach	roc
right/ful	rtf	road	rd
rigid	rjd	road/side	rdsd
rigidity	rjd)	road/ster	rdS
rig/ma/role	rg, rgrl	road/way	rdwa
rigor	rg	roam	ro
rig/or/ous	rgx	roam/ing	ro_
rile	ril	roar	ro
rim	r	roast	ro,
rime	rī	rob	rb
rind	rī—	rob/bery	rby
ring	rg	robe	rob
rink	rq,	robin	rbn
rinse	r/	robot	rbt
riot	rıt	robust	rb,
riot/ous	rıtx	rock	rc
rip	rp	rocky	rce
ripar/ian	rpyn	rococo	rcco
ripe	rıp	rod	rd
ripen	rpn	rode	rd
riposte	rpo,	rodent	rd—
rip/ple	rp	rodeo	rdo
rip/saw	rpsa	roent/gen	r-jn
rise	rz	rogue	roq
ris/ing	rz_	roguish	rqs
risk	rsc	roil	ryl
risk/ing	rsc_	rois/ter	ryS
ris/qué	rsca	role	rol
ris/sole	rsl	roll	rol
rite	rı	roller	rl
ritual	rtul	rol/lick	rlc
rival	rvl	romance	rm/
river	rv	Romanian	rmen
river/side	rvsd	roman/tic	rm-c
rivet	rvt	roman/ti/cism	rm-sz

roman/ti/cism

rule

word	shorthand	word	shorthand
romp		round/about	
rood		roun/de/lay	
roof		round/house	
roof/less		rout	
rook		route	
room		rou/tine	
room/mate		rou/tinely	
roost		rove	
rooster		row	
root		row/boat	
rope		rowdy	
rosary		rowel	
rose		royal	
rose/mary		roy/al/ist	
rosette		roy/alty	
rosin		rub	
ros/ter		rub/ber	
ros/trum		rub/ber/ize	
rot		rub/bish	
rotary		rub/ble	
rotate		rubric	
rotat/ing		ruby	
rota/tion		rud/der	
rote		ruddy	
rotor		rude	
rot/ten		rudi/ment	
roto/gra/vure		rudi/men/tary	
rotund		rue	
rotunda		rue/ful	
rotun/dity		ruff	
rough		ruf/fian	
rough/age		ruf/fle	
roughen		rug	
roughly		rug/ged	
rough/neck		ruin	
rou/lade		ruin/ous	
rou/lette		rule	

rye

ruler
rul/ing
rum
rum/ble
rumi/nant
rumi/nate
rumi/na/tion
rum/mage
rumor
rump
rum/ple
rum/pus
run
runa/bout
runa/way
rung
run/nel
run/ner
runt
run/way
rupee
rup/ture
rural
ruse
rush
rus/set
Russian
rust
rus/tic
rus/ti/cate
rus/tle
rusty
rut
ruth/less
rye

S

Sabbath *sbl*	sac/ro/sanct *sCsg*
sab/bati/cal *sblcl*	sacrum *sC*
saber *sb*	sad *sd*
sable *sb*	sad/dle *sdl*
sabot *sbo*	sad/dler *sdl*
sabo/tage *sblz*	sadly *sdl*
sac *sc*	sad/ness *sd'*
sac/cha/rin *sCn*	safari *sfe*
sachet *ssa*	safe *saf*
sack *sc*	safe/guard *sfgd*
sack/cloth *sccl*	safe/guard/ing *sfgd-*
sack/ing *sc-*	safe/keep/ing *sfcp*
sac/ra/ment *sC-*	safely *sfl*
sac/ra/men/tal *sC-l*	safer *sf*
sacred *sCd*	safety *sf)*
sac/ri/fice *sCfs*	saf/fron *sfn*
sac/ri/fi/cial *sCfx*	sag *sq*
sac/ri/fi/cing *sCfo*	saga *sga*
sac/ri/lege *sCly*	saga/cious *sgx*
sac/ri/le/gious *sClyx*	sagacity *sgb)*
sac/ris/tan *sCsn*	sage *saj*
sac/risty *sCs)*	said *sd*

265

sani/tized

sail s
sail/boat sbo
sail/cloth scl
sail/ing s̲
sailor s̄
saint sa-
saint/li/ness sa-l'
saintly s-l
sake sc
salaam sl
sala/bility sb)
sal/able sb
sala/cious slx
salad sld
sala/man/der sl—
salami slre
sala/ried slj̄
salary sly
sale s
sale/able sb
sales/man ss—
sales/man/ager ssmj̲
sales/man/ship ss—s
sales/men ssm
sales/room ssr
sales/woman ss—)—
sali/cylic slslc
sali/ence sle/
sali/ent sle-
saline sln
saliva slva
sali/vary slvy
sal/low slo
salmon sm
salon sln
saloon sln
salt slt

salt/water slt
salu/bri/ous slbx
salu/tary slty
salu/ta/tion slty
salu/ta/to/rian slutyn
salute slu
salut/ing slu̲
sal/va/tion slvy
salve sv
sal/ver slv
salvo slvo
same sa
sami/sen sarsn
sam/ite sru
sam/ple sa—
sam/pling sa—
sana/to/rium snty
sanc/ti/fi/ca/tion sgfcj
sanc/tify sgf
sanc/ti/mo/ni/ous sg mx
sanc/tion sgj
sanc/tity sg)
sanc/tu/ary sgcy
sanc/tum sg
sand s—
san/dal s—l
san/dal/wood s—l wd
sand/blast s—b,
sand/paper s—pp
sand/wich s—wc
sane sn
sang sg
san/gui/nary sgrny
san/guine sgrn
sani/tary snty
sani/ta/tion sntj
sani/tized sntz

sanity	sn)
sank	sq
sans	snz
sap	sp
sapid	spd
sapi/ent	spe-
saponify	spnf
sap/phire	sfr
sar/casm	Scz
sar/cas/tic	Scsc
sar/coma	Scra
sar/cophagi	Scfgi
sar/copha/gus	Scfgx
sar/dine	Sdn
sar/donic	Sdnc
sar/to/rial	Styl
sash	ss
sat	st
satanic	stnc
sat/chel	sCl
sate	sa
sateen	stn
sat/el/lite	slli
sati/ate	sSa
sati/ety	sti)
satin	stn
sat/ire	sti
satiri/cal	stcl
satir/ist	st,
sati/rize	stz
sat/is/fac/tion	sal
sat/is/fac/to/rily	sal
sat/is/fac/tory	sal
sat/isfy	sal
sat/is/fy/ing	sal
satrap	stp
satu/rate	sCra
satu/ra/tion	sCry
Saturday	st
sat/ur/nine	stnin
satyr	s
sauce	ss
sau/cer	ss
saun/ter	s
sau/sage	ssj
sauté	sta
sav/age	svj
savanna	svna
savant	sv-
save	sv
saver	sv
sav/ing	sv
sav/ior	sv
savor	sv
savory	svy
saw	sa
saw/dust	sad,
saxo/phone	sxfn
say	sa
say/ing	sa
says	sz
scab	scb
scab/bard	scBd
scaf/fold	scfol
scaf/fold/ing	scfol
scald	scld
scale	scal
scal/lion	scln
scal/lop	sclp
scalp	sclp
scal/pel	sclp
scaly	scl
scamp	scrp
scam/per	scrp

267

scor/pion

scan	scn	schizo/phre/nia	sczfna
scan/dal	sc—l	scholar	scl
scan/dal/ize	sc—lz	schol/arly	scdl
scan/dal/mon/ger	sc—lng	schol/ar/ship	scdS
scan/dal/ous	sc—lx	scho/las/tic	sclsc
Scandinavian	sc—nven	school	scl
scan/ning	scn	school/book	sclbc
scant	sc-	school/boy	sclby
scantily	sc-l	school/girl	sclgl
scanty	sc-e	school/house	schh
scape/goat	scpgo	school/ing	scl
scapula	scpla	school/mate	sclma
scapu/lar	scpl	school/room	sclr
scar	scr	school/teacher	scllc
scarab	scb	school/work	sclc
scarce	scs	schooner	scn
scar/city	scs)	sci/atic	slc
scare	sca	sci/at/ica	slca
scarf	scf	sci/ence	sc/
scari/fi/ca/tion	scfc	sci/en/tific	sc—fc
scarify	scf	sci/en/tist	sc—,
scar/la/tina	scllna	scin/tilla	s-la
scar/let	scll	scin/til/late	s-la
scathe	scal	scion	sn
scat/ter	sc/	scis/sors	sz//
scav/en/ger	scvg	scle/ro/sis	sCss
sce/na/rio	snyo	scoff	scf
scene	sn	scold	scol
scenery	sny	scoop	scup
sce/nic	snc	scooter	scu
scent	s-	scope	scop
scep/ter	sp	scorch	sCC
scep/tic	spc	score	sco
sched/ule	scdl	scor/ing	sco
sched/ul/ing	scdl	scorn	sCn
scheme	sce	scorn/ful	sCnf
schism	sz	scor/pion	sCpen

scotch	scC	scuba	scba
scoun/drel	scu— rl	scuf/fle	scfl
scour	scu	scul/lery	scly
scourge	sCj	scul/lion	sclyn
scout	scut	sculp/tor	sclp
scout/ing	scut	sculp/ture	sclpC
scow	scu	scum	sc
scowl	scul	scurf	sCf
scrab/ble	sCb	scur/ril/ous	sClx
scram/ble	sCrb	scurry	scy
scrap	sCp	scurvy	sCve
scrap/book	sCpbc	scut/tle	sctl
scrape	sCap	scythe	sit
scratch	sCC	sea	se
scratches	sCCs	sea/board	sebd
scrawl	sCal	sea/coast	seco,
scrawny	sCne	sea/farer	sefa
scream	sCe	sea/food	sefd
screech	sCeC	sea/go/ing	seq
screen	sCn	seal	sel
screen/ing	sCn_	seal/ing	sel_
screw	sCu	seam	se
scrib/ble	sCb	sea/man	sen—
scribe	sCib	seam/stress	seS?
scrim/mage	sCy	sé/ance	sa/
scrimp	sCrp	sea/plane	sepn
scrip	sCp	sea/port	sept
script	sCp	sear	se
scrip/ture	sCpC	search	sC
scroll	sCol	searches	sCs
scrub	sCb	search/ing	sC
scrub/bing	sCb_	sea/shore	seSo
scruff	sCf	sea/sick	sesc
scru/ple	sCp	sea/son	szn
scru/pu/lous	sCpx	sea/son/able	sznb
scru/ti/nize	sCtnz	sea/sonal	sznl
scru/tiny	sCtne	seat	se

selec/tivity

seat/ing
sea/way
sea/wor/thy
seba/ceous
secant
secede
seces/sion
seclude
seclu/sion
sec/ond
sec/ond/arily
sec/ond/ary
sec/ondly
secrecy
secret
sec/re/tarial
sec/re/tariat
sec/re/tary
secrete
secre/tion
secre/tive
sect
sec/tarian
sec/tion
sec/tional
sec/tor
secu/lar
secure
securely
secur/ing
security
sedan
sedate
seda/tive
sed/en/tary
sedi/ment
sedi/tion

sedi/tious
seduce
seducer
seduc/tion
seduc/tive
sedu/lous
see
seed
seed/ing
seed/ling
seek
seek/ing
seem
seem/ingly
seemly
seen
seep
seep/age
seer/sucker
see/saw
seethe
seg/ment
seg/re/gate
seg/re/ga/ting
seg/re/ga/tion
sei/gneur
seis/mic
seis/mo/graph
seiz/able
seize
sei/zure
sel/dom
select
select/ing
selec/tion
selec/tive
selec/tivity

September

select/man
selector
sele/nium (Se)
self
self-addressed
self-confidence
self-conscious
self-contained
self-control
self-defense
self-esteem
self-government
self-importance
self-interest
self/ish
self/less
self-possessed
self-protection
self-sacrifice
sell
sell/out
sel/vage
seman/tic
sema/phore
sem/blance
semes/ter
semi/annual
semi/annually
semi/circle
semi/colon
semi/con/scious
semi/final
semi/monthly
semi/nar
semi/nary
sen/ate
sena/tor

sena/to/rial
send
send/ing
senile
senility
sen/ior
sen/iority
sen/sa/tion
sen/sa/tional
sense
sense/less
sen/si/bility
sen/si/ble
sen/si/tive
sen/si/tivity
sen/si/tize
sen/sory
sen/sual
sen/su/ous
sent
sen/tence
sen/ten/tious
sen/tient
sen/ti/ment
sen/ti/men/tal
sen/ti/men/tality
sen/ti/nel
sen/try
sepa/ra/ble
sepa/rate
sepa/rately
sepa/rat/ing
sepa/ra/tion
sepa/ra/tor
sepia
sep/sis
September

271

sep/tet *spt*	ser/vile *svl*
sep/tic *spc*	ser/vility *svl)*
sep/tum *sp*	ser/vi/tor *sv*
sepul/chral *splcl*	ser/vi/tude *svld*
sequel *sql*	ses/ame *ssre*
sequence *sq/*	ses/sion *sf*
sequen/tial *sqx*	set *st*
sequen/tially *sqx*	set/tee *s)*
seques/ter *sqs*	set/ter *s*
seques/trate *sq5a*	set/ting *st*
sequin *sqn*	set/tle *stl*
ser/aph *sf*	set/tle/ment *stl-*
seraphic *sfc*	setup *stp*
sere/nade *snd*	seven *7*
serene *sn*	seven/teen *17*
serenity *sn)*	sev/enth *7l*
serf *sf*	sev/enty *70*
ser/geant *sf-*	sever *sv*
serial *syl*	sev/eral *sv*
series *syz*	sev/er/ance *sv/*
serif *sf*	severe *sve*
seri/ous *syx*	severity *sv)*
seri/ously *syx*	sew *so*
ser/mon *sm*	sew/age *suf*
ser/mon/ize *smz*	sewer *sw*
ser/pent *sp-*	sex *sx*
ser/pen/tine *sp-n*	sex/tant *sx-*
ser/rate *sa*	sex/tet *sxl*
ser/ra/tion *sf*	sex/ton *sxn*
serum *s*	shab/bi/ness *sbe'*
serv/ant *sv-*	shabby *sbe*
serve *sv*	shack *sc*
serv/ice *svs*	shackle *scl*
serv/ice/able *svsb*	shade *sd*
serv/ice/man *svs-*	shadow *sdo*
serv/ice/men *svsn*	shad/owy *sdoe*
serv/ing *sv*	shaft *sf*

shaggy Sge	sheer Se
shake Sc	sheet Se
shaker Sc/	shelf Slf
shakily Scl	shell Sl
shall S	shel/lac Slc
shal/low So	shel/ter Sl
sham Sr	shel/ving Slv
sham/ble Srb	shep/herd Sōd
shame Sa	sher/bet Srbt
shame/ful Saf	sher/iff Srf
shame/less Sal'	sherry Sy
sham/poo Srpu	shield Sld
sham/rock Srrc	shift Sf
shank Sq	shift/ing Sf
shan/ties S-es	shift/less Sfl'
shanty S-e	shil/ling Slg (Sh)
shape Sap	shim/mer Sr
shape/less Spl'	shin Sn
shape/less/ness Spl"	shine Sin
share Sa	shin/gle Sgl
share/holder Sahol	ship S
sharp Srp	ship/ment S-
sharp/ener Srpn	ship/per S
sharp/ening Srpn	ship/shape SSp
sharper Srp	ship/wreck Src
sharply Srpl	ship/yard Slfd
sharp/shooter SrpSu	shirk Src
shatter S	shirr S
shave Sa	shirt Srt
shawl Sal	shirt/ing Srt
she S	shiver Sv
sheaf Sef	shoal Sol
shear Se	shock Sc
sheathe Sel	shod Sd
shed Sd	shoddy Sde
sheen Sn	shoe Su
sheep Sep	shone Sn

side/walk

Word	Shorthand	Word	Shorthand
shook	Sc	shrew	Su
shoot	Su	shrewd	Sd
shoot/ing	Su_	shriek	Sec
shop	Sp	shrill	Sl
shop/keeper	Spcp	shrimp	Srp
shop/lifter	Splf	shrine	Srn
shop/per	Sp'	shrink	Sq
shop/walker	Spwc	shrink/age	Sqj
shop/worn	Spwn	shrive	Sv
shore	So	shrivel	Svl
shorn	Srn	shroud	Srd
short	Srt	shrub	Sb
short/age	Srtj	shrub/bery	Sby
short/com/ing	Srtck_	shrug	Sg
short/cut	Srtct	shrunk	Sq
shorten	Srtn	shrunken	Sqn
short/ening	Srtn_	shud/der	Sd
short/hand	Srth—	shuf/fle	Sfl
shortly	Srtl	shun	Sn
shot	St	shunt	S-
shot/gun	Stgn	shut	St
should	Sd	shut/down	Stdn
shoul/der	Sold	shut/ter	S'
shout	Sut	shut/tle	Stl
shove	Sv	shy	Su
shovel	Svl	sibi/lant	sbl-
show	So	sick	sc
show/case	Socs	sicken	scn
show/down	Sodn	sickle	scl
shower	Sur	sick/li/ness	scl'
showily	Sol	sick/ness	sc'
show/ing	So_	side	sd
shown	Sn	side/band	sdb—
show/room	Sorn	side/board	sdBd
showy	Soe	side/long	sdlq
shrap/nel	Spnl	side/track	sdtc
shred	Sd	side/walk	sdwc

274

side/ways sdwas	silt sll
sidle sdl	sil/ver slv (ag)
siege sej	sil/ver/ware slvra
sienna sena	sil/very slvy
siesta sesa	simi/lar srl
sieve sv	simi/larity srl')
sift sf	simi/larly srll
sift/ing sf	sim/ile srl
sigh si	simili/tude srlld
sight si	sim/mer sr
sight/less sil'	simo/nize smz
sight/see sise	sim/per srp
sight/see/ing sise	sim/ple srp
sign sin	sim/plest srp,
sig/nal sgnl	sim/ple/ton srpln
sig/na/tory sgnly	sim/plex srpx
sig/na/ture slg	sim/plicity srps)
signer sin'	sim/pli/fi/ca/tion srpfc
sig/net sgnl	sim/pli/fy/ing srpf
sig/nifi/cance sgnfc/	sim/ply srp
sig/nifi/cant sgnfc-	simu/late srla
sig/nifi/cantly sgnfc-l	simu/la/tion srly
sig/nify sgnf	simu/la/tor srla
sign/post sinpo,	simul/ta/ne/ous srllnx
silence sl/	simul/ta/ne/ously srllnx
silent sl-	sin sn
silex slx	since s/
sil/hou/ette shrl	sin/cere s/e
silica slca	sin/cerely s/el
sili/cate slca	sin/cerity s/r)
sili/cone slcn	sinew snu
silk slc	sin/ful snf
silken slcn	sing sg
silky slce	singe sj
sill sl	singer sg
silly sl	sin/gle sgl
silo slo	sin/gle/ton sglln

slang

sin/gly	sgl	ski	sce
sin/gu/lar	sgl	skid	scd
sin/is/ter	sns	skill	scl
sink	sg	skill/ful	sclf
sinu/ous	snx	skill/fully	sclf
sinus	snx	skim	scm
sip	sp	skimp	scmp
siphon	sfn	skimpy	scmpe
sir	s	skin	scn
sire	se	skin/ning	scn_
siren	sn	skip	scp
sir/loin	slyn	skip/per	scp
sirocco	sco	skir/mish	scrs
sirup	sp	skirt	scl
sisal	ssl	skit	scl
sis/ter	ss	skit/tish	scls
sister-in-law	sSnla	skive	scv
sit	sl	skulk	sclc
site	se	skull	scl
situ/ate	scva	skull/cap	sclcp
situ/ation	sul	skunk	scq
six	6	sky	sce
six/teen	16	sky/light	scli
sixty	60	sky/rocket	scvrcl
siz/able	szb	sky/scraper	scvscp
size	sz	sky/ward	scvvd
siz/zle	szl	sky/way	scvva
skate	sca	slab	— sb
skein	scn	slack	— sc
skele/ton	scln	slacken	— scn
skep/tic	scpc	slag	— sq
skep/ti/cal	scpcl	slain	— sn
skep/ti/cism	scpsz	slake	— sc
sketch	scc	slam	— s
sketchily	sccl	slan/der	— s—
sketchy	scce	slan/der/ous	— s — rx
skewer	scv	slang	— sq

small/est

slant	s-	slip	sp
slant/ing	s=	slip/per	sp
slap	sp	slip/pery	spy
slash	ss	slit	sl
slat	sl	slither	sr
slate	sa	sliver	sv
slat/tern	srn	slob/ber	sb
slaugh/ter	s	slo/gan	sgn
slave	sa	slop	sp
slav/ery	say	slope	sop
slay	sa	sloppy	spe
slay/ing	sa_	slot	sl
sleazy	sze	sloth	sl
sled	sd	sloth/ful	slf
sledge	sj	slouch	svc
sleek	sec	slough	sf
sleep	sep	sloven	svn
sleeper	sp	slov/enly	svnl
sleep/less	spl'	slow	so
sleet	se	slow/down	sodn
sleeve	se	slower	so
sleigh	sa	slowly	sol
sleight	sv	sludge	sj
slen/der	s—/	slug	sg
slept	sp	slug/gard	sgd
sleuth	svl	sluice	sus
slew	sv	slum	s
slice	svs	slum/ber	svb
slick	sc	slump	svp
slide	sd	slung	sg
slid/ing	sd_	slur	s
slight	sv	slush	ss
slightly	svl	sly	sv
slim	s	smack	s-c
slime	sv	small	s-a
sling	sg	smaller	s-a
slink	sg	small/est	s-a,

277

social/ism

smart	*srt*	sneer	*sne*
smart/est	*srt,*	sneeze	*snz*
smash	*sns*	snicker	*snc*
smash/ing	*sns_*	snide	*snd*
smat/ter/ing	*srt_*	sniff	*snf*
smear	*sre*	snip	*snp*
smell	*srl*	snivel	*snvl*
smelt	*srll*	snob	*snb*
smelter	*srl/*	snob/bery	*snby*
smile	*sml*	snob/bish	*snbs*
smirch	*smrc*	snoop	*snup*
smirk	*smrc*	snooze	*snz*
smite	*smt*	snore	*sno*
smith	*srt*	snor/kel	*sNcl*
smock	*smc*	snort	*sNt*
smog	*sg*	snout	*snut*
smoke	*smoc*	snow	*sno*
smoker	*smc*	snow/blind	*snobc —*
smoky	*smce*	snowy	*snoe*
smol/der	*smol*	snub	*snb*
smooth	*smut*	snuff	*snf*
smoothly	*smtl*	snuf/fle	*snfl*
smor/gas/bord	*sgsBd*	snug	*sng*
smother	*smt*	so	*so*
smudge	*smj*	soak	*soc*
smug	*sg*	soap	*sop*
smug/gle	*sgl*	soapi/ness	*spe'*
smutty	*sm)*	soapy	*spe*
snack	*snc*	soar	*so*
snag	*sng*	sob	*sb*
snail	*snal*	sober	*sb*
snake	*snc*	sobri/ety	*sBe)*
snap	*snp*	sobri/quet	*sBca*
snare	*sna*	soc/cer	*sc*
snarl	*sNl*	socia/ble	*sSb*
snatch	*snC*	social	*sx*
sneak	*snec*	social/ism	*sxz*

song

social/ist *sx,*	solici/tor *sls*
social/ize *sxz*	solici/tous *slsx*
socially *sx*	solici/tude *slsd*
soci/ety *ssi)*	solid *sld*
soci/olo/gist *ssel,*	soli/darity *slD)*
soci/ology *sselje*	solidify *sldf*
sock *sc*	solidity *sld)*
socket *scl*	solilo/quize *sllqz*
sod *sd*	solilo/quy *sllq*
soda *sda*	soli/taire *slta*
sod/den *sdn*	soli/tary *slty*
sodium *sde (na)*	soli/tude *sltd*
sofa *sfa*	solo *slo*
soft *sf*	sol/stice *slss*
sof/ten *sfn*	solu/ble *slb*
sof/tly *sfl*	solu/tion *sly*
soggy *sge*	solve *slv*
soil *syl*	solv/able *slvb*
soi/ree *si-ra*	sol/vency *slv /*
sojourn *sjn*	sol/vent *slv -*
sojourn/ing *sjn*	sol/ving *slv_*
sol/ace *sls*	som/ber *srb*
solar *sl*	som/brero *sBro*
solarium *sly*	some *s*
sold *sol*	some/body *srbde*
sol/der *sd*	some/day *srd*
sol/dier *sly*	some/how *srhu*
sole *sol*	some/one *s /*
sole/cism *slsz*	some/thing *s ?*
solely *sol*	some/time *srlu*
sol/emn *sl*	some/what *srut*
solem/nity *slm)*	some/where *srur*
sol/em/nize *slmz*	som/no/lent *sml -*
sole/noid *slnyd*	son *sn*
solicit *slst*	sonar *snr*
solici/ta/tion *slsty*	sonata *snla*
solici/ting *slst_*	song *sq*

279

song/stress
sonic
son-in-law
son/net
sono/rous
soon
sooner
soon/est
soot
soothe
sooth/ing
sooth/sayer
sop
soph/ism
sophis/ti/cate
sophis/ti/ca/tion
soph/istry
sopho/more
sopo/rific
soprano
sor/cerer
sor/cery
sor/did
sore
sorority
sor/rel
sor/row
sor/row/ful
sorry
sort
sor/tie
sor/ting
sot
sou/brette
souf/flé
sought
soul

soul/ful
soul/less
sound
sounded
sound/ing
soundly
sound/ness
soup
soup/çon
sour
source
souse
south
south/east
south/ern
Southerner
south/ward
south/west
sou/ve/nir
sov/er/eign
sov/er/eignty
soviet
sow
soy
spa
space
spa/cious
spade
spa/ghetti
span
span/drel
span/gle
Spaniard
span/iel
spank
spar
spare

spark
spar/kle
spar/kling
spar/row
sparse
spasm
spas/modic
spas/tic
spat
spate
spa/tial
spat/ter
spatula
spawn
speak
speaker
speak/ing
spear
spear/head
spe/cial
spe/cial/ist
spe/ciali/za/tion
spe/cial/ize
spe/cially
spe/cialty
spe/cie
spe/cific
spe/cifi/cally
spe/ci/fi/ca/tion
specify
speci/fy/ing
speci/men
spe/cious
speck
spec/tacle
spec/tacu/lar
spec/tacu/larly

spec/ta/tor
spec/ter
spec/tral
spec/tro/scope
spec/trum
specu/late
specu/la/tion
specu/lum
speech
speeches
speech/less
speed
speedily
speed/ome/ter
spell
spend
spend/thrift
spent
sperm
sphere
spheri/cal
sphe/roid
sphinc/ter
sphinx
spice
spic/ule
spicy
spi/der
spigot
spike
spill
spill/age
spilt
spin
spin/ach
spi/nal
spin/dle

sprin/kler

spine
spine/less
spinet
spin/ster
spi/ral
spire
spirit
spir/it/less
spiri/tual
spiri/tu/al/ist
spiri/tu/ous
spit
spite
spite/ful
spit/tle
spit/toon
splash
splat/ter
splay
spleen
splen/did
splen/dor
sple/netic
splice
splic/ing
splint
splin/ter
split
split/ting
splotch
splurge
spoil
spoiler
spoke
spo/ken
spokes/man
spo/lia/tion

sponge
spon/sor
spon/sor/ing
spon/ta/neity
spon/ta/ne/ous
spon/ta/ne/ously
spoof
spook
spool
spoon
spoon/ful
spoor
spo/radic
spore
sport
sports/man
sports/man/ship
sports/men
sports/wear
spot
spot/less
spot/light
spouse
spout
sprain
sprang
sprawl
spray
spread
spread/ing
spree
sprightly
spring
springi/ness
spring/time
sprin/kle
sprin/kler

sprint
sprite
sprocket
sprout
spruce
sprung
spry
spume
spun
spunk
spur
spu/ri/ous
spurn
spurt
sput/nik
sput/ter
sputum
spy
squab/ble
squad
squad/ron
squalid
squall
squalor
squan/der
square
squash
squat
squaw
squawk
squeak
squeal
squeam/ish
squee/gee
squeeze
squelch
squib

squint
squire
squirm
squir/rel
squirt
stab
sta/bility
sta/bi/lize
sta/bi/lizer
sta/ble
stac/cato
stack
stack/ing
sta/dium
staff
stag
stage
stag/ger
stag/nant
stag/nate
stag/na/tion
staid
stain
stain/less
stair
stair/case
stair/way
stair/well
stake
sta/lac/tite
sta/lag/mite
stale
stale/mate
stalk
stall
stal/lion
stal/wart

steep

sta/men	states/man
stamina	state/wide
stam/mer	static
stamp	sta/tion
stam/pede	sta/tion/ary
stamper	sta/tioner
stance	sta/tion/ery
stanch	sta/tis/ti/cal
stan/chion	stat/is/ti/cian
stand	sta/tis/tics
stand/ard	statu/ary
stand/ard/ize	statue
standby	statu/esque
stand/point	statu/ette
stand/still	stat/ure
stanza	sta/tus
sta/ple	sta/tus quo
star	stat/ute
starch	statu/tory
stare	staunch
stark	stave
star/let	stay
star/light	stay/ing
star/ling	stead
star/lit	stead/fast
starry	steadily
start	steady
starter	steak
star/tle	steal
star/tling	stealth
star/va/tion	steam
starve	steam/boat
state	steamer
state/hood	steam/ship
stately	steed
state/ment	steel
state/room	steep

stee/ple
steer
steer/age
steer/ing
stein
stel/lar
stem
stench
sten/cil
ste/nog/ra/pher
steno/graphic
ste/nog/ra/phy
sten/to/rian
step
step/child
step/father
step/ladder
step/mother
step/son
ste/reo
ste/reo/pho/nic
ste/reo/type
ster/ile
ste/rility
ster/il/ize
ster/ling
stern
ster/num
ster/to/rous
stetho/scope
ste/ve/dore
stew
stew/ard
stew/ard/ess
stick
sticker
stick/ler

sticki/ness
stiff
sti/fle
stigma
stig/ma/tize
stile
sti/letto
still
stilt
stimu/lant
stimu/late
stimu/la/tion
stimuli
stimu/lus
sting
stin/gi/ness
stingy
stink
stint
sti/pend
stip/ple
stipu/late
stipu/la/tion
stir
stir/rup
stitch
stock
stock/ade
stock/bro/ker
stock/holder
stock/room
stodgy
stoic
stoke
stole
stolen
stolid

string

stom/ach		strap	
stone		strata	
stonily		strata/gem	
stood		stra/te/gic	
stooge		strate/gist	
stool		strategy	
stoop		stratify	
stop		stra/to/sphere	
stop/gap		stra/tum	
stop/per		straw	
stop/ping		straw/berry	
stor/age		stray	
store		strayed	
store/house		streak	
store/keeper		stream	
store/room		stream/ing	
storm		stream/line	
stormy		street	
story		strength	
stout		strengthen	
stove		strength/en/ing	
stow		strenu/ous	
stow/age		strep/to/coc/cus	
stow/away		strep/to/my/cin	
strad/dle		stress	
strag/gle		stretch	
straight		stretch/ing	
straighten		strew	
strain		stria/tion	
strain/ing		stricken	
strait		strict	
strand		stric/ture	
strange		stride	
stran/ger		stri/dent	
strangely		strife	
stran/gle		strike	
stran/gu/late		string	

sub/jec/tive

string/ing	stuffi/ness
strin/gent	stul/tify
strip	stum/ble
stripe	stump
strive	stumped
striv/ing	stun
stro/bo/scope	stunt
strode	stunted
stroke	stu/pefy
strok/ing	stu/pen/dous
stroll	stu/pen/dously
strong	stu/pid
stronger	stu/pidity
strong/hold	stu/por
strongly	sturdy
strop	stur/geon
strove	stut/ter
struck	sty
struc/tural	style
struc/ture	styl/ish
strug/gle	sty/lus
strug/gling	sty/mie
strum	styp/tic
strung	suave
strut	sua/vity
strych/nine	sub/al/tern
stub	sub/cable
stub/ble	sub/com/mit/tee
stub/born	sub/con/scious
stucco	sub/con/trac/tor
stuck	sub/cu/ta/ne/ous
stud	sub/di/vide
stu/dent	sub/due
stu/dio	sub/edi/tor
stu/di/ous	sub/head
study	sub/ject
stuff	sub/jec/tive

sub/ju/gate
sub/junc/tive
sub/lease
sub/li/mate
sub/li/ma/tion
sub/lime
sub/limi/nal
sub/ma/rine
sub/merge
sub/mer/sion
sub/mis/sive
sub/mit
sub/mitted
sub/nor/mal
sub/or/di/nate
sub/or/di/na/tion
sub/orn
sub/poena
sub/rou/tine
sub/scribe
sub/scriber
sub/scrip/tion
sub/se/quent
sub/se/quently
sub/ser/vi/ent
sub/side
sub/sid/ence
sub/sidi/ary
sub/si/dize
sub/sidy
sub/sist
sub/sis/tence
sub/stance
sub/stan/dard
sub/stan/tial
sub/stan/tially
sub/stan/ti/ate

sub/stan/tive
sub/sti/tute
sub/sti/tu/tion
sub/ter/fuge
sub/ter/ra/nean
sub/tle
sub/tlety
sub/tract
sub/trac/tion
sub/tra/hend
sub/trea/sury
sub/tropi/cal
sub/urb
sub/ur/ban
sub/ver/sion
sub/ver/sive
sub/vert
sub/way
suc/ceed
suc/ceeded
suc/ceed/ing
suc/cess
suc/cess/ful
suc/cess/fully
suc/ces/sion
suc/ces/sive
suc/ces/sor
suc/cinct
suc/cor
suc/cu/lent
suc/cumb
such
suck
sucrose
suc/tion
sud/den
sud/denly

super/fluity

sue
suede
suet
suf/fer
suf/fer/ance
suf/fice
suf/fi/ciency
suf/fi/cient
suf/fix
suf/fo/cate
suf/fo/ca/tion
suf/frage
suf/fra/gette
suf/fuse
suf/fu/sion
sugar
sug/gest
sug/gested
sug/ges/tion
sug/ges/tive
sui/cidal
sui/cide
suit
suit/able
suit/ably
suit/case
suite
suitor
sulfa
sulk
sulki/ness
sul/len
sully
sul/phate
sul/phide
sul/phite
sul/phur

sul/tan
sul/tana
sul/try
sum
sum/ma/rily
sum/ma/rize
sum/mary
sum/ma/tion
sum/mer
sum/mer/time
sum/mit
sum/mon
sump/tu/ous
sun
sun/beam
sun/burn
sun/burst
Sunday
sun/dial
sun/down
sun/dry
sun/glass
sunk
sunken
sun/light
sun/rise
sun/set
sun/shine
sun/stroke
sup
super
super/an/nu/ate
superb
super/cargo
super/cili/ous
super/fi/cial
super/fluity

289

super/flu/ous
super/human
super/im/pose
super/in/tend
super/in/tend/ent
supe/rior
supe/ri/ority
super/la/tive
super/man
super/nal
super/natu/ral
super/nu/mer/ary
super/sede
super/sonic
super/sti/tion
super/sti/tious
super/struc/ture
super/vise
super/vi/sion
super/visor
supine
sup/per
sup/plant
sup/ple
sup/ple/ment
sup/ple/men/tal
sup/ple/men/tary
sup/pli/ance
sup/pliant
sup/pli/cant
sup/pli/cate
sup/pli/ca/tion
sup/plier
sup/ply
sup/port
sup/porter
sup/port/ing

sup/pose
sup/po/si/tion
sup/posi/tory
sup/press
sup/pres/sion
sup/pressor
sup/pu/rate
su/premacy
supreme
supremely
sur/cease
sur/charge
sure
surely
surety
surf
sur/face
sur/feit
surge
sur/geon
sur/gery
sur/gi/cal
surly
sur/mise
sur/mount
sur/name
sur/pass
sur/passes
sur/plice
sur/plus
sur/prise
sur/render
sur/rep/ti/tious
sur/ro/gate
sur/round
sur/tax
sur/veil/lance

sur/vey	
sur/veyor	
sur/vival	
sur/vive	
sur/vi/vor	
sus/cep/tible	
sus/pect	
sus/pected	
sus/pend	
sus/pended	
sus/pense	
sus/pen/sion	
sus/pi/cion	
sus/pi/cious	
sus/tain	
sus/te/nance	
sut/ler	
suture	
svelte	
swab	
swad/dle	
swag	
swag/ger	
swal/low	
swam	
swamp	
swan	
swank	
swanky	
swap	
swarm	
swarthy	
swas/tika	
swat	
sway	
sway/ing	
swear	
sweat	
Swede	
sweep	
sweet	
swell	
swel/ter	
swept	
swerve	
swerv/ing	
swift	
swiftly	
swim	
swim/mer	
swin/dle	
swin/dler	
swine	
swing	
swirl	
swipe	
swish	
Swiss	
switch	
swivel	
swol/len	
swoon	
swoop	
sword	
swore	
sworn	
syba/rite	
syca/more	
syco/phant	
syl/labi/cate	
syl/lable	
syl/la/bus	
sylph	
syl/van	

sys/tole

sym/bol
sym/bolic
sym/bol/ize
sym/met/ri/cal
sym/me/try
sym/pa/thetic
sym/pa/thize
sym/pa/thy
sym/phonic
sym/phony
sym/po/sium
symp/tom
syna/gogue
syn/chro/nize
syn/chro/nizer
syn/chro/nous
syn/co/pate
syn/co/pa/tion
syn/cope
syn/di/cate
syn/er/gism
synod
syno/nym
syn/ony/mous
syn/op/ses
syn/op/sis
syn/the/size
syn/thetic
syphon
syringe
syrup
sys/tem
sys/tema/tic
sys/tema/tize
sys/tole

T

tab
tab/er/na/cle
table
tab/leau
tab/leaux
table/cloth
table d'hote
table/spoon
tab/let
table/top
table/ware
tab/loid
taboo
tabor
tabo/ret
tabu/lar
tabu/late
tabu/lat/ing
tabu/la/tion
tabu/la/tor
tachome/ter
tacit

taci/turn
tack
tackle
tack/ling
tact
tact/ful
tac/ti/cal
tac/ti/cian
tac/tic
tac/tile
tact/less
taf/feta
taff/rail
tag
tagged
tag/ging
tail
tail/light
tai/lor
tai/lored
tai/lor/ing
taint

take
taken
take/off
tak/ing
talc
tale
tal/ent
tal/ented
tal/is/man
talk
talka/tive
talker
talk/ing
tall
taller
tal/low
tally
talon
tam/bou/rine
tame
tamp
tam/per
tam/pon
tan
tang
tan/gent
tan/gen/tial
tan/ge/rine
tan/gible
tan/gle
tank
tan/kard
tan/nery
tan/nic
tan/ta/lize
tan/ta/mount
tan/trum

tap
tape
taper
taper/ing
tap/es/try
tar
tardy
tare
tar/get
tar/iff
tar/la/tan
tar/nish
tar/pau/lin
tar/pon
tarry
tart
tar/tan
tar/tar
task
tas/sel
taste
taste/less
tasty
tat/ter
tat/tle
tat/too
tat/too/ing
taught
taunt
tav/ern
taw/dry
tawny
tax
tax/able
taxa/tion
taxi
taxi/cab

taxi/dermy
tax/payer
tea
teach
teacher
teach/ing
team
team/mate
team/ster
team/work
tea/pot
tear
tear sheet
tea/room
tease
tea/spoon
tea/spoon/ful
tea/time
tech/ni/cal
tech/ni/cality
tech/ni/cally
tech/nology
tedi/ous
tedium
tee
teem
teen-ager
tee/pee
tee/ter
teeth
tee/to/taler
tele/cast
tele/caster
tele/gram
tele/graph
tele/graphic
teleg/ra/pher

teleme/try
telepa/thy
tele/phone
tele/phonic
tele/phon/ing
tele/photo
tele/scope
tele/type
tele/vise
tele/vi/sion
tell
teller
tell/ing
tem/blor
temerity
tem/per
tem/pera/ment
tem/per/ance
tem/per/ate
tem/pera/ture
tem/pest
tem/pes/tu/ous
tem/plate
tem/ple
tempo
tem/po/ral
tem/po/rarily
tem/po/rary
tem/po/rize
tempt
temp/ta/tion
tempt/ress
ten
ten/able
tena/cious
tenacity
ten/ancy

ten/ant
tend
tend/ency
tender
tend/ered
tend/er/ing
ten/der/loin
ten/don
ten/dril
tene/ment
tenet
ten/nis
tenon
tenor
tense
ten/sile
ten/sion
tent
ten/tacle
ten/ta/tive
ten/ta/tively
ten/ter/hook
tenth
tenu/ous
ten/ure
tepid
term
ter/mi/nal
ter/mi/nate
ter/mi/nated
ter/mi/na/ting
ter/mi/na/tion
ter/mini
ter/mi/nology
ter/mi/nus
ter/mite
ter/race

terra-cotta
terra firma
ter/rain
ter/ra/pin
ter/res/trial
ter/ri/ble
ter/ri/bly
ter/rier
ter/rific
ter/rify
ter/ri/fy/ing
ter/ri/to/rial
ter/ri/tory
ter/ror
ter/ror/ist
ter/ror/ize
terse
ter/ti/ary
tes/sel/late
test
tes/ta/ment
tes/ta/tor
tester
tes/tify
tes/ti/mo/nial
tes/ti/mony
test/ing
teta/nus
tête-à-tête
tether
text
text/book
tex/tile
tex/ture
tex/tur/ized
Thai
than

thank
thank/ful
thank/ing
thank/less
thanks/giv/ing
that
thatch
that's
thaw
the
thea/ter
the/at/ri/cal
theft
their
the/ism
them
the/ma/tic
theme
them/selves
then
thence/forth
the/oc/racy
the/odo/lite
theo/lo/gian
theo/logi/cal
the/ology
theo/rem
theo/reti/cal
theo/reti/cally
theo/rize
theory
the/oso/phy
thera/peu/tic
thera/pist
therapy
there
there/after

thereby
there/fore
there/from
therein
thereof
thereon
there's
thereto
there/under
there/upon
ther/mal
ther/mite
thermi/onic
ther/mo/dy/namic
ther/mome/ter
ther/mo/nu/clear
ther/mo/stat
the/sau/rus
these
the/sis
thes/pian
they
they'll
they're
they've
thick
thicket
thick/ness
thick/nesses
thief
thieves
thigh
thim/ble
thin
thing
think
thinker

think/ing
thin/ner
third
thirst
this
thirsty
thir/teen
thirty
this/tle
thing
tho/racic
tho/rax
tho/rium
thorn
thor/ough
thor/ough/fare
thor/oughly
thor/ough/ness
those
though
thought
thought/ful
thought/ful/ness
thou/sand
thrall/dom
thrash
thread
thread/bare
threat
threaten
threat/en/ing
three
three/fold
three/score
thresh
thresh/old
threw

thrift
thrift/less
thrill
thrill/ing
thrive
throat
throb
throm/bo/sis
throne
throng
throttle
through
through/out
throw
thrown
thrust
thud
thug
thumb
thump
thun/der
thun/der/bolt
thun/der/cloud
thun/der/head
thun/der/ous
thun/der/shower
thun/der/struck
Thursday
thus
thwart
thyme
thy/mus
thy/roid
tiara
Tibetan
tibia
tic

tick	tin/der
ticker	tine
ticket	tinge
tickle	tin/gle
tick/ler	tinker
tidal	tinkle
tid/bit	tin/sel
tide	tin/smith
tidily	tint
tie	tin/type
tie/line	tin/ware
tier	tiny
tiff	tip
tiger	tip/ping
tight	tip/ple
tighten	tip/ster
tightened	tip/toe
tight/ness	tip/top
tile	tirade
till	tire
till/age	tire/some
tilt	tis/sue
tim/bale	titan
tim/ber	titanic
tim/bre	tithe
time	tit/il/late
time/less	titi/vate
time/li/ness	title
timely	tit/ter
time/piece	titrate
time/table	titra/tion
timid	titu/lar
timidity	to
tim/or/ous	toad
timo/thy	toast
tin	toaster
tinc/ture	toast/mas/ter

tor/por

tobacco	tbco	ton/sil	t/l
tobac/co/nist	tbcn	ton/sil/litis	t/lls
tobog/gan	tbgn	ton/so/rial	t/yl
toc/sin	tcsn	ton/sure	tc
today	td	too	to
tod/dle	tdl	took	tc
toddy	tde	tool	tul
toe	to	tooled	tul-
tof/fee	tfe	tool/ing	tul_
toga	tga	toot	tu
together	tgt	tooth	tut
tog/gle	tgl	tooth/ache	ttac
toil	tyl	tooth/pick	ttpc
toi/let	tylt	top	tp
toi/let/ries	tyltes	topaz	tpz
toi/lette	tlt	top/coat	tpco
token	tcn	toper	tp
told	tol	top/flight	tpft
tol/er/ance	tl/	topic	tpc
tol/er/ant	tl-	topi/cal	tpcl
tol/er/ate	tla	top/knot	tpnt
toll	tol	top/most	tpmo
toma/hawk	tmhc	topog/ra/pher	tpgf
tomato	tmto	topog/ra/phy	tpgfe
tomb	tu	top/ple	tp
tome	to	top/sail	tps
tomor/row	tmro	top/side	tpsd
ton	tn	top/soil	tpsyl
tonal	tnl	torch	Tc
tonality	(tnl)	tore/ador	tydo
tone	tn	tor/ment	T-
tongs	tgs	tor/men/tor	T-/
tongue	tg	torn	Tn
tonic	tnc	tor/nado	Tndo
tonight	tnt	tor/pedo	Tpdo
ton/nage	tny	tor/pid	Tpd
ton/neau	tno	tor/por	Tp

300

train/ing

tor/rent
tor/ren/tial
tor/rid
tor/sion
torso
tor/tilla
tor/toise
tor/tu/ous
tor/ture
toss
tot
total
totali/tarian
totalled
total/ling
totally
totem
tot/ter
touch
tough
tou/pee
tour
tour/ism
tour/ist
tour/ma/line
tour/na/ment
tour/ney
tour/ni/quet
tou/sle
tout
tow
toward
towel
tower
tower/ing
town
town/ship

towns/man
towns/people
toxe/mia
toxic
toxi/cology
toxin
toy
trace
trace/able
tracer
tra/chea
tra/che/otomy
tra/choma
track
track/ing
track/less
tract
trac/table
trac/tile
trac/tion
trac/tor
trade
trade/mark
trades/man
tra/di/tion
tra/di/tional
tra/di/tion/ally
tra/duce
traf/fic
tra/ge/dian
tragedy
tragic
trail
trailer
train
trainee
train/ing

301

treach/ery

trait
trai/tor
trai/tor/ous
tra/jec/tory
tram
tram/mel
tramp
trample
trance
tran/quil
tran/quil/izer
trans/act
trans/ac/tion
trans/at/lan/tic
tran/scend
tran/scend/ent
tran/scribe
tran/scriber
tran/script
tran/scrip/tion
tran/sept
trans/fer
trans/fer/ring
trans/fig/ure
trans/fix
trans/form
trans/for/ma/tion
trans/former
trans/fuse
trans/gress
trans/gres/sion
trans/gres/sor
tran/sient
tran/sis/tor
tran/sis/tor/ized
transit
tran/si/tion

tran/si/tory
trans/late
trans/la/tion
trans/la/tor
trans/lu/cent
trans/mis/sion
trans/mit
trans/mit/tal
trans/mit/ter
trans/mu/ta/tion
trans/mute
tran/som
trans/par/en/cies
trans/pa/rent
tran/spire
trans/plant
tran/spon/der
trans/port
trans/por/ta/tion
trans/pose
trans/po/si/tion
trans/ship
trans/verse
trap
tra/peze
trap/per
trash
trauma
tra/vail
travel
trav/eler
tra/verse
trav/esty
trawl
tray
treach/er/ous
treach/ery

302

trea/cle
tread
trea/dle
tread/mill
trea/son
trea/sure
trea/surer
trea/sury
treat
trea/tise
treat/ment
treaty
treble
tree
tre/foil
trek
trel/lis
trem/ble
tre/men/dous
tre/men/dously
tremolo
tremor
tremu/lous
trench
trench/ant
trend
tre/pan
tre/phine
trepi/da/tion
tres/pass
tres/passer
tress
trestle
triad
trial
tri/angle
tri/an/gu/lar

tribal
tribe
tribu/la/tion
tri/bu/nal
tri/bune
tribu/tary
trib/ute
trick
trick/ery
trickle
trick/ster
tri/color
tri/cycle
tri/dent
tri/en/nial
tri/fle
tri/focal
trig
trig/ger
trigo/nome/try
trill
tril/lion
trilogy
trim
trinity
trin/ket
trio
tri/ode
trip
tripe
tri/ple
tri/plet
tri/plex
trip/li/cate
tri/pod
trip/tych
tri/sect

tui/tion

trite
tri/umph
tri/umph/ant
tri/um/vi/rate
trivet
trivial
tro/che
trod
trog/lo/dyte
troll
trol/ley
trom/bone
troop
trope
tro/phy
tropic
tropi/cal
tro/po/pause
tro/po/sphere
trot
troth
trou/ba/dour
trouble
trou/ble/some
trough
trounce
troupe
trou/sers
trous/seau
trout
trowel
troy
tru/ancy
tru/ant
truce
truck
truckle

trucu/lent
trudge
true
truf/fle
tru/ism
truly
trump
trump/ery
trum/pet
trun/cate
trun/cheon
trun/dle
trunk
truss
trust
trus/tee
trus/tee/ship
trust/wor/thy
trusty
truth
truth/ful
truth/fully
try
try/ing
tryst
tub
tuba
tube
tuber
tuber/cu/lar
tuber/cu/lo/sis
tubu/lar
tuck
Tuesday
tuft
tug
tui/tion

typhus

tulip	*Ulp*	tur/ret	*Il*
tulle	*Iul*	tur/tle	*Iil*
tum/ble	*Lnb*	tusk	*lsc*
tum/bler	*Lnb*	tus/sle	*lsl*
tum/brel	*LBl*	tus/sock	*lsc*
tumid	*Lnd*	tutor	*lu*
tumor	*Ln*	tuto/rial	*ttyl*
tumult	*Lnll*	tuxedo	*ledo*
tumul/tu/ous	*Lnllx*	twad/dle	*hrdl*
tun	*Ln*	twang	*hrg*
tune	*Ln*	tweak	*hrec*
tung/sten	*Lgsn (w)*	tweed	*hrd*
tunic	*lnc*	tweeter	*hre*
Tunisian	*Lnzn*	tweez/ers	*hrz//*
tun/nel	*Lnl*	twice	*hrs*
tur/ban	*Ibn*	twi/light	*hrle*
tur/bid	*Ibd*	twill	*hrl*
tur/bine	*Ibn*	twin	*hrn*
tur/bo/jet	*Ibjl*	twine	*hrn*
tur/bo/prop	*Ibsp*	twinge	*hry*
tur/bot	*Ibl*	twin/kle	*hrgl*
tur/bu/lence	*Ibl/*	twirl	*trl*
tur/bu/lent	*Ibl-*	twist	*hr,*
turf	*If*	twitch	*hrC*
tur/gid	*Iyd*	two	*2*
tur/key	*Ice*	tycoon	*lcn*
tur/moil	*Iryl*	tym/pa/num	*lpnm*
turn	*In*	type	*lp*
tur/nip	*Inp*	type/cast	*lpc,*
turn/out	*Inou*	type/script	*lpsCp*
turn/over	*InO*	type/set/ter	*lps*
turn/pike	*Inpc*	type/write	*lpri*
turn/stile	*Insl*	type/writer	*lpri*
turn/table	*Inlb*	type/written	*lprln*
tur/pen/tine	*Ip-ln*	typhoid	*lfyd*
tur/pi/tude	*Ipld*	typhoon	*lfn*
tur/quoise	*Iqyz*	typhus	*lfx*

305

tyro

typi/cal
typify
typ/ist
typog/ra/pher
typo/graphi/cal
typog/ra/phy
tyran/ni/cal
tyr/anny
tyrant
tyro

U

ubiq/ui/tous
udder
ugly
uku/lele
ulcer
ul/cer/ous
ulna
ul/ster
ul/te/rior
ul/ti/mate
ul/ti/mately
ul/ti/ma/tum
ultra
ul/tra/high
ul/tra/ma/rine
ul/tra/sonic
ul/tra/vio/let
ulu/la/tion
umber
um/bili/cal
um/brage
um/brella

um/pire
un/abashedly
un/able
un/abridged
un/ac/cept/able
un/ac/count/able
un/ac/cus/tomed
un/af/fected
un/afraid
un-American
una/nimity
unani/mous
un/an/swered
un/an/tici/pated
un/ap/plied
un/ap/pointed
un/as/sum/ing
un/at/tended
un/au/thor/ized
un/avail/ability
un/avail/able
un/avoid/able

un/aware
un/bal/anced
un/be/com/ing
un/be/liev/able
un/bend
un/bi/ased
un/bid/den
un/bounded
un/but/ton
un/canny
un/cashed
un/cer/tain
un/cer/tain/ties
un/cer/tainty
un/changed
un/chari/table
un/civi/lized
uncle
un/clean
un/clear
un/col/lected
un/com/fort/able
un/com/fort/ably
un/com/mit/ted
un/con/di/tional
un/con/scious
un/couth
un/cover
un/crossed
unc/tu/ous
un/dated
un/de/liv/ered
un/de/ni/able
under
un/der/brush
un/der/clothes
un/der/cur/rent

un/der/frame
un/der/glaze
un/dergo
un/der/going
un/der/gone
un/der/gradu/ate
un/der/ground
un/der/handed
un/der/line
un/der/lined
un/der/lin/ing
un/der/load
un/der/ly/ing
un/der/mine
un/der/neath
un/der/paid
un/der/pin/ning
un/der/rate
un/der/score
un/der/sea
un/der/sell
un/der/shirt
un/der/signed
un/der/stand
un/der/stand/able
un/der/stand/ing
un/der/stood
un/der/study
un/der/take
un/der/take r
un/der/tone
un/der/value
un/der/wa/ter
un/der/way
un/der/wear
un/der/weight
un/der/world

un/der/write
un/der/writer
un/de/sir/able
un/de/ter/mined
un/dis/closed
un/di/vided
undo
un/doubt/edly
undue
un/du/la/tion
un/duly
un/earned
un/earthly
un/easy
un/eco/nomi/cal
un/em/ploy/ment
un/equal
une/qualled
un/equally
un/equivo/cal
un/err/ing
un/es/cap/able
un/ethi/cal
un/even
un/ex/pected
un/ex/pect/edly
un/ex/pired
un/ex/plain/able
un/ex/posed
un/ex/pressed
un/fair
un/fa/mil/iar
un/fa/vor/able
un/filled
un/fired
unfit
un/fold

un/fold/ing
un/fore/seen
un/for/tu/nate
un/for/tu/nately
un/freeze
un/furl
un/gainly
un/guent
un/happy
un/handi/capped
un/hon/ored
un/hur/ried
uni/cam/eral
uni/fi/ca/tion
uni/fied
uni/form
uni/formity
uni/formly
uni/lat/eral
un/im/por/tant
un/im/proved
un/in/sured
un/in/ter/ested
un/in/ter/rupted
union
unique
uni/son
unit
unite
united
units
unity
uni/ver/sal
uni/ver/sally
uni/verse
uni/ver/sity
un/kempt

309

un/tamed

un/known
un/law/ful
un/less
un/li/censed
un/like
un/likely
un/lim/ited
un/load
un/load/ing
un/locked
un/lucky
un/mailed
un/manly
un/matched
un/ma/tured
un/men/tion/able
un/mer/ci/fully
un/named
un/natu/ral
un/nec/es/sary
un/num/bered
un/ob/tain/able
un/ob/tru/sive
un/oc/cu/pied
un/of/fi/cial
un/opened
un/or/tho/dox
un/pack/ing
un/paid
un/par/al/leled
un/pleas/ant
un/prece/dented
un/preju/diced
un/pre/medi/tated
un/pre/pared
un/pre/ten/tious
un/prin/ci/pled

un/prof/it/able
un/pro/tected
un/proven
un/pub/lished
un/quali/fied
un/ques/tion/able
un/ques/tion/ably
un/ravel
un/real
un/rea/son/able
un/rea/son/ably
un/re/gen/er/ate
un/reg/is/tered
unre/lated
un/re/mit/ting
un/re/solved
un/rest
un/re/stricted
un/safe
un/sat/is/fac/tory
un/sa/vory
un/scru/pu/lous
un/seemly
un/self/ish
unset
un/sightly
un/signed
un/skilled
un/so/cia/ble
un/solved
un/so/phis/ti/cated
un/speak/able
un/spo/ken
un/suc/cess/ful
un/suit/able
un/strung
un/tamed

un/tax/able
untie
until
un/timely
un/told
un/truth/ful
un/used
un/usual
un/usu/ally
un/var/nished
un/wanted
un/war/ranted
un/wary
un/wieldy
un/wind
un/wise
un/wonted
un/worked
un/wor/thy
un/wrin/kled
un/writ/ten
up
up/braid
up/build/ing
up/com/ing
up/date
up/dat/ing
up/grade
up/grad/ing
up/heaval
up/hold
up/holds
up/hol/sterer
up/hol/stery
up/keep
up/land
up/lift

upon
upper
up/per/most
up/range
up/right
up/ris/ing
up/roari/ous
up/root
up/rooted
upset
up/shot
up/side
up/stairs
up/start
up-to-date
up-to-the-minute
up/ward
ura/nium
urban
ur/bane
ur/chin
urge
ur/gent
ur/gently
urg/ing
uric
urn
us
usage
use
used
use/ful
use/ful/ness
use/less
user
uses
usher

311

uxo/ri/ous

using
usual x
usu/ally x
usu/rer
usu/ri/ous
usurp
usurper
usurp/ing
usury
uten/sil
uten/sils
uter/ine
utili/tar/ian
utili/ties
utility
utili/za/tion
uti/lize
uti/liz/ing
ut/most
uto/pia
uto/pian
utter
ut/terly
uxo/ri/ous

va/can/cies *vc//*
va/cancy *vc/*
va/cant *vc-*
va/cate *vca*
va/cated *vcā*
va/ca/tion *vcj*
va/ca/tion/ers *vcj/*
va/ca/tion/ing *vcj+*
va/ca/tions *vcjs*
vac/ci/nate *vcsna*
vac/ci/na/tion *vcsnj*
vac/cine *vcsn*
vac/cines *vcsns*
vac/il/late *vsla*
va/cuity *vcu)*
vacu/ous *vcx*
vacuum *vc∽*
vacu/um/ing *vc∽*
vacuum-packed *vē-pc̄*
vaga/bond *vgb-*
va/gary *vgy*
va/grancy *vg/*

va/grant *vg-*
vague *vag*
vain *vn*
val/ance *vl/*
vale *val*
vale/dic/to/rian *vldcyn*
val/en/tine *vl-in*
valet *vll*
val/iant *vl-*
valid *vld*
vali/date *vlda*
vali/dated *vldā*
vali/dat/ing *vlda*
vali/da/tion *vldj*
va/lidity *vld)*
va/lise *vls*
val/ley *vl*
val/leys *vls*
valor *vl*
val/or/ous *v lx*
valu/able *vlub*
valu/a/tion *vluj*

valu/a/tions
value
val/ued
val/ues
valu/ing
valve
valves
val/vu/lar
vamp
vam/pire
van
van/dal
van/dal/ism
vane
van/guard
va/nilla
van/ish
van/ish/ing
vanity
van/quish
van/tage
vapid
vapor
va/pori/za/tion
va/por/izer
vari/able
vari/ables
vari/ance
vari/ances
varia/tion
varia/tions
vari/col/ored
var/ied
varie/gate
var/ies
va/rie/ties
va/riety

vari/ous
var/nish
vary
vary/ing
vas/cu/lar
vase
Vaseline
vas/sal
vast
vastly
Vatican
vaude/ville
vault
vaults
vec/tor
vec/tors
veer
vege/ta/ble
vege/ta/bles
vege/tarian
vege/tate
vege/ta/tion
ve/he/mence
ve/he/ment
ve/hi/cle
ve/hi/cles
ve/hicu/lar
veil
veils
vein
vel/lum
ve/locity
ve/lour
vel/vet
vel/vet/een
venal
vend

ven/detta
ven/dor
ve/neer
ve/neers
ven/er/able
ven/er/ate
Venetian
ven/geance
venge/ful
ve/nial
veni/son
venom
ve/nous
vent
vented
ven/ti/late
ven/ti/lat/ing
ven/ti/la/tor
vent/ing
ven/tral
ven/tri/cle
ven/trilo/quist
vents
ven/ture
ven/tures
ven/ture/some
ven/tur/ous
venue
ve/ra/cious
ve/racity
ve/randa
verb
ver/bal
ver/ba/tim
ver/bi/age
ver/bose
ver/bo/ten
verbs
ver/dant
ver/dict
ver/dure
verge
veri/fi/ca/tion
veri/fied
veri/fi/ers
verify
veri/fy/ing
veri/ta/ble
verity
ver/mi/celli
ver/mi/form
ver/mi/fuge
ver/mil/ion
ver/min
ver/nacu/lar
ver/nal
ver/nier
ver/sa/tile
ver/sa/tility
verse
versed
ver/sify
ver/sion
ver/sions
ver/sus
ver/te/bra
ver/te/brae
ver/te/brate
ver/tex
ver/ti/cal
ver/tigi/nous
ver/tigo
verve
very

vine

vesi/cle	vscl
ves/per	vs
ves/sel	vsl
ves/sels	vsls
vest	v,
ves/tal	vsl
vested	v,-
ves/ti/bule	vsbl
ves/tige	vsj
ves/tigial	vsjl
vest/ment	vs-
ves/try	vSe
vet/eran	vrn
vet/er/ans	vrns
vet/er/in/arian	vrnyrn
vet/er/in/ary	vrny
veto	vto
vex	vx
vexa/tion	vxj
via	va
via/ble	vab
via/duct	vadc
vial	vl
viand	vu —
vi/brant	vB-
vi/brantly	vB-l
vi/brate	vBa
vi/bra/tion	vBj
vicar	vc
vi/cari/ous	vcyx
vice	vs
vice-president	vP
vice-presidential	vPx
vice/re/gal	vsrgl
vice/roy	vSy
vice versa	vsa vsa
vi/cinity	vsn)

vi/cious	vx
vi/cis/si/tude	vssld
vic/tim	vc
vic/tim/ize	vc-z
vic/tim/ized	vc-z
vic/tims	vcs
vic/tor	vc
vic/to/ria	vcya
vic/tory	vcy
vict/ual	vtl
video	vdo
vie	vu
Vietnamese	veln-z
view	vu
viewed	vu
view/ers	vu//
view/ing	vu
view/point	vupy-
views	vus
vigil	vjl
vigi/lant	vjl-
vigi/lante	vjl-e
vi/gnette	vnyl
vigor	vg
vig/or/ous	vgx
vig/or/ously	vgx
vile	vl
vilify	vlf
villa	vla
vil/lage	vlj
vil/lain	vln
vil/lain/ous	vlnx
vin/ai/grette	vngl
vin/di/cate	v—ca
vin/di/ca/tion	v—cj
vin/dic/tive	v—cv
vine	vn

vocal

vine/gar
vin/tage
vinyl
viol
viola
vio/late
vio/lated
vio/lates
vio/lat/ing
vio/la/tion
vio/lence
vio/lent
vio/let
vio/lin
viper
vi/rago
vir/gin
vir/ile
vir/tual
vir/tu/ally
vir/tue
vir/tues
vir/tu/osity
vir/tuoso
vir/tuo/sos
vir/tu/ous
viru/lent
virus
visa
vis/age
visas
vis-à-vis
vis/cera
vis/cid
vis/cose
vis/cosity
vis/count

vis/cous
vise
visi/bility
visi/ble
vi/sion
vi/sion/ary
visit
visi/ta/tion
vis/ited
vis/it/ing
visi/tor
visi/tors
vis/its
visor
vista
visual
visu/al/ize
visu/ally
vital
vi/tality
vi/tally
vi/ta/min
vi/ta/mins
vi/ti/ate
vit/re/ous
vit/rify
vit/riol
vi/tu/pera/tion
vi/tu/pera/tive
vi/va/cious
vi/vacity
vivid
viv/idly
vivi/sec/tion
vixen
vo/cabu/lary
vocal

vul/ture

vo/cal/ist
vo/cal/ize
vo/ca/tion
vo/ca/tional
voca/tive
vo/cif/er/ous
vodka
vogue
voice
voiced
voice/less
void
vola/tile
vol/cano
vo/li/tion
vol/ley
volt
volt/age
volu/ble
vol/ume
vol/umes
vo/lu/mi/nous
vol/un/tarily
vol/un/ta/rism
vol/un/tary
vol/un/teer
vol/un/teered
vol/un/teer/ing
vol/up/tu/ary
vo/lup/tu/ous
vomit
vo/ra/cious
vo/racity
vor/tex
vo/tary
vote
voted

voter
vot/ing
vo/tive
vouch
voucher
vouch/ers
vouch/safe
vow
vowel
voy/age
vul/can/ize
vul/gar
vul/garity
vul/ner/able
vul/ture

318

W

wad
wade
wafer
waf/fle
waft
wag
wage
wager
wa/gers
wa/ger/ing
wagon
wa/gons
waif
wail
wain
wain/scot
waist
wait
waited
waiter
wait/ers
wait/ing

wait/ress
waive
waived
waiver
waiv/ers
wake
walk
walkie-talkie
walk/ing
walks
wall
wall/board
wall/cov/er/ing
wal/let
wal/lets
wal/let/size
wal/lop
wal/lop/ing
wal/low
wall/pa/per
walls
wal/nut

wal/rus
wan
wand
wan/der
wane
wan/gle
want
wanted
want/ing
wan/ton
wants
war
war/ble
ward
warden
ward/robe
ware
ware/house
ware/houses
ware/hous/ing
war/fare
war/head
warily
war/like
warm
warmer
warm/est
warmly
warmth
warn
warned
warn/ing
warp
warp/age
warp/ing
warped
war/rant

war/ran/tor
war/rants
war/ranty
war/ren
war/rior
wars
war/ship
war/time
wart
wary
was
wash
wash/ability
wash/able
wash/bowl
wash/cloth
washed
washer
wash/ing
wash-n-wear
wash/room
wasn't
wasp
was/sail
waste
waste/bas/ket
wasted
waste/ful
waste/pa/per
wast/rel
watch
watches
watch/ful
watch/ing
watch/maker
watch/man
watch/men

wel/com/ing

watch/tower
water
wa/ter/fall
wa/ter/fowl
wa/ter/log
wa/ter/melon
wa/ter/proof
wa/ter/proof/ing
wa/ter/tight
wa/ter/way
wa/tery
watt
watt/age
wave
waver
wax
waxen
waxes
way
way/lay
way/bill
way/bills
ways
way/side
way/ward
we
weak
weaken
weak/ened
weak/ling
weak/ness
weak/nesses
wealth
wealthy
weaned
weapon
weap/ons

wear
wear/able
wearer
wea/ri/ness
wea/ri/some
weary
wea/sel
weather
weath/er/proof
weave
weaver
web
we'd
wed
wed/ding
wedge
wed/lock
Wednesday
weed
week
week/day
week/end
weekly
weeks
weep
weep/ing
wee/vil
weigh
weigh/ing
weighs
weight
weights
weighty
weird
wel/come
wel/comed
wel/com/ing

321

wherein

weld	wend
weld/able	went
welded	wept
welder	were
weld/ing	we're
weld/ments	west
wel/fare	west/erly
well	west/ern
we'll	west/erner
well-balanced	west/ward
well-being	wet
well-bred	we've
well-deserved	whale
well-developed	whales
well-done	whal/ing
well-equipped	wharf
well-formulated	wharves
well-fortified	what
well-frozen	what/ever
well-informed	what/so/ever
well-kept	wheat
well-known	whee/dle
well-lighted	wheel
well-maintained	wheel/bar/row
well-planned	wheel/chair
well-proven	wheeled
well-received	wheels
well-respected	when
well-rewarded	whence
well-rounded	when/ever
wells	when/so/ever
wells/ite	where
well-suited	where/abouts
well-taken	whereas
well-tempered	whereby
well-trained	where/fore
wel/ter	wherein

whereof
wher/ever
whether
whet/stone
whey
which
which/ever
whiff
while
whim
whim/per
whim/si/cal
whine
whip
whip/lash
whip/pet
whirl
whirl/pool
whirl/wind
whisk
whisker
whis/key
whis/per
whist
whis/tle
whit
white
white/wall
whither
whit/tle
who
who/dunit
who/ever
whole
whole/hearted
whole/heart/edly
whole/sale

whole/saler
whole/some
wholly
wholly owned
whom
whom/ever
whoop
whop/per
whose
who/so/ever
why
wick
wicked
wicker
wicket
wide
widely
widen
wider
wide/spread
wid/est
widow
wid/ows
width
wield
wife
wig
wig/gle
wild
wil/der/ness
wild/fire
wild/life
will
willed
will/ful
will/ing
will/ing/ness

wolves

wilt	wires
wily	wir/ing
win	wis/dom
wince	wise
wind	wise/acre
wind/break	wish
wind/fall	wished
wind/lass	wishes
wind/mill	wish/ing
win/dow	wisp
win/dows	wist/ful
win/dow/pane	wit
wind/pipe	witch/ery
wind/shield	with
wind/storm	with/draw
windy	with/drawal
wine	with/draw/als
win/ery	with/drawn
wing	with/held
wings	with/hold
wing/ing	with/hold/ing
wink	with/hold/ings
wink/ing	within
win/ning	with/out
win/ners	with/stand
win/now	wit/ness
wins	wit/nessed
win/some	wit/nesses
win/ter	wit/ti/cism
win/ters	witty
win/ter/ized	wives
win/ter/time	wiz/ened
wipe	woe
wiped	woe/be/gone
wire	woke
wired	wolf
wire/less	wolves

woman
wom/an/hood
wom/an/kind
wom/an/like
womb
women
won
won/der
won/dered
won/der/ful
won/der/fully
won/der/ing
won/der/ment
won/ders
won/drous
won't
wood
wood/cut
wooden
wood/work
wood/work/ing
woofer
wool
word
word/ing
words
wore
work
work/able
work/book
work/day
worked
worker
work/ers
work/ing
work/man
work/man/like

work/man/ship
work/men
work/out
work/room
work/sheet
work/shop
world
world/fam/ous
world/wide
worm
worm/hole
worn
worn-out
worry
worse
wor/ship
worst
wor/sted
worth
worthi/ness
worth/less
worth/while
wor/thy
would
would-be
wouldn't
wound
wounded
wove
woven
wow
wraith
wran/gle
wrapped
wrap/per
wrap/ping
wraps

wrath
wreath
wreck
wrecker
wrench
wres/tle
wres/tler
wretched
wrig/gle
wring
wringer
wrin/kle
wrin/kles
wrist
wrists
writ
write
writer
writ/ers
write-up
writ/ing
writ/ings
writhe
writ/ten
wrong
wrong/ful
wrote
wrought
wrung
wry

xenon
xe/ro/graphic
xe/rog/ra/phy
Xerox
x-ray
x-rays
xy/lo/graph
xy/lo/phone

Y

yacht *yt*
yak *yc*
yam *y*
yank *yg*
Yankee *yqe*
yard *yd*
yard/age *ydg*
yards *yds*
yard/stick *ydsc*
yarn *yn*
yaw *ya*
yawl *yal*
yawn *yn*
yea *ya*
year *y*
year/book *ybc*
year/books *ybcs*
year/end *ye —*
year/ling *ylg*
yearly *yl*
year-round *yru —*
yearn *yn*

years *ys*
yeast *ye,*
yell *yl*
yel/low *ylo*
yeo/man *y —*
yes *ys*
yes/ter/day *ysd*
yet *yt*
yew *u*
yield *yeld*
yielded *yeld*
yields *yelds*
yoke *yoc*
yokel *ycl*
yolk *yoc*
yon/der *y —*
yore *yo*
you *u*
you'd *ud*
you'll *ul*
young *yg*
younger *yg*

329

yule

young/ster
young/sters
your
yours
your/self
your/selves
youth
youths
youth/ful
you've
yowl
yule

Z

zany
zeal
zeal/ous
zebra
ze/nith
zephyr
zep/pe/lin
zero
zest
zig/zag
zinc
Zion
Zionism
zip
zip code
zip codes
zip/per
zip/pers
zir/con
zir/co/nium
zither
zo/diac

zo/dia/cal
zone
zones
zon/ing
zoo
zoom
zoo/logi/cal
zo/ology
zwie/back
zy/mase
zy/motic

331

APPENDIX A
SUMMARY OF PRINCIPLES

WRITING VOWELS

1. Write long vowels in one-syllable words: *goal* gol ; *huge* huy ; *wife* wf ; *league* leg

2. Write INITIAL and FINAL short vowels: *asset* asl ; *egg* eg ; *ice* is ; *quota* goa ; *editor* ed ; *formula* fla

3. When a word ends in the sound *ate, eet, ite, ote,* or *ute,* write the vowel and omit the *t*: *date* da ; *meet* me ; *light* li ; *vote* vo ; *suit* su

4. When a word ends in the sound of *ave, eve, ive, ove,* or *uve,* write the vowel and omit the *v*: *gave* ga ; *leave* le ; *arrive* ari ; *drove* do ; *groove* gu

5. When a word ends in the sound of *ame, eem, ime, ome,* or *ume,* write the vowel and omit the *m*: *same* sa ; *extreme* xe ; *lifetime* lfti ; *home* ho ; *presume* pzu

6. When a word ends in the sound of *air, eer, ire, ore,* or *ure,* write the vowel and omit the *r*: *repair* rpa ; *appear* ape ; *acquire* aqi ; *explore* xpo ; *insure* nsu

7. When *ing* or *ed* is added to an outline that contains a long vowel, retain the vowel in the outline: *hoping* hop ; *teaching* tec ; *filed* fil (Recap and Prevue: Vowels).

8. When the outline of a root word begins or ends in a vowel, retain that vowel when a prefix or suffix is added to it: *high* hi ; *highly* hil ; *true* tu ; *truly* tul ; *pay* pa ; *payroll* parl ; *renew* rnu ; *renewal* rnul ; *react* rac ; *reelect* relc ; *reopen* rop

9. When a long vowel is followed by a mark of punctuation, retain the vowel: *moment* mo- ; *truant* tu- ; *duty* du) ; *consumer* ksu

334 Summary of Principles

10. Write *ol* for the sound of *old: golden* goln ; *boulder* bol ; *folder* fol

11. Write *i* for the INITIAL sound of *im: imitate* ila ; *impossibility* ipsb)

12. Write *u* for the INITIAL sound of *un: undoubtedly* udtl ; *unfortunately* ufCntl

13. Write *in* for the sound of *ine: combine* kbin ; *consignee* ksine

14. When a word contains two MEDIAL pronounced consecutive vowels, write the first vowel only: *trial* til ; *annual* aul ; *diameter* dir

15. When a word contains two FINAL pronounced consecutive vowels, write the last vowel only: *create* ca ; *graduate* gda

16. Write *al* for the FINAL sound of *all: install* nsal ; *football* ftbal

17. Write *a* for the INITIAL and FINAL sound of *aw: all* al ; *alter* al ; *law* la ; *saw* sa

OMITTING VOWELS

1. Omit all MEDIAL short vowels: *citizenship* slznß ; *finish* fnß ; *yellow* ylo ; *knowledge* nlj

2. Omit all MEDIAL long vowels in words of more than one syllable: *obtain* obln ; *procedure* psj ; *belief* blf

3. Write *c* for the MEDIAL and FINAL sounds of *ake: make* mc ; *lakeside* lcsd ; *taking* lc

4. Omit the vowel and write *d* for the MEDIAL and FINAL sounds of *ade, ede, ide, ode,* and *ude: made* md ; *cede* sd ; *side* sd ; *reload* rld ; *crudely* cdl

5. Omit the vowel and write *z* for the MEDIAL and FINAL sounds of *aze, eze, ize, oze,* and *uze: phase* fz ; *reason* rzn ; *wisely* zl ; *chosen* czn ; *chooses* czs

6. Write *m* for the prefix *em: emphatic* mfc ; *emblem* mb ; *employer* mpy

7. Omit the vowel and write *n* for the sounds of *ane, een, one,* and *une: train* tn ; *seen* sn ; *loan* ln ; *soon* sn

Summary of Principles 335

8. Write *y* for the MEDIAL or FINAL sound of a vowel + *ry*: *various* ; *machinery* ; *inquiry* ; *territory* ; *hurry*

9. Write *n* for the prefix *en*: *enclosure* ; *endure* ; *engine*

10. When a word contains two MEDIAL pronounced consecutive vowels, omit the second vowel: *trial* ; *annual* ; *diameter*

11. When a word contains two FINAL pronounced consecutive vowels, omit the first vowel: *create* ; *graduate*

12. Write *l* for the FINAL sound of *lee*: *efficiently* ; *originally* ; *early*

13. Write for the MEDIAL or FINAL sounds of a vowel + *shun*: *qualifications* ; *completion* ; *competition* ; *promotions*

14. Write a *)* for the FINAL sound of *tee*: *duty* ; *quantities* ; *ability* ; *authority*

COMBINATION SOUNDS

1. Write for the sound of *wh*: *what* ; *when* ; *which*

2. Write *C* for the sound of *ch*: *attachment* ; *chiefly* ; *much* ; *nature*

3. Write *S* for the sound of *sh*: *issuing* ; *insurance* ; *sufficient*

4. Write for the MEDIAL and FINAL sounds of *ow*: *allowance* ; *doubt* ; *now*

5. Write *l* for the sound of *th*: *them* ; *method* ; *health*

6. Write a hyphen on the INITIAL letter of an outline to indicate the INITIAL combination-*r* sounds: *broke* ; *crashed* ; *dropped* ; *free* ; *group* ; *privilege* ; *travel* ; *through* ; *argue* ; *earn* ; *or* ; *urge* ; *shred*

To express a MEDIAL combination-*r* sound, capitalize the letter

Summary of Principles

that precedes the *r* and omit the *r* from the outline: *fabric* ___ ; *increase* ___ ; *refresh* ___ ; *agreement* ___ ; *approach* ___ ; *attractive* ___

7. Write ___ for the sound of *oi: appointment* ___ ; *oil* ___ ; *toy* ___

8. Write ___ for the sound of *kw: frequently* ___ ; *acquainted* ___ ; *quit* ___ ; *quite* ___ ; *adequate* ___

9. Write a dash on the INITIAL letter of an outline to indicate the INITIAL combination-*l* sounds: *block* ___ ; *clients* ___ ; *element* ___ ; *flight* ___ ; *glad* ___ ; *ill* ___ ; *plan* ___ ; *slow* ___ ; *ultimate* ___ ; *alibi* ___ ; *else* ___

When the combination-*l* sound is MEDIAL, omit the *l* and write the letter that precedes it: *application* ___

10. Write a comma (,) for the INITIAL and FINAL sound of *st: largest* ___ ; *listings* ___ ; *introduced* ___ ; *study* ___ ; *stands* ___

11. Write ___ for the MEDIAL sound of *st: mistake* ___ ; *instead* ___

12. Write ___ for the sound of *nk: frankly* ___ ; *thinking* ___

13. Write ___ for the FINAL sounds of *bul* and *blee: able* ___ ; *favorably* ___

14. Write ___ for the FINAL sounds of *pul* and *plee: simple* ___ ; *simply* ___

15. Write a small printed ___ for the sound of *sp: spend* ___ ; *respect* ___ ; *grasp* ___

16. Write a disjoined slant for the sounds of *nse* and *nsy: expense* ___ ; *responsible* ___ ; *fancy* ___

17. Write ___ for the sound of *zh: treasure* ___ ; *treasury* ___

18. Write a capital printed ___ for the sound of *str: distribute* ___

19. Write a dash (—) for the MEDIAL or FINAL *nd: recommend* ___ ; *brand* ___

20. Write ___ for *sub: submit* ___

21. Write ___ for *trans: transfer* ___

PUNCTUATION MARKS

1. Use an underscore to indicate the addition of *ing* or *thing* to a word: getting ____ ; recommending ____ ; anything ____

2. Use an overscore to indicate the addition of *ed* to form a past tense: added ____ ; occurred ____ ; wanted ____ ; mended ____ ; announced ____

3. Use a hypen for the MEDIAL and FINAL sounds of *nt* and *ment*: resident ____ ; didn't ____ ; judgment ____ ; rental ____

4. Use a joined slant to indicate the FINAL sounds of *er* and *ter*: favor ____ ; feature ____ ; officers ____ ; errors ____ ; center ____

5. Use a dash for the sound of *nd*: recommend ____ ; brand ____

6. Use an apostrophe to indicate a FINAL *ss* and *ness*: regardless ____ ; addresses ____ ; illness ____

7. Use a quotation mark to indicate a FINAL *ssness*: hopelessness ____ ; helplessness ____

8. Use a comma to indicate the INITIAL and FINAL sounds of *st*: largest ____ ; listings ____ ; introduced ____ ; study ____ ; stands ____

9. Use a blend ( ) to indicate the FINAL sound of *tee*: duty ____ ; abilities ____

10. Use a disjoined slant to indicate the sounds of *nse* and *nsy*: expense ____ ; responsible ____ ; fancy ____ ; and ____ for *self* and *selves*: selfish ____ ; myself ____ ; themselves ____

CAPITALIZATION

1. To express a MEDIAL combination-*r* sound, capitalize the letter that precedes the *r* and omit the *r* from the outline: fabric ____ ; increase ____ ; refresh ____ ; agreement ____

2. To express the MEDIAL vowel and *r*, capitalize the outline that precedes the sound: liberally ____ ; report ____ ; accordingly ____ ; modern ____ ; furniture ____ ; regard ____ ; certainly ____ ; determine ____ ; converse ____ ; reserved ____ ; thorough ____

338 Summary of Principles

3. For the FINAL sound of *ther* write a capital *t: author* a͞T ; *farther* fT͞
4. Write C for the sound of *ch: cheap* Cep ; *reach* reC
5. Write ȿ for the sound of *sh: issue* iȿu ; *rush* rȿ
6. Write n for the sounds of *enter* and *inter: entertain* nUn ; *interest* n,

MISCELLANEOUS

1. Write ꜱ to form plurals of outlines ending in a letter of the alphabet: *groups* gups ; *today's* ldꜱ ; *joins* jynꜱ
2. Repeat the punctuation mark to form plurals of outlines ending in punctuation marks: *mailings* nal= ; *events* ev-- ; *abilities* ab)) ; *expenses* xpll ; *invests* nv,,
3. Write C for the sound of *k: cashier* cȿe ; *keynote* cenl ; *booklet* bcll ; *walk* uc
4. Write v for MEDIAL and FINAL *tiv: effective* efcv ; *tentative* t-v ; *positively* pzvl
5. Write k for the sounds of *com, con,* and *coun: combination* kbny ; *convenient* kvn- ; *counters* k//
6. Write S for the sounds of *str, star, ster,* and *stor: distribute* dSbu ; *start* Sl ; *registered* rjS ; *story* Se
7. Write x for the sounds of *aks, eks, iks, oks,* and *uks: accident* xd- ; *extent* xl- ; *fix* fx ; *box* bx ; *deluxe* dlx
8. Write 1 for the sounds of MEDIAL and FINAL *shun*, vowel + *shun*, and *nshun: national* njl ; *invitations* nvlyꜱ ; *attention* aly
9. Omit *n* before the sounds of *g, j,* and *ch: bring* bq ; *length* lgl ; *exchange* xCj ; *ranch* rC
10. Write x for MEDIAL and FINAL sounds of *us, usly, shus, shusly, shul, shully, nshul,* and *nshully* in words of more than one syllable: *bonus* bnx ; *officially* ofx ; *anxious* agx ; *financially* fnx
11. Omit *t* after the sounds of *k, p, f,* and *x* and omit *pt* after *m: act* ac ; *except* xp ; *draft* df ; *next* nx ; *prompt* p
12. Omit *d* before *m* and *v: admit* aml ; *advance* avl
13. Write *f* for *ful, fully,* and the final sound of *fy: carefully* caf ; *beautiful* blf ; *notify* nlf

WRITING SPECIFIC SOUNDS IN DIFFERENT POSITIONS

1. Write a hyphen on the INITIAL letter of an outline to indicate the INITIAL combination-*r* sound; capitalize the letter that precedes this sound in a MEDIAL position: *brick* ; *fabric* ; *crease* ; *increase* ; *drama* ; *melodrama* ; *fresh* ; *refresh* ; *gram* ; *program* ; *print* ; *reprint* .

2. Write a dash on the INITIAL letter of an outline to indicate the INITIAL combination-*l* sound; omit the *l* and write the letter that precedes the MEDIAL combination-*l* sound: *block* ; *glad* ; *plan* ; *apply* ; *duplicate* .

3. INITIAL *er* is indicated ; FINAL *er* and *ter* are indicated with a joined slant; and MEDIAL vowel + *r* is indicated by capitalizing the letter that precedes the sound: *earn* ; *cover* ; *after* ; *different* .

4. INITIAL and FINAL *st* are indicated by a comma; MEDIAL *st* is indicated by writing : *style* ; *just* ; *mistake*

APPENDIX B
SUMMARY OF BRIEF FORMS

about	ab	by	b
above	bv	call	cl
acknowledge	ak	came	k
advantage	avj	can	c
again, st	ag	charge	Cg
almost	lro	circumstance	cl
already	lr	collect	cc
also	lso	come	k
always	l	committee	k
am	⌒	conclusion	kclj
an	a	consider	ks
appreciate	ap	continue	ku
are	r	contract	Kc
around	r	correct	Kc
as	3	country	c
ask	sc	customer	K
at	a	deal	dl
auto	a	declare	dec
be	b	definite, ly	dfn
because	cs	deliver	dl
been	b	delivery	dl
began	bg	describe	des
begin	bg	description	des
benefit	bnf	develop	dv
between	bt	difficult	dfk
both	bo	difficulty	dfk
business	bs	direct	D
busy	bg	during	du
but	b	easy	eg
buy	b	entitle	ntl

342 Summary of Brief Forms

word	shorthand	word	shorthand
even	vn	is	s
evening	vn-	it	l
ever	E	keep	cp
every	E	kind	ci
extra	X	known	no
extraordinary	Xo	letter	L
fail	fl	life	lf
feel	fl	like	lc
field	fld	line	li
find	fi	little	ll
fine	fi	man	⌒-
fire	fr	many	⌒
firm	F	member	⌒B
for	f	move	⌒v
full	fu	necessarily	nec
fully	fu	necessary	nec
future	fC	not	n
given	gv	note	nl
go	g	object	ob
good	g	of	v
great	g	on	o
had	h	once	c/
has	as	only	nl
have	v	open	op
he	h	opinion	opn
held	hl	opportunity	opl
help	hp	order	O
him	h	organization	og
his	s	organize	og
hole	hl	other	J
hour	r	our	r
idea	id	out	ou
immediate, ly	ida	over	O
important	ip	particular, ly	P
in	n	perhaps	pps
individual, ly	ndv	please	p
initial, ly	ix	poor	po

Summary of Brief Forms

price		the	
probable, ly		their	
prove		there	
public		they	
publish		this	
pull		those	
pupil		thought	
purchase		throughout	
put		to	
real, ly		too	
reel		under	
regular, ly		until	
regulation		up	
result		upon	
sale		usual, ly	
sample		very	
satisfaction		was	
satisfactory		we	
satisfy		well	
save		were	
school		where	
several		while	
shall		whole	
she		whom	
ship		why	
situation		will	
small		with	
stop		without	
subject		woman	
success		world	
successful, ly		would	
that		your	

APPENDIX C
SUMMARY OF STANDARD ABBREVIATIONS

absolute, ly	abs	dollar, s	d
administrate	ad	East	E
administration	ad	envelope	env
advertise	adv	establish	est
America, n	A	federal	fed
a.m.	a	feet	ft
amount	amt	figure	fg
and	&	foot	ft
approximate, ly	apx	government	gvt
associate	asso	hundred	H
avenue	ave	inch	in
average	av	independent	ind
billion	B	intelligence	int
boulevard	blvd	intelligent, ly	int
bureau	Bu	invoice	inv
capital	cap	junior	jr
catalog	cal	magazine	mag
cent, s	c	manufacture	mfr
certificate	cert	maximum	max
certify	cert	memorandum	memo
child	ch	merchandise	mdse
children	chn	mile	mi
Christmas	Xms	million	M
company	co	minimum	min
corporation	corp	minute	min
credit	cr	miscellaneous	misc
day	d	month	mo
department	dpt	mortgage	mtg
discount	dis	Mr.	M
doctor	dr	Mrs.	Ms

346 Summary of Standard Abbreviations

North	*n*	room	*r*
number	*no*	second	*sec*
o'clock	*o*	secretary	*sec*
ounce	*oz*	senior	*sr*
page	*p*	signature	*sig*
paid	*pd*	South	*S*
pair	*pr*	square	*sq*
parcel post	*pp*	street	*st*
percent	*pc*	subscribe	*sub*
place	*pl*	subscription	*sub*
p.m.	*p*	superintendent	*supt*
popular	*pop*	telephone	*tel*
post office	*po*	thousand	*Td*
pound	*lb*	total	*tot*
president	*P*	vice-president	*VP*
question	*q*	volume	*vol*
railroad	*rr*	warehouse	*whs*
railway	*ry*	week	*k*
represent	*rep*	West	*W*
representative	*rep*	year	*y*

APPENDIX D
SUMMARY OF GEOGRAPHICAL TERMS

THE UNITED STATES

Alabama (AL)	Montana (MT)
Alaska (AK)	Nebraska (NB)
Arizona (AZ)	Nevada (NV)
Arkansas (AR)	New Hampshire (NH)
California (CA)	New Jersey (NJ)
Colorado (CO)	New Mexico (NM)
Connecticut (CT)	New York (NY)
Delaware (DE)	North Carolina (NC)
District of Columbia (DC)	North Dakota (ND)
Florida (FL)	Ohio (OH)
Georgia (GA)	Oklahoma (OK)
Hawaii (HI)	Oregon (OR)
Idaho (ID)	Pennsylvania (PA)
Illinois (IL)	Rhode Island (RI)
Indiana (IN)	South Carolina (SC)
Iowa (IA)	South Dakota (SD)
Kansas (KS)	Tennessee (TN)
Kentucky (KY)	Texas (TX)
Louisiana (LA)	Utah (UT)
Maine (ME)	Vermont (VT)
Maryland (MD)	Virginia (VA)
Massachusetts (MA)	Washington (WA)
Michigan (MI)	West Virginia (WV)
Minnesota (MN)	Wisconsin (WI)
Mississippi (MS)	Wyoming (WY)
Missouri (MO)	

Summary of Geographical Terms

AMERICAN CITIES

City	Shorthand	City	Shorthand
Akron	aCn	Evansville	evnzvl
Albany	albne	Flint	f-
Albuquerque	abCce	Fort Wayne	ft n
Amarillo	rlo	Fort Worth	ft rt
Annapolis	apls	Frankfort	frft
Atlanta	al-a	Gary	gy
Augusta	agsa	Grand Rapids	g— rpds
Austin	asn	Greensboro	gnzBo
Baltimore	bel ro	Harrisburg	HsBg
Baton Rouge	bln ruz	Hartford	HtFd
Birmingham	Brgh	Helena	hlna
Bismarck	bz rc	Honolulu	hnllu
Boise	byze	Houston	hsn
Boston	bsn	Indianapolis	ndenpls
Bridgeport	byrl	Jacksonville	jcsnvl
Buffalo	bflo	Jefferson City	(fsn s)
Cambridge	kBy	Jersey City	jze s)
Camden	c rdn	Juneau	jno
Carson City	Csn s)	Kansas City	Czs s)
Charleston	Crlsn	Lansing	ll/g
Chattanooga	Cnga	Lincoln	lgn
Cheyenne	Sin	Little Rock	ll rc
Chicago	Scg	Long Beach	lg beC
Cincinnati	snsn)	Los Angeles	ls ajls
Cleveland	cvl	Louisville	lubl
Columbia	Cl ba	Madison	rdsn
Columbus	Cl bs	Memphis	mfs
Concord	kCd	Miami	mre
Dallas	dls	Milwaukee	lce
Dayton	dln	Minneapolis	mepls
Denver	dnv	Montgomery	n- gy
Des Moines	de myn	Montpelier	n- pl/
Detroit	dryt	Nashville	nsvl
Dover	dv	Newark	nllc
El Paso	E pso	New Haven	nu hvn
Erie	Ee	New Orleans	nu olnz

Summary of Geographical Terms

New York	*nu Yc*	San Diego	*sn deg*
Norfolk	*nfc*	San Francisco	*sn fnsco*
Oakland	*ocl—*	San Jose	*sn hza*
Oklahoma City	*och—a s)*	Santa Fe	*s-a fa*
Olympia	*o—pa*	Savannah	*svna*
Omaha	*o—ha*	Seattle	*sell*
Paterson	*p—en*	Shreveport	*Svsl*
Philadelphia	*fldlfa*	South Bend	*S b—*
Phoenix	*fnx*	Spokane	*sc*
Pierre	*pa*	Springfield	*sgfld*
Pittsburgh	*plsBg*	Syracuse	*Scz*
Portland	*pll—*	Tacoma	*tc—a*
Providence	*pvd/*	Tallahassee	*llhse*
Raleigh	*rl*	Toledo	*lldo*
Richmond	*rC—*	Trenton	*T-m*
Rochester	*rCS*	Tucson	*tsn*
Sacramento	*sC-o*	Tulsa	*llsa*
St. Louis	*sa-lus*	Washington	*sgtn*
St. Paul	*sa-pal*	Wichita	*Cla*
St. Petersburg	*sa-ptsBg*	Worcester	*S*
Salem	*sl—*	Yonkers	*yg—*
Salt Lake City	*sll lc s)*	Youngstown	*ygstn*
San Antonio	*sn atno*		

CANADIAN PROVINCES AND TERRITORIES

Alberta	*aBla*	Ontario	*o-yo*
British Columbia	*BtS cl—ba*	Prince Edward Island	*p/edrd cl—*
Manitoba	*mlba*	Quebec	*qbc*
New Brunswick	*nu bnz—c*	Saskatchewan	*sscC—n*
Newfoundland	*nf—l—*	Yukon Territory	*uk Tly*
Northwest Territory	*nt Tly*		
Nova Scotia	*nva scSa*		

CANADIAN CITIES

Alma	*a—a*	Arvida	*avda*
Amherst	*H,*	Barrie	*by*

Summary of Geographical Terms

Place	Shorthand	Place	Shorthand
Belleville	blvl	Kitchener	cKn
Brampton	b—m	Lachine	lSn
Brandon	b—n	LaSalle	lsl
Brantford	b-fd	La Tuque	la luc
Brockville	bcvl	Lauzon	lzn
Calgary	clgy	Laval-des-Rapides	lvldrpd
Cap-de-la-Madeleine	cpd—dln	Leaside	lsd
Charlottetown	Srltt—n	Lethbridge	llBy
Chicoutimi	schre	Lindsay	l—ze
Cornwall	Cn—al	London	l—n
Cote-St.-Michel	clsa—Sl	Long Branch	lg bC
Dartmouth	Dt—i	Magog	mgg
Drummondville	d—n—vl	Medicine Hat	mdsn hl
Edmonton	ed—n-m	Mimico	mco
Edmundston	ed—n—sn	Moncton	mgn
Fairville	Fvl	Montreal	mtal
Flin Flon	fn fn	Moose Jaw	mus ja
Forest Hill	f, hl	Nanaimo	nn—o
Ft. William	fl wl	New Toronto	nu T-o
Ft. William-Pt. Arthur	fl wl, pl at	New Westminster	nu—ms
Fredericton	fdcn	Niagara Falls	nga fals
Galt	gll	North Bay	n ba
Glace Bay	gas ba	North Vancouver	N vnco
Granby	gnb	Orillia	ola
Guelph	gulf	Oshawa	oSa
Halifax	hlfx	Ottawa	ota
Hamilton	h—lln	Owen Sound	on s—
Hull	hl	Pembroke	p Bc
Jacques-Cartier	zcCla	Penticton	p-cn
Jasper-Place	j Spl	Peterborough	pTBo—b
Joliette	zlel	Pointe-aux-Trembles	pt—o
Jonquiere	zce	Pointe-Claire	p—c
Kenogami	cng—e	Portage la Praire	plgby
Kenora	cNa	Port Alberni	pl—aBne
Kingston	cgsn	Port Arthur	pl at
Kirkland Lake	Ccl—lc	Port Colborne	pl clBn
		Prince Albert	pl—aBl

Prince George	
Prince Rupert	
Quebec	
Red Deer	
Regina	
Rimouski	
Riverside	
St. Boniface	
St. Catharines	
St. Hyacinthe	
St. James	
St. Jean	
St. Jerome	
St. John's	
St. Lambert	
St. Laurent	
St. Michel	
St. Thomas	
Ste. Foy	
Sarnia	
Saskatoon	
Sault Sainte Marie	
Shawinigan Falls	
Sherbrooke	
Sillery	
Sorel	
Stratford	
Sudbury	
Swift Current	
Sydney	
Thetford Mines	
Timmins	
Toronto	
Trail	
Trenton	
Trois-Rivieres	
Truro	
Valleyfield	
Vancouver	
Verdun	
Victoria	
Victoriaville	
Ville-Jaques-Cartier	
Waterloo	
Welland	
Whitehorse	
Windsor	
Winnipeg	
Woodstock